H.L.A. Hart, Second Edition

Neil MacCormick

STANFORD LAW BOOKS

AN IMPRINT OF STANFORD UNIVERSITY PRESS

STANFORD, CALIFORNIA

Stanford University Press
Stanford, California
© 2008 by the Board of Trustees of the
Leland Stanford Junior University
All rights reserved.

First edition © Neil MacCormick 1981
Originating publisher: Edward Arnold (Publishers) Ltd., London, 1981

Library of Congress Cataloging-in-Publication Data

MacCormick, Neil.
   H.L.A. Hart / Neil MacCormick. — 2nd ed.
     p. cm. — (Jurists : profiles in legal theory)
   Includes bibliographical references and index.
   ISBN 978-0-8047-5678-5 (cloth : alk. paper)
   ISBN 978-0-8047-5679-2 (pbk. : alk. paper)
   1. Jurisprudence.   2. Hart, H. L. A. (Herbert Lionel Adolphus),
1907– 3. Hart, H. L. A. (Herbert Lionel Adolphus), 1907––
Bibliography.   I. Title.

K230.H3652M3 2008
340'.1—dc22   2007044945

Printed in the United States of America
on acid-free, archival-quality paper

Typeset by Newgen in 10/13 Galliard

Contents

Preface

If this book has one particular message, it is a message about method in legal study. Law is an aspect of human society, and 'human society is a society of persons' (p. 184 below) whose activities and institutions are understandable only through interpretation of their meaning to those engaged in them. The method of understanding legal and other human institutions by reference to their meaning from an insider's or an 'internal' point of view is central to Herbert Hart's work. That method I argue to be the correct one. Where I criticize more detailed aspects of his theories about law, I do so mainly on the ground that he has not always taken his own method far enough. The corrections and extensions which I propose, as against other critics, involve pressing Hartian arguments further than Hart pressed them.

His work has fascinated me since I first read *The Concept of Law* and attended his lectures in Oxford in the years 1963–65 while adding legal studies to my prior studies at Glasgow in philosophy and literature. As a Fellow of Balliol College from 1967 till 1972, I got to know Hart as a senior Oxford colleague whom I had cause both to like and to admire. If as a result my judgment of his work is flawed by the bias of friendship, there may be some offsetting gain by way of insight into his line of thought.

He very kindly gave me advice about the biographical part of the first chapter. I then had the pleasure of giving him a copy not only of that chapter but of the whole typescript, but this was not done with a view to my seeking nor, from his point of view, to his giving any kind of *imprimatur*. The book stands or falls as its author's, not its subject's, view of a leading contribution to jurisprudence.

As well as to Herbert Hart, I have other large debts of gratitude. To William Twining as general editor; to Sarah Cohen and Helen Tuschling as publisher's editors; to Michael Machan, Robert Moles, David Nelken, and Jes Bjarup as acute critics and advisers; to Sheila Macmillan, Sheila Smith, Kim Chambers, Annette Stoddart, and Moira Seftor as clear typists of obscure manuscripts; and to my family as tolerant victims of neglect, I owe and give unstinted thanks.

Neil MacCormick
Edinburgh, February 1981

FURTHER WORDS ON THE SECOND EDITION

The reasons for producing a second edition are sufficiently stated in the Introduction (Chapter 1). It is now fifteen years since Herbert Hart's death, and one hundred since his birth. So it is a good time to attempt, even in a short introductory way, a comprehensive account and assessment of his work both as jurist and as moral critic of positive law. The passage of time has also given the opportunity to take a longer perspective on the subject matter of the book, acknowledging that I have come to characterise my own work as decidedly post-positivist, and my position much less closely aligned with that of Hart than in 1981. I thank Max Del Mar for help in preparing the text.

Neil MacCormick
Edinburgh, June 2007

List of Main Works by H.L.A. Hart

This is a chronological list of the works of H. L. A. Hart most frequently cited in this book. For convenience of citation, the abbreviations [in brackets] are used in the text. Number 12 is printed also as chapter 7 of *E.o.B.*; numbers 2, 5, 10, and 13 are printed also as chapters 1, 2, 9, and 11 (respectively) of *E.J.P.*

A full bibliography of Hart's publications (and of most of the significant commentaries on them) appears in N. Lacey, *A Life of H.L.A. Hart: The Nightmare and the Noble Dream* (Oxford Univ. Press, Oxford, 2004), pp. 394–403.

1. "The Ascription of Responsibility and Rights." (1948/1949) 49 *Proceedings of the Aristotelian Society*, 171–94.

2. *Definition and Theory in Jurisprudence* (Inaugural lecture, Clarendon Press, Oxford, 1953). Also published in (1953) 70 *Law Quarterly Review*, 37. [*D.T.J.*; page references are to the Oxford edition.]

3. "Are There Any Natural Rights?" (1955) 64 *Philosophical Review*, 175–91. Also published in *Political Philosophy*, ed. A. Quinton (Oxford Univ. Press, Oxford, 1967), pp. 53–66. [*A.A.N.R.?*; page references are to the Quinton volume.]

4. "Analytic Jurisprudence in Mid-twentieth Century; a Reply to Professor Bodenheimer." (1957) 105 *Univ. of Pennsylvania Law Review*, 953–75. [*A.J.M.C.*]

5. "Positivism and the Separation of Law and Morals." (1958) 71 *Harvard Law Review*, 593–629. [*P.S.L.M.*]

6. *Causation in the Law*, jointly with A. M. Honoré (Clarendon Press, Oxford, 1959; 2nd ed., by Honoré, 1986). [*Causation*]

7. *The Concept of Law* (Clarendon Press, Oxford, 1961; 2nd ed., with Postscript, edited by P. P. Bulloch and J. Raz, 1994). [*C.L.*; page references are to the second edition. The Postscript is cited as *Postscript*.]

8. *Law, Liberty and Morality* (Oxford Univ. Press, London, 1963). [*L.L.M.*]

9. *The Morality of the Criminal Law* (Magnes Press, Hebrew Univ., Jerusalem; Oxford Univ. Press, London, 1965). [*M.C.L.*]

10. "Social Solidarity and the Enforcement of Morality." (1967/1968) 35 *Univ. of Chicago Law Review*, 1–13. [*S.S.E.M.*]

11. *Punishment and Responsibility: Essays in the Philosophy of Law.* (Clarendon Press, Oxford, 1968). [*P.R.*]

12. "Bentham on Legal Rights," *Oxford Essays in Jurisprudence, Second Series*, ed. A. W. B. Simpson (Clarendon Press, Oxford, 1973), pp. 171–91. [*B.L.R.*]

13. "Between Utility and Rights," *The Idea of Freedom*, ed. A. Ryan (Oxford Univ. Press, Oxford, 1979), pp.77–98. Also published in (1979) 79 *Columbia Law Review*, 827–46. [*B.U.R.*]

14. *Essays on Bentham: Jurisprudence and Political Theory.* (Clarendon Press, Oxford, 1982). [*E.o.B.*]

15. *Essays in Jurisprudence and Philosophy.* (Clarendon Press, Oxford, 1983). [*E.J.P.*]

16. "Comment," *Issues in Contemporary Legal Philosophy: The Influence of H.L.A. Hart,* ed. R. Gavison (Oxford Univ. Press, Oxford, 1987), pp. 35–42.

H.L.A. HART, SECOND EDITION

CHAPTER ONE

Introduction to the Second Edition

SOME PERSONAL REFLECTIONS

This is a book about the philosophical ideas of a great thinker who transformed the study of jurisprudence in the English-speaking world and beyond. His impact was great in practice as well as in theory. By his arguments, writings, personal standing, and eminence, he contributed markedly to the liberalisation of law in the United Kingdom—and to the liberation of attitudes beyond these shores—in relation to human sexuality and aesthetic celebrations of it. He had a remarkable career, encompassing eight years of successful practice at the English chancery bar (during which he also discovered a taste for riding to hounds), the 1939–45 war years working as an official in British intelligence, the following eight years teaching philosophy in New College Oxford and becoming a significant figure in the Oxford 'philosophical revolution' of that period, then sixteen years from 1952 as Professor of Jurisprudence in Oxford University after his somewhat surprising appointment to the chair, matched by an equally surprising early retirement in 1968 that led into a period of editorial work on Jeremy Bentham's papers while also holding office as a Monopolies Commissioner, and finally the Principalship of Brasenose College Oxford from 1972 till 1978. He remained active in retirement and was the focus of much scholarly activity till shortly before his death in December 1992.

He was married throughout nearly all this period to the brilliant but wayward Jenifer Williams, a high-flying civil servant in the Home Office before and during the 1939–45 war and an Oxford don after the war. They had four children, the youngest of whom sadly had suffered brain damage at birth. The marriage was famously a somewhat tempestuous and open one, but it was a partnership that endured for life and sustained both the partners through many vicissitudes. Its last years became mired in controversy, even scandal. While Herbert Hart was in wartime intelligence, Jenifer Hart was a civil servant in the Home Office (after the war, she too moved to Oxford, to an academic post first in Nuffield College, subsequently as a Fellow of St Anne's College). But during the thirties she had been a member of the Communist Party, like many other young people shocked by the rise of fascism and the apparent impotence of the democracies of the West.[1] By 1939, her membership had petered out, and she had ceased to have any contact with the party member who had been her contact in her early days in the Home Office. No attempt had been made to recruit her into spying. In the sixties, there was a series of revelations about spying in wartime, and Jenifer (like others who had had some engagement with communism in the thirties) was twice questioned in great detail by officials from the Security Service ('MI5') long before any public storm broke. She always maintained tenaciously that her early position as a potential 'sleeper' within the Home Office never came to anything but fizzled out along with her membership of and interest in the Communist Party during the period of the Molotov–Ribbentrop Pact, or shortly after. Break the storm did, however, in 1983. And it broke with a vengeance.

In 1983, Jenifer had given a (not uncharacteristically) indiscreet interview to a journalist at a time of public anxiety and speculation concerning spies at the heart of the British establishment. In the following furore, Herbert Hart became implicated as someone who allegedly might have passed secret intelligence information to his wife who in turn would have passed it on to her spymasters. As a respected figure in a pretty exalted position in the 'establishment', Hart was profoundly shocked to be faced with this innuendo or even accusation. It devalued in his own eyes the glowing record of the preceding years. And it was completely false. (So he robustly maintained throughout his ordeal of adverse publicity, and those who knew him considered him to be a person of rigid attachment to the truth.) He suffered a severe mental collapse, not cured until after a period of very unhappy hospitalisation culminating in electroconvulsive therapy.

The last public engagement at which I had the opportunity to meet him occurred some months after this unhappy episode. The occasion was a seminar in his honour held in Jerusalem in 1984 at the initiative of admirers of his in the senior ranks of the law faculty of the Hebrew University. He seemed to me to have recovered much of his sparkle, though still with an underlying sadness. He took a fairly low-key role at the seminar itself, while contributing a written response to a paper by Ronald Dworkin in the resulting volume edited by Ruth Gavison.[2] By that time, it was three years since the publication of the first edition of the present book, which Hart had largely welcomed while not fully agreeing with some parts of my reading of his work. We remained on very friendly terms since the time when I had worked alongside of him in the Oxford law faculty, though I was never a member of his inner circle of close friends, nor one of his doctoral supervisees. My abiding memory of the Jerusalem visit is of his enthusiastically urging me to see the sights of the Old City. He wanted me to share his appreciation of the Islamic as well as the Jewish and Christian significance of the place and its wonderful gates and monuments, above all the Dome of the Rock and the Wailing Wall. It struck me how much more aesthetic experience mattered to him than religious observance, though his upbringing as an observant Jew was something he never belittled or disowned however far he moved into a stance of liberal agnosticism on religious questions.[3]

We met once or twice after that at meetings of the British Academy and during working visits of mine to Oxford. In 1992, when he was becoming very frail, the Trustees of the Hart Lectures in Oxford invited me to give the 1993 Hart Lecture, hoping that a tribute from a former student and self-confessed follower of Hart might be a source of pleasure in the evening of his days. Alas, he died some weeks before the time set for the lecture, and my tribute became a posthumous one. Jenifer Hart spoke to me very kindly after it, and I called on her at her house in Manor Road, Oxford. She said that my lecture[4] had for the first time made *The Concept of Law* seem fully comprehensible to her, but perhaps on this one occasion her lifelong propensity for unvarnished truthfulness was overridden by the graciousness of a hostess. When her own autobiography *Ask Me No More*[5] was published, I eagerly bought and eagerly read it. My sense of Hart's eminence as a leader in the academic field in which I had also made a life's work remained undimmed. I was very specially gratified to receive in 1994 a copy, signed by Jenifer, of the newly published second edition of Hart's *Concept of Law*, which had been edited at her request by Joseph Raz and Penny Bulloch, assisted by Timothy Endicott.

Quite a few years later, I heard from another valued friend, Professor Nicola Lacey of the London School of Economics, that she was embarking on a biography of Hart and inquiring if I had any information that might be of interest to her. I was then embroiled in what turned out to be a single five-year mandate as a Member of the European Parliament for Scotland. So far as I could recall, I had nothing of interest to add to what was contained in this very book, *H.L.A. Hart*, in its first edition, and I reported so from my rather frantically busy office in Brussels. Anyway, I was somewhat surprised that Niki should divert herself from the main stream of legal scholarship to an essay in biography, perhaps rather vainly thinking that my own book had exhausted the market for sympathetic studies of Hart and his work.

How very wrong I was. Nicola Lacey's *A Life of H.L.A. Hart: The Nightmare and the Noble Dream*[6] burst upon the world in 2004 and was a runaway success. It confirmed the greatness of Hart's work as educator, jurist, philosopher, and scholar and the value of his public contributions to significant debates during a time of change in public sensibilities. But it revealed an astonishing level of private self-doubt and spiritual turmoil, including an abiding ambiguity of sexual orientation with resulting tensions in conjugal relations and other tensions in the relations of the Harts to various of their friends. Many readers had thought, certainly I had thought, that Hart had written his very influential *Law, Liberty and Morality* from a stance of deep but essentially detached sympathy with those whose sexual predilections and activities popular morality pilloried and the law denounced as criminal. This was, after all, not the case. Behind the vigour of his writing there lay a personal sense of felt suffering as well as a cool rationalism concerning proper uses of the criminal law.

What I had not originally realised about Lacey's biographical activity was that she was working on Hart's life with the encouragement of Jenifer Hart, having been a close friend of both Herbert and Jenifer when they were all three working in Oxford, and that Jenifer had given her the free run of all Herbert Hart's hugely voluminous papers and diaries. There, all his inner turmoil was fully disclosed. Such turmoil contrasted sharply with the awareness most people had of the public person, with its sometimes aloof gravitas, its wise and rational stance on philosophical and practical issues, including issues of university governance, and its essentially benign view of fellow humans and their follies and foibles.

Lacey's biography has provoked controversy. Some consider that Jenifer betrayed Herbert in letting his papers be used in this way.[7] Some consider that Lacey has made too much of the private record in a way that besmirches the public memory. Many, and I for certain among them, take a strongly opposed view. Lacey's honest account of Hart's own honest self-doubt increases, not diminishes, my respect both for Herbert and for Jenifer and the deep affection in which I shall always hold the memory of each of them. Even the great have their points of vulnerability, perhaps especially the great. But we all have our private dragons to slay, and a biography like Lacey's of Hart can encourage any reader to believe that however fierce one's personal dragons may be, much that is of true worth can be accomplished while they are held at bay or even partially tamed.

Anyway, despite superficial appearances, Hart's life was not without its dramatic or even exotic aspects. The Lacey biography enables one to understand these. But this is not the place to rake over the same ground. The mundane details of Hart's life matter perhaps more, or certainly matter as much, for the purposes of a book aimed at explaining his contribution to Jurisprudence. We shall attend to these now.

THE PUBLIC PERSON

Born in 1907 of Jewish parents, he was educated briefly at Cheltenham College (which he hated) and Bradford Grammar School (which he loved, and where his appetite for ideas was whetted). He then proceeded to New College Oxford, where he performed brilliantly in the study of classics and ancient history and philosophy, taking a first in 'Greats' in 1929. As for many others, success in Greats was for him a prelude to a legal career. He read for the Bar Examinations, and was called to the Bar in 1932. For the next eight years he practised as a Chancery barrister establishing a successful junior practice in such complicated matters as trusts, family settlements, and succession and related questions of taxation. His ambitions were for success in the law, and although during this period he was invited to return as a philosophy tutor to New College where he had been taught by H. W. B. Joseph, he chose to stay in the world of legal practice.

Upon the outbreak of war, he became a civil servant working in military intelligence. During this period, his never wholly dormant interest in philosophy was rekindled in a new form, partly through his working association with two Oxford philosophers in a connected department of intelligence, Gilbert Ryle and Stuart Hampshire. During intervals in their intelligence work, conversation among those three turned to philosophy.

After the war, New College renewed its invitation to him to return to Oxford as a Fellow and Tutor in philosophy, and this time he accepted the invitation. He then saw himself as giving up all legal interests in favour of the more profound intellectual challenge to be found in testing the new philosophical approaches against old philosophical fascinations of his own about perception, about the reconciliation of scientific and commonsense beliefs, and about Plato's work, in which H. W. B. Joseph's work had engaged his interest even through his years of legal practice. After sixteen years of intensely practical work in the law and then in war service, he returned to the academic life.

The Oxford to which he returned was in a state of philosophical effervescence, with claims in the air about the 'philosophical revolution'[8] that was perceived both to be necessary and to be under way. Leading figures were Gilbert Ryle and J. L. Austin, but they were by no means the only important figures in the new Oxford philosophy of the postwar years. Others with whom Hart came into close contact on his return to Oxford and to philosophy after his sixteen years' absence were Friedrich Waissman and G. A. Paul, from the latter of whom he obtained his first sight of Wittgenstein's still unpublished 'Blue Book'.[9] These two were participants in regular Saturday morning philosophical discussions in Austin's rooms, as were also J. O. Urmson, A. D. Woozley, R. M. Hare, P. F. Strawson, Geoffrey and Mary Warnock, Philippa Foot, A. M. Honoré the jurist, and of course Hart himself. (Isaiah Berlin, the closest of Hart's philosophical friends and the one through whom he had been kept aware of newer philosophical developments during his years of legal practice, did not take part in these discussions.) In a work such as the present, no adequate account can be given of the range or quality of the work done by all the above named. Suffice it to say only that the galaxy of talent represented was a formidable one. Nevertheless, one should also acknowledge that in the perspective of a half-century later some of the claims of the 'revolution' (as so often with revolutions of all kinds) have proved to be somewhat overstated. The school of 'ordinary language philosophy' has dissolved into many different philosophical strands, some of which have involved rediscovering works that the revolutionaries treated with disdain.

However that may be, Hart's aims in returning to academia had nothing to do with applying philosophy to legal problems. Indeed, he saw himself as abandoning law in favour of philosophy. One can scarcely conceive of his having at that time accepted an appointment as a law tutor or even law professor, for that would have seemed a very low-grade alternative to legal practice. In those days, lawyers in practice, and especially those whose route to practice was through a university education in some subject other than law, regarded academic law with a certain disdain, as a very ancillary kind of activity in comparison to the real business of law. Such an attitude is by no means unfamiliar to this day. Philosophy in the universities was seen quite differently, clearly engaging the minds of brilliant people at the forefront of the world of ideas.[10]

As it turned out, however, Hart's legal experience in the Chancery barrister's manipulation of words to practical ends was particularly relevant to the current concerns of his fellow philosophers. The study of the uses of language in practical as well as theoretical ways had assumed a new urgency for them, as we shall see in due course. Hence Hart's legal experience came to be drawn into his philosophical work, despite his exchange of the barrister's for the academic's gown. Yet the law in a way reclaimed him.

In 1952 A. L. Goodhart resigned from the Chair of Jurisprudence in Oxford. Although Hart had not yet published extensively, he was a respected member of the new school of postwar Oxford philosophers. Alone among them, he was a man of law as well as of philosophy. He was elected to the vacant Chair, but undertook his tasks very much in the style of a philosopher among lawyers, not as a lawyer with philosophical interests. His inaugural lecture on "Definition and Theory in Jurisprudence" put him at once in controversy when he announced the relevance of the new philosophy to long-standing juristic controversies over the nature of legal concepts. Instead of building theories on the backs of definitions, he argued, jurists must work at analysing the use of legal language in the practical workings of the law. From the United States, he was denounced by Professor Edgar Bodenheimer for reducing jurisprudence to the repetition of lawyers' talk and for diverting juristic attention from more urgent sociological inquiries. Hart rejoined[11] that the sociologists themselves could do with applying more rigorous conceptual analysis in their own work and that at least the starting point for juristic study ought to be the careful study by lawyers and law students of the linguistic fabric of their own enterprise.

Hart's analysis of law and legal concepts has sometimes been criticized for the rather detached, value-neutral approach it exhibits with regard to the law. This can plausibly be linked to the fact that, as we have seen, he had made a quite deliberate decision to break with the law and go over to philosophy. That break survived in his stance as one who inquires about law from the outside, not as one committed to finding practical solutions to current problems within it. It may be doubted whether this is really the stance of one who seeks to stand right outside the ordinary world and to find an 'Archimedean point' from which to cast doubt on all that lies below.[12] It implies a choice of standpoint or of method of study, and one that is certainly understandable in the light of Hart's own life-course. In the final chapter, the appropriateness of this methodological choice will be considered more closely.

The fruits of Hart's way of working did not become available to a wider public (beyond his well-attended Oxford lectures, which alternately stimulated and puzzled the law students present) until the publication in 1959 of *Causation in the Law*. This was a joint work with A. M. Honoré, which had been prefigured in a series of *Law Quarterly Review* articles.[13] Questions of causation have wide-ranging importance in law where questions of civil or criminal liability are at stake. (Did Smith's act cause damage to Jones's property? Did it cause Macdonald's death?) They are also of philosophical and scientific concern. And they bulk large in the affairs of ordinary life and in commonsense speech. *Causation* was a masterly and detailed elucidation of the legal uses of a concept with its roots in everyday thought and speech, and it certainly vindicated Hart's—and Honoré's—jurisprudence from any plausible charge of triviality.

It was soon followed, in 1961, with the publication of Hart's central work, *The Concept of Law*, which offers an analysis of the concepts of law and of legal system through a discussion of the way in which rules of human conduct are used as social standards of behaviour. These are sometimes combined together into complex systematic wholes within which the concepts of legal discourse make sense and become applicable in appropriate social contexts. *The Concept of Law* can keep company even with the massively erudite and acutely perceptive works of the great Austrian jurist Hans Kelsen, among the great works of twentieth-century jurisprudence. It is a work of international eminence, and even its strongest critics have acknowledged it as a masterpiece worth at least the compliment of careful refutation.

Although such a work aims at universality of application, being supposedly as relevant to quite alien legal traditions as to the author's own, every jurist is apt to bear the marks of his own historical and geographical locality. Hart's work, though it is not directed particularly at British institutions and though he claimed that it applied to legal systems quite generally, is nevertheless clearly recognizable as the work of an English lawyer of the twentieth century.

Perhaps everywhere there is a line that can be drawn between 'law' and 'politics', but one of the more obvious facts of cross-cultural comparisons is that it gets drawn differently in different places. The British parliamentary tradition right up till the end of the twentieth century was one in which questions of fundamental rights and of justice fell primarily and permanently in the political sphere. It belonged primarily to the political nation—citizens, journalists, parties, politicians, parliamentarians, and statesmen—to settle and secure the rights of the people and to determine the framework of social justice. Under the constitution, whatever the political nation determined through proper parliamentary process issued forth as binding law. It was not then for judges and lawyers as such to pass a judgment of superior wisdom upon the decisions of the political nation. Their proper role was wise and faithful application of the law as it issued from those political decisions. They needed to have criteria for what counted as law, but in interpreting and applying whatever counted as law by these criteria, they were not themselves to be bothered with issues of political theory in the grand manner.

The criteria in question were of course 'constitutional' in nature. But in a system that entrusted so much to the wisdom of the political nation, there seemed scarcely any room for grand notions of fundamental law, 'basic norms' which cement together the whole legal and political edifice, founts of all rightful authority. How different had to be the assumptions built into different traditions. Jurists in the European continental tradition have in their background in modern times constitutions and basic laws which are, as it were, the legally uncaused cause of all legal effects. In this context, the greatest of modern European jurists, Hans Kelsen, postulated the idea of a 'basic norm' or *'Grundnorm'* as a presupposition of all legal and juristic thinking, under which the actual historical act of determining a constitution is transformed into a source of *normative* authority determining what *ought* to be done, as distinct from what merely *is* done.

Jurists in the tradition of the United States work against a background of constitutionally guaranteed rights so general in their initial statement that theories of just relations between government and people are essential to implementing them. What, for example, is to be understood by a guarantee of "equal protection of the laws" for all citizens? Does this or that state or federal enactment infringe "equal protection"? What is "due process of law"? When is a punishment "cruel or unusual"? Such questions fall to be contested before and determined by courts of law, and ultimately the Supreme Court. Their determination leads judges inexorably into framing and acting upon political theories as an intrinsic element of constitutional law. Jurists and jurisprudence must then have something to say about theories of just government since they are intrinsic to the administration of such a system of law.

Yet from a British standpoint, the same matters seemed in Hart's day to be issues of political morality *v* questions of law. Deciding such issues was a matter for the political nation. The outcome of the decision was an act of lawmaking. But the law, once made, was binding law, which the courts had to apply even if they thought the political theories that justified it to be wild nonsense.

Great changes have come over the legal traditions of the United Kingdom since the time of Hart's flourishing. Entry in 1973 into the European Economic Community (itself, since 1992, one 'pillar' of the European Union) has wrought deep changes, yet changes that were little noticed in the jurisprudence of the following decade. The unitary United Kingdom has been made quasi-federal with the devolution of power to a reestablished Scottish Parliament, a National Assembly for Wales, a new power-sharing Northern Ireland Assembly, and an elected Greater London Authority. (Plans for devolving power to regional assemblies in other parts of England have, however, been abandoned through lack of public demand for them). The European Convention for the Protection of Human Rights and Fundamental Freedoms has been largely made justiciable before British courts under the Human Rights Act 1998, though in a way that does preserve the last-resort supremacy of Parliament in relation to upholding the Convention rights. The development of public law has led to a far greater degree of judicial scrutiny of executive action than was ever practised before.

At the time of Hart's death in 1992, nearly all of this lay in the future, or at any rate had not yet impinged deeply on ideas about legal theory. Beyond doubt or denial, Hart's theory of law bears some of the marks of the previously prevailing unspoken assumptions of the English lawyer (to some extent shared also by Scots lawyers) as to the line that fell between the legal and the moral-cum-political. In turn, certain criticisms of his theories may indicate the concerns which seem more salient to legal thinkers grounded in other traditions. A German critic,[14] for example, has characterized Hart's and other similar works as *'Rechtstheorie ohne Recht'* —a rightless theory of the legally right, as one might falteringly translate the play on the German word *Recht*. In a partly similar way, American critics have attacked the absence from Hart's jurisprudence of any elucidation of the 'inner morality' which one of them, Lon L. Fuller, considered an intrinsic element of anything we can recognize as law. A landmark of Anglo–American juristic debate in the late 1950s was the publication in the *Harvard Law Review* of a controversy[15] between Fuller and Hart upon the question whether law is or is not essentially moral in its inner nature. Neither convinced the other, and each subsequently extended his argument in a powerfully argued book. Somewhat later, Ronald Dworkin, also of course an American, found in Hart's jurisprudence a failure to 'take rights seriously'[16] since it fails to build up any theory of the way in which basic principles of right come to be bodied forth in the 'black letter law' of statutes and judicial precedents.

These criticisms are perhaps not unrelated to some of the criticisms which some sociologists of law and sociologically minded jurists, including 'Critical Legal Scholars', have in their turn directed against Hart's way of elucidating the concept of law and related concepts.[17] The gravamen of the sociological complaint is that analytical work upon legal ideas takes for granted the ideological scheme within which lawyers in general and, *a fortiori*, lawyers within a particular national tradition do their work. The task of understanding law is a task of seeing it as a manifestation of ideology located within a larger politico-economic framework of which it is but a part. This cannot be achieved within the four corners of an 'analytical jurisprudence' which elucidates lawyers' concepts from inside the taken-for-granted assumptions either of legal systems at large or of a single legal system.

Again, there may in any event be a gap between the concepts and rules that lawyers, judges, and administrators of law manipulate in their debates and arguments, and the way in which they actually conduct the business they are authorized to do. Understanding a legal system requires us, as 'American realists' and their sociologically minded successors in jurisprudence have insisted, to look behind the linguistic and conceptual smoke screen and find out what really goes on in the name of 'law'.[18]

Great though Hart's distinction as a jurist is, greater than that of any other twentieth-century British jurist, one cannot claim for his work that it is flawless or that it presents an entire and complete view of law. Like all great work it has gaps and defects, like all great work it bears the marks of place and time, and like all great work it is eminently open to criticism and owes some at least of its importance to the criticisms it has provoked.

Hart's work has another side to it, beyond the contribution it makes to analytical jurisprudence. His way of drawing the line between issues of law—moral-cum-political questions about the law and its conformity to ideas of freedom and justice—undoubtedly reveals some of the characteristically British assumptions of his own times concerning where that line falls. But he did not restrict himself to one side only of the line. He made powerful contributions to debate upon justice and good law as well as to descriptive analytical jurisprudence. He characterized these contributions as works of "critical morality", aimed at expounding principles for the just and proper uses of law in a civilized society. In this field he concentrated mainly on matters of criminal law and punishment, on which his position was set out in works published subsequently to *The Concept of Law*, namely *Law, Liberty and Morality* (1963), *The Morality of the Criminal Law* (1965), and *Punishment and Responsibility* (1968).

Both in his analytical and in his critical work, Hart drew heavily on the British tradition of liberal utilitarianism and legal positivism. (Legal positivism can for the moment be sufficiently defined as the theory that all laws owe their origin and existence to human practice and decisions

concerned with the government of a society and that they have no necessary correlation with the precepts of an ideal morality.) The utilitarian/
positivist line of thought starts with the work of philosophers such as
Thomas Hobbes and David Hume, but the more direct influence on Hart
came from Jeremy Bentham (1748–1832) and John Austin (1790–1859) and
their disciple John Stuart Mill (1806–73). As will be seen, Hart's critical
moral theory restates liberal ideas about liberty under law, though at the
same time adapting them to a social democratic political philosophy. On
the other hand, his analytical work is founded on a critique of Bentham's
and Austin's theories of law as always deriving from a sovereign's will. His
interest in their work is manifested not only in many scholarly articles,[19]
but also in acting as editor of their work. In 1954 he published an introduction to an edition of John Austin's *Province of Jurisprudence Determined*, and
later in his professional career he was instrumental in putting in train the
vast project of editing the huge mass of (partly unpublished) papers left by
Bentham. For his part in this project, he acted as editor together with J. H.
Burns of Bentham's *An Introduction to the Principles of Morals and Legislation*
and *Comment on the Commentaries and Fragment on Government* and as sole
editor of Bentham's *Of Laws in General*.

Such was the burden of this editorial work, coupled with the duties
he had undertaken as a member of the (UK) Monopolies Commission,
that in 1968 he resigned from the Oxford Chair of Jurisprudence, being
in due course succeeded as professor by Ronald Dworkin. For the next
four years he held a Senior Research Fellowship at University College
Oxford, then in 1972 he was elected Principal of Brasenose College, an
office which he held until his retirement in 1978. During a period of student unrest in the 1960s, Hart had acted as chairman of a committee appointed by Oxford University to look into relations between junior and
senior members of the university. The committee's report recommended
a series of liberalizing reforms in university discipline and related matters, reforms mostly enacted by the university's legislative forum in the
late 1960s. So he was by no means a stranger to the problems of academic
government when he took up the Principalship of Brasenose in the somewhat quieter days of the 1970s. Even after his retirement, he remained active in scholarship and writing and in the formal and informal supervision
and assistance of younger scholars. The 'Oxford spy' scandal, his break-
down, and his hospital treatment affected him quite badly and probably
diminished his vigour and appetite for controversy. Anyway, for what-

ever reason, he never completed the *Postscript* to *The Concept of Law* in the form that he had hoped it would take.

WHY A NEW EDITION?

The first edition of this book appeared in 1981, to a generally rather favourable reception, and it seems quite largely to have stood the test of time. At least Nicola Lacey has been kind to it in referring to it as one useful source for her far more massive work. But much has happened in the intervening years, and the present second edition of *H.L.A. Hart* must take due account of things that have changed. This edition follows its predecessor after a lapse of twenty-six years, and fifteen years after Hart's death. The corpus of Hart's work is complete, and there have been some years for reflection upon it. The first edition was written as a friendly/critical introductory account of a great jurist's work, aimed at sympathetic reconstruction of Hart's main ideas in a way that would be easily accessible to readers unfamiliar with jurisprudence in general and Hart's work in particular. I undertook it in the hope that, notwithstanding its relative modesty of aim, it could also make a significant contribution in its own way to shedding light on the very important topics it necessarily covers. The new edition remains faithful to the original conception.

Since 1981, however, there have been developments that any book about H.L.A. Hart's contribution to jurisprudence has to take into account. Hart himself added significant thoughts about his theoretical position as a whole in the context of the two volumes of collected papers (*Essays on Bentham, Essays in Jurisprudence and Philosophy*) that he produced in 1982 and 1983.[20] The former was a blue book, the latter a brown, perhaps in a deliberate graphic echo of the celebrated blue and brown books of Ludwig Wittgenstein.[21] Each contained a substantial reflective introduction that discussed the content of the papers included and expressed a new, or a somewhat adjusted, orientation to the themes he had addressed over the years. He took part in the previously mentioned Jerusalem seminar about his work, making responses in the published proceedings to some of the critical comments on his work. He also attempted in his later years to survey the huge volume of comment his work had called forth and to respond to it. He did, however, once remark to me that there was simply too much of it for him to cope with it. He had mountains of volumes and offprinted articles sent to him by admirers and by critics, and he did try to read these and come to some sort of position in relation to them; however, taking a synoptic view was out of the question.

After his death, the fruits of some of his later labours came to the surface in the form of a draft *Postscript* to his magnum opus, *The Concept of Law*. His great friend and former student Joseph Raz, together with Penny Bulloch, as requested by Jenifer Hart, edited this for publication as the concluding part of a new, posthumous edition of *C.L.* The editors record that the *Postscript* was incomplete relative to its author's own intention, for he had only completed the first part of what he hoped to achieve and even that was still in draft form, requiring sympathetic editorial intervention to work it up for publication. This first part, in six sections, consisted of a fairly detailed response to Ronald Dworkin's criticisms of Hart's jurisprudence coupled, naturally, with a critique by Hart of what he considered defects in Dworkin's own work. A hoped-for second section dealing with, and in some cases accepting, comments and criticisms from other scholars lay quite unfinished in merely skeletal note form. So it remains a matter for speculation what Hart would have said about other scholars (and perhaps even about this book's first edition) had he been able to fulfil his own intention.

Certainly though, the *Postscript*, even in its never-completed form, reveals how much his attempt to come to terms with and respond to the ideas and the critical observations of his Oxford successor had absorbed his intellectual energy in his last years. The *Postscript* is not a broad reflection on legal philosophy in the light of the huge and multifarious response generated by his work. It is a response to Dworkin, with a few subsidiary references to one or two other significant figures.

Nicola Lacey's biography also shows from the private papers to what an extent Hart's intellectual and personal relationship with Dworkin came to dominate his thought in his last years. In 1968, Hart had been unusually active, contrary to the normal convention, in seeking to influence the appointment of his successor after he retired (early) from the Oxford Jurisprudence Chair. Though still relatively little known in the United Kingdom or even in the United States, Ronald Dworkin was his preferred candidate, and in due course Dworkin was indeed appointed. Yet after the most mutually cordial of beginnings, the atmosphere between them became, over time, one of mutual noncomprehension, and their early friendship cooled considerably. This was a matter of particular regret to Dworkin, whose intellectual disagreements with Hart never disrupted personal regard and indeed respect for the man and the thinker.

Beyond doubt, the intellectual gulf between them was a deep one. Hart believed it possible to give a philosophical analysis of law that was straightforwardly descriptive of a significant social institution to be found in varying forms in many different states or societies. This account acknowledged that participants in the institution had necessarily a value-laden engagement with it and that relevant values might therefore be highly relevant to any rich description of it. They were not, however, the values of, nor need they be values shared by, the descriptive theorist. They were simply the (observed and described) values of active participants in the system. Hart's insistence on the possibility and intellectual desirability of a detached, descriptive, and positivistic jurisprudence was more sharply stated in his *Postscript* than ever before. This approach necessarily discountenanced certain readings of Hart's work that stressed his own basis in values. Such accounts suggested that the best argument for Hart's positivistic approach was one that appealed to moral values. The first edition of the present book stated (and the present edition repeats) a rather vigorous case in favour of such a reading. It is therefore one among the readings of his work on which a shadow was cast by Hart in his own concluding thoughts.

For his part, in his Hart Lecture of 2001,[22] Dworkin confessed himself simply unable to grasp what there is for this supposedly descriptive theory to describe. In his view, all political and social theorising, legal theory included, has to express some 'value-commitment' made by the theorist, since all attempts to grasp any social practices or institutions must be interpretative of them. The best interpretation of a practice is the one that makes the best sense of it, and this means constructing the most evaluatively attractive version that is faithful to the pre-interpretive materials brought into view in the process of constructing the meaning of the practice as a whole.

The relative merits of the two sides of this argument will be taken up later in this book. For the moment, the point is only to confess that Hart's later work effectively, though not explicitly, rejected one part of the interpretation of his work offered in the first edition of the present book. William Twining, general editor of the series to which the present book belongs, recalls a conversation on the train between Oxford and London. In response to a question by Twining about his reaction to the first edition of this book, Hart "indicated general approval, but said emphatically that he considered himself to be more of a hardened positivist than MacCormick had depicted".[23] The *Postscript* certainly underlines this self-conception of Hart's, and indeed Hart once remarked to me that I made him out to be more of a natural lawyer than he wanted to be.

This has an inevitable bearing on the task here undertaken of producing a new edition. All useful interpretation of an author's work is indeed a kind of 'constructive' interpretation [24] that reads the text and tries to construct or construe the ideas discerned in it in the most attractive and persuasive way possible. Yet a living author always has the right to reject someone else's interpretation and offer her or his preferred counterinterpretation. In turn, the interpretative commentator must revise the originally offered interpretation to encompass the new self-interpretation offered by the target author.

This second edition mainly sustains the arguments and interpretations offered in the first edition. Yet adjustments have been made that allow for Hart's subsequent disowning of works on which the first edition relied, and others have been made in response to criticisms of the first edition where these seemed just. At some points, the reading that is here offered of the texts remains apparently less 'positivistic' than their author would have thought appropriate. At such points, a warning note is entered to that effect. A new final chapter, the Epilogue, has been added to take up some of the specific issues of positivistic methodology raised by Hart's later writings and to take a little account of subsequent writing about him.

There have been many major contributions to Hart scholarship in the quarter century between 1981 and 2007 and also two other full-length critical studies of his whole body of work, both carried through in greater depth and detail than is appropriate to this book.[25] Responses to the *Postscript* have produced a major collection of important and wide-ranging essays.[26] There is such a mountain of material to be considered that one can barely encompass it in thought. To do it anything like full justice in what remains by design a short and relatively simple introduction to a great philosophical contribution is simply impossible. In other recent works, I have discussed much of it, more than is possible or desirable in this book. These are works that have taken up themes originally sketched in this book's first edition and developed them in ways that reveal an intellectual inheritance from Hart while nevertheless reaching conclusions divergent from his on many important points.[27] They add up to an 'institutional theory of law' of a markedly post-positivist kind. The most recent of them, *Institutions of Law*, includes at full strength an alternative view to that of Hart's on many of the issues covered in this book, acknowledging nevertheless a huge debt to Hart's work and influence.

CHAPTER TWO

Hart: Moral Critic and Analytical Jurist

INTRODUCTION: ON JURISPRUDENCE

Jurisprudence is the theoretical study of a practical subject. Its object is to achieve a systematic and general understanding of law. The business of law is the organization and ordering of human communities, the protection and regulation of human beings as members of communities. Theoretical study of this practical business can follow several lines. For example, it may overlap with and draw from moral and political philosophy in trying to establish principles of justice and of good law against which to criticize actual laws, legal practices, and modes of government. Or it may overlap with and draw from history, sociology, or descriptive political science in trying to depict the working of the legal system as one element within the entirety of social and political order. Or it may overlap with and draw from analytical philosophy in trying to analyse and elucidate the concepts and ideas through which the practical business of law articulates itself. Or it may overlap with and draw from logic and rhetoric in studying the modes and forms of argument used in the conduct of legal business. Or it may apply all or any of these lines of inquiry to more detailed case studies of particular institutions or branches of the law. None of these ways of theorising about law can be entirely independent of any other, and a complete view of law would in some form comprehend them all—and perhaps others besides. For Hart, however, jurisprudence was primarily a branch of philosophy, involving the application of philosophical ideas and methods both to the criticism of law and to the conceptual analysis of law, legal systems, and legal concepts. The strength of his commitment to the philosophical approach is easily comprehensible in view of the biographical details recounted in the preceding chapter.[1]

HART AS MORAL CRITIC OF LAW

During the fifteen years from 1955 to 1970, there was in the United Kingdom a substantial movement toward liberalization of the law. Obscene publications, abortion, and homosexual and heterosexual acts between adults in private were in part liberated from previous criminal restraints. The death penalty was abolished for murder. Divorce lost some of its quasi-penal implications and its moral stigma. Debate in Parliament and outside it be-came much concerned with methods to achieve greater humaneness in the penal system and the legal system generally.

No one who lived through those years would deny that during them the moral climate underwent great change. The value of enabling people to 'do their own thing' became more and more accepted and emphasized. Old restraints and taboos were questioned and overturned. The 1960s were celebrated as the 'swinging sixties' by the popularizers of the new morality. Nor were these changes peculiar to the United Kingdom. Equally obvious and in some ways farther reaching changes of a similar kind went ahead throughout the Western democracies, perhaps most notably in the United States and the small, predominantly Protestant countries of the north—the Netherlands, Denmark, Sweden, and Norway.

Such changes might well be ascribed to 'liberalism' in its classical sense. They involved the removal of restraints on individual freedom of action in matters where the individual or freely associating groups of individu-als should be permitted to pursue what they see as good, not what other people define as good for them. Individuals and groups should be left free to do as they will, except for such acts as involve doing harm to others without their consent; and the mere fact that what I do goes against your moral standards is not admitted as an instance of harm done by me to you. So says classical liberalism, certainly in the form set out in John Stuart Mill's famous *Essay on Liberty*.

On the other hand, the postwar period up to and including the 1960s saw a vast extension in the powers of intervention of the state in previously private fields of activity. This stemmed from a commitment to maintain-ing full employment through economic management. This commitment was considered in some cases as requiring the state to take control of the 'commanding heights' of an industrial economy, instead of leaving the fate of individuals and the hope for economic growth to the free play of market forces. Closely parallel to this was a commitment to extending and improving health and welfare services on a universal rather than selective basis, protecting public amenity through controls on private development of land, and extending and so far as possible equalizing opportunities for all through the public educational system.

The circumstances of economic growth of the times encouraged a substantial flow of brown and black British subjects and Commonwealth citizens from former colonies and imperial possessions into Britain. As a response to a growth in racial tensions and antagonisms, race relations legislation was introduced limiting freedom in private transactions by prohibiting various forms of discriminatory behaviour. At the same time, in a manner which some found contradictory, Parliament legislated to stem the flow of further brown and black immigrants into the country, performing remarkable legislative contortions with a view to wrapping up that purpose in a bundle of ostensibly nondiscriminatory provisions for the control of immigration. In due course, the protections against racial discrimination in housing, employment, and provision of services were extended to cover sexual discrimination and to strike a blow at the 'male chauvinism' ingrained in social mores that had been inherited from the Victorian patriarchs. A good deal later, this attack on discrimination was extended to protect sexual orientation as well as gender.

A similar sensitivity to problems of race and gender was no less marked in other democratic states. Nowhere was this more dramatically obvious than in the United States, where from 1954 onward the civil rights movement won important judicial and legislative changes in law and attitude on behalf of ethnic minorities, many of whose members descended from African slaves. There also, the women's movement built its case on top of the victories of the civil rights movement. By a curious inversion of previous usage, economic and social reforms or changes of this further kind are sometimes also ascribed to liberalism though in fact they involve restraints upon individual freedom of acting in order to maintain public standards of welfare and decency. To European ears it is perhaps more easy to speak of such reforms as social democratic than as liberal. But we need not too much trouble ourselves here with niceties of usage, for the important point to make is that according to a powerful body of modern thought, the liberalizing and the welfare equalizing trends of modern legislation and modern state practice are fully compatible each with another.

H.L.A. Hart provided a vocabulary to express that compatibility. He suggested a distinction between the *existence* of legal or constitutional liberty and its *value* to individuals, a distinction which John Rawls also took up to considerable effect.[2] A law securing freedom of the press, for example, may be so framed as to be absolutely universal in its terms and thus to confer an identical and equal liberty on all citizens. But in fact this liberty will mean more and be worth more to those who have achieved literacy through education and who can afford to buy books and newspapers and have leisure to read them than to those who are lacking in all or any of these good fortunes. Those who own and control newspapers and publishing houses are, on the other hand, yet more favoured. The same general point can be made in respect of legal and constitutional liberties in all their manifestations, i.e., in all instances in which people are left free to do as they will without legal interference. Thus it can be argued that the original programme of classical liberalism needs to be revised by superimposing on it a social democratic strategy aimed at narrowing the grosser inequalities in the value of liberties. But the fundamental importance of liberties as propounded by classical liberalism remains a basic tenet of the social democrat.

This view is susceptible to attack from at least two sides. Some see a fundamental contradiction in programmes that seek to enhance the value of liberty through a diminution of the extent of liberty, especially economic liberty. Further, they see an attack on the inviolability of the human person or on the basic rights of human beings in schemes that force some people through taxation to transfer their resources and earnings to others. Additionally, it is argued that at the economic level it is both contradictory and self-defeating to pursue general welfare by restricting the only long-run effective system for securing economic growth (viz., a market economy).

On the other side, out-and-out socialists, especially Marxist-socialists, may well agree with market philosophers such as Hayek,[3] Nozick,[4] or Friedman[5] in their critique of the mistakes and contradictions allegedly intrinsic to the liberal/social democratic philosophy. They, however, ascribe these contradictions to capitalism itself both in its classical form and in the 'late capitalist' system of which social democracy is conceived to be the ideological reflection. Hence the proper path of progress is revolutionary change which will substitute full, positive, socialist liberty and equality for the merely formal and negative legal or constitutional liberty lauded by classical liberals and essential to the capitalist mode of production in all its manifestations.[6]

These controversies over the liberal/social democratic philosophy and its politico-legal practice require no more than brief allusion. But a reminder concerning them is essential to any proper appreciation of the thought and the writing of H.L.A. Hart. As thinker and as writer, Hart was one of the most important and influential contributors of the postwar period to the liberal/social democratic way of thought and action. He made powerful contributions to the philosophical arguments in favour of the liberalizations of criminal law mentioned in the first paragraph of this section and in favour of a particular conception of humaneness in punishment. These contributions are to be found in his books *Law, Liberty and Morality*; *The Morality of the Criminal Law*; and *Punishment and Responsibility*. His essay "Are There Any Natural Rights?", which propounds the thesis that there is at least one natural right—the right to equal personal freedom of each individual—was disowned by Hart in his later writing on its main point but still contains elements of value that cannot be overlooked.

As advocate of these positions on the liberal front, Hart nevertheless held firm also to the social democratic political and economic philosophy, which was so powerful in the postwar period within the British Labour Party—in whose right wing a prominent role was taken by some of his closest friends and associates. In this context, one should particularly mention Hart's friendship since undergraduate days with the late Douglas Jay, a former member of Parliament and minister and leading contributor to the theory of social democracy.⁷ As evidence of Hart's adherence to the social democratic rather than the classical variant of liberal thought, one may cite his critique of the American political philosopher Robert Nozick. In a book called *Anarchy, State and Utopia*, Nozick purports to establish a conclusive argument in favour of restoring the 'minimal state' favoured by classical liberalism. His argument is grounded in a reassertion of the fundamental character of each individual's rights to 'life, liberty, and estate' as John Locke set this forth three hundred years previously.⁸

Nozick holds, for example, that a system of compulsory income tax is equivalent to partial slavery. (In every five days, a man works three days for himself and two for the state, which compulsorily redistributes its two-fifths part to other men.) By contrast, Hart in "Between Utility and Rights" argued that this was, in effect, a reduction to absurdity of Nozick's own first principles. What is more, Nozick, he said, actually departs from Locke's own version of those first principles, since Locke's version includes the principle that every person has a right to the basic necessities of bodily survival. Hart accepts that the collectivist mode of utilitarian political theory subsumed within much social democratic thought is open to some criticism such as that of Nozick and (in a different vein) of Ronald Dworkin for ignoring the distinctness and individuality of each person. He himself argues that utilitarianism must be qualified and supplemented by independently established principles of justice, as is shown in chapter 12 of the present book. But he found the theories of individual rights advanced by these writers to be (in their different ways) even less convincing at key points than the utilitarianism that they reject. And he remained to the end convinced that a case can be made for the view I have here called 'social democratic'.

If Hart made no other claim on our attention, he would be a significant figure simply for his contribution to the ideology of liberal social democracy. As ideologist he contributed a particularly powerful statement of the liberal element in that way of thinking, exercising considerable influence on the thinking of his contemporaries and juniors, far beyond the normal influence exercised by professors and teachers.

Nobody who reads or thinks about Hart's work dares ignore the fact that he lived through the 1930s and the years of war from 1939 to 1945 and observed, as an intellectual of Jewish family origins, the growth and then the destruction of Fascism and Nazism and their British copies. During his time as a barrister, he lived in an intellectual milieu chiefly of persons committed to competing variants on the socialist theme as the desirable answer to Fascism, to tyranny, and to the injustice of man to man. The weight of his commitment to a certain conception of human liberty is to be seen against that background. His is comparable with the philosophy of Sir Isaiah Berlin,[9] his closest friend.

His commitment to that idea of liberty led him earlier than many of his own generation in the 1930s to a hostility toward the tyranny of Marxist regimes no less blunt than his hostility to Fascism and even to merely conservative moralism. Thus, unlike many contemporaries including Jenifer Williams, his friend and subsequently his wife, he was never even briefly persuaded of the virtues of the Communist party as an alternative to the Fabian or social democratic approach to politics. Apart, however, from work he did helping refugees from Nazi Germany during the 1930s and giving seminars on loopholes in the tax law to Labour Party groups organized by Douglas Jay, his political beliefs and commitments took no public form until after the war. Indeed, his main statements of position in these matters were not published until the early 1960s.

Their roots, however, lie deep in his experience of life, and their importance for an appreciation of his whole achievement as a jurist must not be underestimated. While much of his work aims to be descriptive or purely analytical (and thus requires a deliberate disengagement from issues of personal commitment in matters of morals and politics), that ought not to obscure the seriousness of the commitments he expresses in his other work. No one can be surprised about that seriousness once taking account of the experiences against which the commitments were formed. To be fully aware of this is essential as a prelude to considering the background and the nature of his analytical work.

ANALYTICAL JURISPRUDENCE AND
LINGUISTIC PHILOSOPHY

Hart's position of preeminence among British jurists of the twentieth century rests even more on his analytical work than on his work as a philosophical critic of legal institutions and practices. Let us consider the intellectual context to which his analytical jurisprudence belongs and the end to which it is directed.

The aim of analytical jurisprudence is an improved understanding of law and legal ideas, both for its own sake and for the practical value of such understanding. It is natural that throughout the long history of juristic studies, much attention has always been given to terms and concepts. The reason is not far to seek. Law, the subject matter of jurisprudence, concerns human actions not simply as natural processes but as the social actions of thinking and speaking animals. Law is essentially and irreducibly, though not only, linguistic. Laws are formulated and promulgated in words. Legal acts and decisions involve articulate thought and public utterance—often also public argument. A complicated conceptual framework and indeed a large and partly specialized vocabulary are essential to the structuring of the wide range of practices and activities which constitute a legal order. Hence, the understanding of law requires elucidation and analysis of the complex conceptual framework involved. Not merely is jurisprudence an activity conducted linguistically through private thoughts as well as the written and spoken word; that which it studies is an activity that is also conceptual and linguistic in its very essence. So Hart's, like anyone else's, attempt to clarify the nature of legal order is inevitably, in part at least, linguistic in focus and concern.

It is, nevertheless, a special feature of Hart's work that it is linguistic in a stronger sense, for he was one of the leading proponents of what is sometimes called 'linguistic analysis' or 'ordinary language philosophy'. This makes it necessary to give a brief account of the philosophical school in which Hart developed his approach to analytical jurisprudence. Whereas 'reform' is the watchword of his critical morality, we have already noted that 'revolution' was the philosophical banner raised by Hart and his colleagues in postwar Oxford.[10] They claimed to be effecting a revolution in philosophy by rescuing it from a series of misunderstandings about language. Clear ideas needed clarification of speech, not elaborate constructions of philosophical systems.

A famous text illustrating this approach is Gilbert Ryle's *The Concept of Mind*,[11] whose title Hart's own main book, *The Concept of Law*, was later to echo. Many of the questions central to the philosophy of western Europe since its beginnings in classical Greece have focused on the nature of the human mind and its relation to the physical universe. Since questions of philosophy have at their centre questions about what there really is and how we can know what there really is—how our minds can apprehend 'reality'—questions about the mind and its relationship to matter have an obvious importance. Equally, in moral and political philosophy, the question of how minds can control physical human bodies is vital. The issues of responsibility for acts and of freedom of the will seem fundamental to any view of human beings as moral agents whose acts really are *their* acts and are not merely elements in a physical process over which they have, at best, an illusion of being in control.

Ryle's thesis was that the way philosophers had traditionally gone at the question of the existence and working of the mind was itself the source of the problems they sought to resolve. The invention of and concentration on nouns like *soul, mind, intention, will,* and so forth conjured up a seemingly irresistible belief in the existence of a 'ghost in the machine' which in turn made it seem highly problematic how the ghost made the machine work. The answer was not to go on beavering away at constructing theories of the ghost but to start afresh with new questions. The new questions take us back to ordinary nonphilosophical speech. What do we mean when we say "Smith did that intentionally", "Jones did that of his own free will", "Macdonald has it in mind to take a holiday in France this year"? Do not ask what 'mental condition' is involved in 'being happy', 'being angry', 'being sad', or the like. The notion of a 'mental condition' is a philosophical invention by way of bogus explanation of these states of affairs, and it actually itself generates the problem of the ghost in the machine. Ask rather in what conditions we can truly say in ordinary English that someone 'is happy', 'is angry', 'is sad', or whatever. That is all that there is to be explained. There is no problem of the mind over and above a recognition of all the ways we ordinarily have as English (or German, or French) speakers for talking about people's acts, expressions of attitude, and so forth.

An even more influential colleague of Hart's was J. L. Austin, who (after war service as an army intelligence officer) returned to his prewar position as Fellow in philosophy at Magdalen College, becoming White's Professor of Moral Philosophy in Oxford University from 1952 until his early death in 1960. Much of his most important work was posthumously published in the next few years on the basis of lecture notes.[12] In his *Sense and Sensi-*

bilia, Austin challenged the basis of much previous work on the theory of perception. Philosophical talk about 'sense data' and such simply misrepresented the way people talk about seeing and hearing things. Philosophers treat nouns like *reality* or *truth* as names calling for investigation of what 'lies behind' them—what is reality, what is truth? But they would do better to go back to adjectives. What distinctions do we draw when we call some things *real*, others *unreal*? What are we doubting if we ask whether this is a real duck? Are we concerned about its being an optical illusion or about its being a decoy duck? When can we say that some sentence is true or not true? What are the conditions for making such judgments? That is worth knowing by contrast with pursuing investigations into truth as such.

> What needs discussing . . . is the use, or certain uses, of the word 'true'. *In vino*, possibly, '*veritas*' but in a sober symposium '*verum*'.[13]

To one who takes seriously consideration of the conditions for the truth or falsity of what people say, a striking fact appears, namely that by no means everything that anyone says is either true or false. This is not just a matter of distinguishing expressive or emotive or poetic utterances from ordinary observations of fact. The point, as Austin put it in an influential paper,[14] is that many utterances are 'performative'. To *do* certain things you have to *say* certain words, for example, to make a promise ("I promise to meet you tonight"), to name a ship ("I name this ship *Titanic*"), to convict a person ("Guilty") or acquit him ("Not guilty"). The insight was one he shared with Hart.[15] These ways of using words are just as important and just as worthy of philosophical attention as statements, though *true* and *false* apply only to statements.

To begin with, Austin presented this as a distinction between performative and non-performative utterances. Later however (in the posthumously published lectures *How to Do Things with Words*), he improved and extended the doctrine. He drew attention to the fact that to utter *any* words is to perform an act—the act of making a statement, or of promising, or of recording a verdict, or of conferring a name; his name for such an act was a 'speech act'. The study of these types of acts required reflection on and clarification of the social rules or conventions that make possible the performance of any such acts when a person utters certain articulate sounds. Hence such philosophizing is not a merely trivial matter of verbal questions and disputes. It is the discovering and making plain of the social context that give words their sense. It is a matter of attending to words in order to find out about the world.

Austin's approach parallels the work pursued at more or less the same time in Cambridge by Ludwig Wittgenstein and his circle, work which became known to the world at large with the publication of *Philosophical Investigations* [16] in 1953. This book represented Wittgenstein's reaction against his own earlier work (in association with Bertrand Russell). In this, he had adopted the notion of the world as a vast aggregation of 'atomic facts' that could be grasped only by the construction of a logically perfect language, which would faithfully depict every fact and nothing else. Dissatisfied with this 'picture' theory of language, Wittgenstein directed his later attention to the real uses of everyday speech and philosophical speech. Speaking a language, he concluded, is not a matter of setting out to produce a series of verbal pictures of 'facts'. There might indeed be a kind of 'language-game' that could be constructed with a view to doing simply that; but it would be a special game with rules of its own, and it would coexist with a whole range of other already existing 'language-games' each with rules of their own. His talk of 'games' was not a wilful trivialization of his subject matter. Rather, it was a way of getting at the point that every language expresses a 'form of life', a collaboration of individuals made possible by their sharing in a common way of life structured by partly explicit and partly inexplicit but commonly understood conventions. Hence the analogy of games.

So there was a convergence in ideas between Wittgenstein and his Cambridge followers and the proponents of 'linguistic analysis' in the Oxford mode. They shared the view that philosophers must be alert to the way in which language, and particularly the technical jargon employed in traditional approaches to philosophy, can itself be the very source of philosophers' problems about the nature of the world. Words do not always and necessarily 'stand for' things, so before we dash into inquiries about the supposed things for which they stand, we must carefully work out the ways in which and the conditions under which words are used meaningfully in the languages we speak. A chief task for philosophy is therefore that of working toward an interpretive understanding of normal human discourse in its normal social settings.

For present purposes, enough has been said to fill out a point mentioned earlier, concerning the way in which the new philosophical movement that Hart joined was one to which his practising experience of law had an important relevance. Although the interests quickened by his wartime reading of works of G. E. Moore, L. S. Stebbing, Schlick, Isaiah Berlin, and A. J. Ayer had seemed to lead him clean away from any sort of legal concerns, he was soon enough led back to them. It is easy to explain why this came about.

Among the questions raised by Ryle's *Concept of Mind* are questions about the nature of 'mental states', and the new school of thought interpreted these questions as requiring reflection on the proper use of such terms as *intention, motive*, and the like. But to understand the use of such terms, it is necessary to reflect on the contexts in which they are characteristically used. A famous illustration of this is the "Plea for Excuses",[17] which J. L. Austin made in his Presidential Address to the Aristotelian Society in 1956 (the argument in the paper having been developed earlier in a seminar jointly run by Hart and Austin at Oxford during the 1950s).

Austin's thesis was that concern over whether someone has or had a certain intention is characteristically raised in a context where moral blame or legal punishment is in issue. The context is one in which an untoward occurrence has come about, and we want to know who, if anyone, was to blame. Did some act of this or that person cause the accident? If it did, the person concerned is apt to be held responsible and blameworthy— but not if he had a justification or a good excuse. A possible good excuse is that he did the deed in question *unintentionally*. To generalize, the primary point of references to intention or the lack of it is by way of rebutting or (as the case may be) establishing excuses for ostensibly blameworthy acts. So the proper inquiry for someone who wants to understand about 'intention' is an inquiry into the range of excusing conditions that are accepted as eliding or mitigating responsibility for one's acts. The same would go for concepts like that of 'will', as related to the notice that some acts are 'wilful', others not—again in the context of decisions about responsibility and blameworthiness.

To take this line is necessarily to treat lawyers' practices as highly significant for philosophy. The very terms like *intent* or *intention* in which the criminal law is framed by legislators and applied by judges and lawyers are key terms for philosophers. These terms are used in the context of a social practice that gives them sense and that is publicly available for scrutiny and analysis. No doubt lawyers' theoretical analyses of *intention, will*, and such like terms might have defects akin to—even inherited from— those of traditional mental philosophy. But a study of the practical legal use of the terms, as distinct from lawyers' abstract theorizings about them, must be a key to a new understanding of the meaning of *mind*. Likewise, from the point of view of an interest in how people 'do things with words', an interest in such legal activities as conveyancing, contracting, or legislative drafting—all ways of making words 'operative', as Hart has put it—is unavoidable.

It is therefore not at all surprising to find that an early fruit of Hart's return to philosophy was the presentation in 1949 of his seminal, but subsequently disowned, essay on 'The Ascription of Responsibility and Rights'.[18] His point here was that *responsibility* or *rights* are not *descriptive* features of human beings, but are *ascribed* to them in contexts determined by legal or other social rules. Hence the character of such ascription has to be considered, and upon consideration it is found both to be dependent upon rules and yet to have a *defeasible* character. There is a range of settled grounds for ascribing to persons responsibility for some act or state of affairs and for ascribing to them rights over something or other. But one can defeat such ascriptions by showing that some exceptional circumstances exist, and in practice it appears that the list of exceptional circumstances is not necessarily a closed one. Rules for ascription are hence open-ended, since the ascription holds good only if nothing has vitiated it, and the conditions of such defeasance need not be—perhaps cannot be—exhaustively listed in advance of the particular cases that come up for decisions.

Interesting though this essay was as an example of the new style of philosophy and of its natural concern with legal questions, it was not of itself a work of such evident preeminence as to make its author the obvious candidate for the vacant Chair of Jurisprudence in 1952. To those outside the particular circle of younger philosophers and jurists who knew him and his work, Hart's appointment must at the time have seemed a surprising one. Yet, as I have already said, it did not take long for his work to stir up interest and controversy.

In the inaugural lecture that provoked so strong a response from Professor Bodenheimer, Hart set about showing the relevance of the new philosophy to long-standing problems in jurisprudence. In the case of concepts like *right* and *corporation*, lawyers no less than philosophers had gone head-on at questioning what such things are as if definitions could solve the difficulties to which such terms give rise. This had resulted in 'the growth of theory on the back of definition'. The aim of such work was a laudable 'effort to define notions actually involved in the practice of a legal system'. Unhappily the result was one of failure 'to throw light on the precise work they do there'. A fresh and more fruitful approach would be to elucidate the conditions in which true statements are made in legal contexts about rights, corporations, etc. and the point that such statements have in these practical contexts. Here was an obvious case for applying the linguistic philosophers' programme of studying the use of words in context rather than the pursuit of mysterious essences or the construction of theories to justify definitions.

The same approach was carried on in the joint work with A. M. Honoré on *Causation in the Law*.[19] There again we find a two-handed attack both on arid formalism, the elaboration of high-level conceptual constructs inept for practical application, and on any excessive so-called realism that seeks to portray every legal ascription of cause to effect as nothing other than a mere act of judicial policy making tailored to a judge's hunch or prejudice about the fair outcome of a case. *Causation* deserves recognition both for its exhaustive scholarly scrutiny of a huge range of civil and criminal case law drawn from many English-speaking jurisdictions and for the contribution its authors made to improving and refining a necessary conceptual tool for lawyers. It also represents the partial fulfilment of Hart's hope to reconcile scientific and commonsense modes of thought. It has perhaps been unduly overshadowed by the success of *The Concept of Law*, in which Hart's analytical jurisprudence was finally brought to the point of a general analysis of the nature of law itself.

Of the philosophical context to which Hart responded and contributed, enough has been said. Of the legal, there is, perhaps, less to be said. Hart's view of law was primarily formed by experience in practice, not in the academic world. This is no doubt reflected in the way he tried to build a bridge directly from linguistic philosophy to practical law in his inaugural lecture and in the criticisms he offered of prior legal theory in the same lecture (though even in that he was already paying tribute to the analytical insights he found in Bentham's early writings). Yet others ahead of him—as he readily acknowledged in a review article [20] of the same period—had stepped out upon juristic paths similar to his own, none more noticeably than Professor Glanville Williams in a series of articles on 'Language and the Law'. [21]

In the main, however, jurisprudence, as the general study of law and legal ideas by contrast with the particular scholarly study of major areas of positive law, was in the doldrums in Britain in 1952. Two great movements in nineteenth-century thought had gone stale. On the one hand there was a tradition of analytical jurisprudence, Benthamite in intellectual inspiration but based immediately on John Austin's *Province of Jurisprudence Determined* and *Lectures on Jurisprudence*. On the other hand there was the school of historical jurisprudence stemming from Sir Henry Maine's *Ancient Law*, itself in part a reaction against Austinian theory. The former tended to pre-dominate in academic teaching and writing but in a way that cut it adrift from its philosophical roots. Lawyers had stopped being interested in philosophy, philosophers in law. Jurisprudence in the universities had become a routine reading and rereading of a canon of texts and textbooks. Excepting a handful of brilliant exceptions, the subject was moribund.

Hart certainly succeeded in regenerating excitement and interest in jurisprudence. He did so not by abandoning traditional areas of conceptual study, as the American realists did in the law schools of the United States in the 1930s, but by redefining and reexamining the traditional questions in the style and spirit of the new philosophy. Thereby he excited the legal imagination to reconsideration of the philosophical significance of legal problems, while at the same time forcefully recalling philosophers to an awareness of legal problems as vital ones both for analytical philosophy and for moral and political philosophy. The reexamination of the traditional questions involved a reexamination of the traditional texts, above all Austin's *Province of Jurisprudence Determined*. It is not at all surprising to find that Hart's *Concept of Law* spends three initial chapters teasing out difficulties about Austin's jurisprudence before announcing a fresh start. The fresh start was made from a station in which the locomotive of British jurisprudence seemed to have broken down. Naturally and rightly, the man who did most to get things moving again became for English-speaking jurists the focal figure of the succeeding fifty years.

Some subsequent work has in different ways explored and refined the insights of Hartian positivism. Some work has sought to restate more traditional natural law theory in a way that takes account of Hart's work. Some work has aimed at the pursuit of 'law in context', some, such as my own, at a kind of post-positivist legal institutionalism. Reaction to the claim in the preface of *C.L.* that it is in part a work of 'descriptive sociology' of law has involved a ferment of essentially anti-Hartian sociology of law, paralleled in a way by the Critical Legal Studies Movement. As noted earlier, Ronald Dworkin's 'interpretive' account of law and legal thought emerged from a critique of Hartian positivism. Legal theory (jurisprudence, philosophy of law, sociology of law, socio-legal studies, law, and economics) presents a hugely changed intellectual landscape from that of 1952. Hart is, of course, not entitled to credit for all of that, but it is difficult not to give him credit for having had a huge catalytic effect, and for having made a major contribution, some of whose elements will endure for many years yet.

CHAPTER THREE

Hart's Conception of Law

The task of this book is to give a constructive critique of Hart's jurisprudence, so there will have to be close scrutiny of its elements. As a preliminary to that, it seems desirable to present in this chapter a concise description of Hart's main positions unencumbered for the present with any critical comment on these. A résumé in plain terms of the whole will provide at least a sketch-map against which to check the succeeding critical investigation of its parts.

A RÉSUMÉ OF HART'S JURISPRUDENCE

The main text for consideration as presenting Hart's general legal theory is, of course, *The Concept of Law*. The theory there presented is of a legal system as a system of social rules, social in a double sense: both in that they govern the conduct of human beings in societies and in that they owe their origin and existence exclusively to human social practices. As social rules, they belong to a general class to which also belong such diverse other types of rule as rules of morality, of manners and etiquette, of games, of speech, etc. Two features differentiate them from this general class. The first is that, like moral rules, they are concerned with 'obligations' or 'duties', that is, they make certain conduct 'obligatory' or 'binding'. As such, they amount to a kind of 'peremptory' reason for action. The second is that, unlike moral rules, they have a systemic quality depending on the interrelationship of two kinds of rules, 'primary rules' and 'secondary rules' as Hart calls them.

The primary rules are those that establish obligations and duties and proscribe the forms of wrongdoing that we call *crimes, offences, torts*, or *delicts*. Rules of the other kind are 'secondary' in that they do not themselves constitute binding standards of obligatory conduct. Rather, these other rules relate in various ways to the primary ones, and in this special kind of relationship lies the *systemic* quality of law. For example, there are rules that confer competence on certain people to pass judgment on cases of alleged wrongs (i.e., breaches or infractions of primary rules). This power to adjudicate can be, and in modern states is, coupled with a further power either to order the performance of some remedial action by wrongdoers (e.g., payment of damages) or to impose punishments on them. These might take the form of an order to another competent person or persons to take away their liberty or even life or to punish them physically in some other way. Such rules involving the competence of officials do not impose duties but confer powers, powers of judging and of law enforcement. Compendiously, Hart calls these rules about judging and law enforcement 'rules of adjudication'.

In modern law, both the primary rules of obligation and the secondary rules of adjudication (like almost all other legal rules) are susceptible to deliberate change by legislative amendment and repeal, by the enactment of new rules, and possibly also by judicial decisions or even social customs. This process of change is itself rule regulated, in the sense that there are rules, secondary rules again, which confer on individually or generically identified persons or groups (such as parliaments, presidents, ministers) power to enact legislation by specified and more or less complex procedures.

These 'secondary rules of change' have a parallel in lower order secondary rules that empower ordinary individuals to make various changes in the legal position or legal relationships of themselves and others. To do so, they must have the requisite legally defined characteristics in the way of legal status and legal capacity. One may undertake duties by making contracts; one may alter the incidence of the laws prohibiting theft by exercising a power to give or to sell a certain piece of property to another. One may impose obligations on others (trustees) by giving them property subject to certain trusts, or on yet others (executors) by making a will which they are duty bound to implement. One may get married or form a partnership or a limited company. The possibility of all such exercises of private power depends on the existence of relevant power-conferring secondary rules, whose existence may itself derive from the exercise by a legislator of the public power of legislative change.

In addition to primary rules of obligation and secondary rules of adjudication and change, every legal system includes a further secondary rule essential to its distinct existence as a legal system. This is what Hart calls a 'rule of recognition'. The rule of recognition lays down the criteria that determine the validity of all the other rules of a particular legal system. Whereas the secondary rules of adjudication and change are power-conferring, the rule of recognition lays down duties binding on those who exercise public and official power, especially the power to adjudicate. If those who have power to act as judges are also duty bound as judges to apply all and only those rules that satisfy certain more or less clearly specified criteria of validity, then the whole body of rules which those judges have power to administer has a relatively determinate or determinable content.

That relatively determinate group of rules is the one these judges must apply to all those over whom they have jurisdiction (i.e., power to adjudicate). For that population and within a certain territorial area, there is then a 'legal system'. It is the system made up of the rule of recognition and all those other rules of adjudication and change (public and private) and of obligation or duty that are valid by reference to the criteria of validity contained in the rule of recognition. For example, a certain group of judges having jurisdiction over everyone in territory T is held to be duty bound to apply all unrepealed rules enacted by a certain legislature L, all judicial precedents of those judges and their predecessors except the ones that conflict with rules enacted by L, and all customary rules observed in T except the ones that conflict either with rules enacted by L or with binding judicial precedents. All rules that satisfy any of these three criteria then belong to the legal system of T, and the legal system comprises that rule of recognition (here, the rule that judges must apply every rule satisfying the three criteria) and all those other rules.

But the legal system in question 'exists' as the legal system of T only if it is effectively in force. For this it is a necessary condition that the bulk of the inhabitants of T do, most of the time, comply with the primary rules requiring them to do certain things and to omit others. Some may do so willingly because they regard the rules as 'binding law'; others may do so only reluctantly and for fear of sanctions (criminal punishments and civil remedies) enforced by officials having both legal powers of adjudication and that collective force which organized groups of people can deploy. Almost the whole population could even be in this state of passive and coerced obedience.

The officials themselves, however, must have a somewhat different view. For, as we saw, the 'legal system' requires by definition a rule of recognition, a rule prescribing official duties to apply certain rules as 'law'. But for that rule itself to exist, it is necessary that the officials at least observe it as a binding social rule. They must accept it and observe it 'from the internal point of view'. This is a key phrase of Hart's, as we shall see.

That entails, of course, that they do, as a matter of duty, apply more or less faithfully all those other rules which are 'valid' precisely because they satisfy the relevant criteria of recognition. The rule of recognition, if it is to exist at all, exists only as a shared social rule *accepted as a binding common standard of behaviour* by those whose official power as a 'legal power' is dependent ultimately upon that very rule. It is possible, but not necessary, for citizens at large (few, some, many, or even, in a limiting case, all) to share in the attitude of support for the ultimate rule of recognition. But it is sufficient that only governors and officials so accept it, provided that by some means they can procure obedience and conformity in large measure to the other rules that it validates.

A system of rules that is, in this sense, effectively in force in a territory is, according to Hart, the central case of a legal system. But although it is the central case falling within the concept of law, there are other cases. There are instances of primitive forms of human social community whose members acknowledge a common set of primary rules of obligation, without having yet developed any power-conferring rules setting up some of their number as adjudicators of alleged breaches of duty, far less any power-conferring rules enabling anyone by any process to procure deliberate legislative change in the basic rules by which the community lives. An almost parallel case is presented by modern international law, which lacks any central adjudicative organ with compulsory powers and lacks any method other than the cumbersome one of multilateral treaties for procuring changes in the rules of law to meet perceived changes in the circumstances of interaction among states. There may be, or may have been, many cases intermediate between such rudimentary modes of social coexistence and the complex and highly integrated form of legal system found within modern states, comprising a 'union of primary and secondary rules' effectively in force among a population within a territory. All are in some sense instances of law.

There are, however, important differences of form and structure between primitive forms of law and developed legal systems. These differences exhibit themselves, for example, in the inapplicability in primitive law of terms and concepts essential in the description of modern states and daily current in everyman's speech, terms such as *power, right, official, judge, penalty, corporation, trust, legislature*, and indeed *state* itself. A self-proclaimed virtue of Hart's analysis is that it provides an analytical framework for the elucidation of such 'legal concepts' with which generations of legal and political thinkers had more or less ineffectually wrestled.

Despite these differences of form and structure there are essential similarities of *content* and *function* as between the primitive and the developed cases. These similarities make it natural to think of the concept *law* as including *primitive law* and *international law* alongside the more central instance of the developed legal system of a territorial state. As to content, all such social orderings contain among their primary rules certain basic prohibitions on interpersonal violence, deception, free taking and use of valued things, dishonesty, breaches of promise, and such like. The explanation for this is in terms of social function. Human beings, having the physical and emotional makeup they have and living in the kind of terrestrial environment they inhabit, need to coexist in social groups if they are to survive as most of them most of the time wish to do. But individual and group survival of such beings so circumstanced depends on common observance of common rules covering at least the matters mentioned. What is more, in most but not all forms of society, successful maintenance of that rule observance depends on some organized practice of enforcing conformity to the rules by imposing sanctions on miscreants in order that those who are prepared to cooperate voluntarily do not fall victim to those who would exploit their complaisance.

In this statement of the basic point of legal order in all its manifestations, Hart sees a germ of truth in what have come to be known as theories of 'natural law'. There are natural features of human existence which make it necessary for human beings (those who have a drive for survival) to participate in social orderings. This provides the basis for a minimum content of natural law essential to collective survival.

Just because such rules are important to human beings, they also feature as elements in any code of conduct that might be considered a moral code. The basic legal rules are also, from almost any point of view, basic moral rules. To that extent, there is an inevitable overlap between *law* and *morality*. What is more, since moral values represent profound commitments for individuals who hold them, those who exercise legal powers of adjudication and change in developed societies may see reason to secure that the law expresses sound morality according to their view of it. In a perhaps conflicting way, they will surely see reason also to avoid affronting the moral commitments of any sizeable group among the citizenry. Otherwise the system's efficacy may be put seriously at risk. So even where law and morality have become differentiated as a result of the evolution of a legal system, there is always some overlap in the content of legal and moral orders and considerable reciprocal influence between them.

True as all that is, it does *not* mean that law is in any sense *derived* from moral principles as a preexisting higher order of normative system governing humanity. Nor is it the case that there is some necessary *conceptual* link between the legal and the moral. There are many and various contingent links dependent on functional similarity. There is even the possibility that (as in the legal systems within the United States since 1787 and the Federal Republic of Germany since 1949) the rule of recognition of some states may explicitly include certain moral principles as governing principles for that legal order.

Because of his insistence on the absence of any necessary conceptual link between law and morality, Hart holds himself to be a legal 'positivist'. Positivists deny that law as such is essentially moral and affirm that the existence of a law is always a conceptually distinct question from that of its moral merit or demerit. Hart, like all positivists, rejects the tenets of 'natural law' theorizing as propounded by thinkers as diverse as Aristotle, Aquinas, Grotius, Locke, Kant, Stammler, L. L. Fuller and, most recently, John Finnis.

In adopting the positivist position on this point, Hart deliberately follows the line of the two greatest English jurisprudents of the past, Jeremy Bentham and John Austin. Just as they do, Hart affirms that natural lawyers' moralization of the concept of law tends either toward a form of extreme conservatism (whatever is law must be moral, therefore all law is morally binding) or toward revolutionary anarchism (since whatever is law must be moral, governments must be disobeyed or even overthrown if what they propound as law is not morally justified). The proper attitude to law is, as against that, one which acknowledges that the existence of law depends on complex social facts and which therefore holds that all laws are always open to moral criticism. For there is no *conceptual* ground for supposing that the law which *is* and the law which *ought to be* coincide.

Indeed, as Hart frankly acknowledges towards the end of his book (*C.L.* ch. 9 pp. 209–10), one basis for adhering to the positivist thesis of the conceptual differentiation of law and morals is itself a moral reason. The point is to make sure that it is always open to the theorist and the ordinary person to retain a critical moral stance in face of the law that actually exists. It might be very bad law indeed, and history is full of examples of cruelly oppressive uses of law. The positivist thesis makes it morally incumbent upon everyone to reject the assumption that the existence of any law can ever itself settle the question what is the morally right way to act.

For that reason it is proper to stress that Hart's analytical description of legal systems is powerfully complemented by his critical moral philosophy. His work as an exponent of the principles of liberal social democracy is his response to the moral demands of his positivist position according to which the law as it is must always be held open to criticism and reform. In the moral criticism of the positive law and in promoting what, by his moral principles, have been highly desirable reforms, Hart played his full part.

Whereas he took the Benthamite-cum-Austinian stance on the absence of a conceptual link between law and morality, and while indeed his critical moral philosophy drew heavily on the utilitarian liberalism of Bentham and John Stuart Mill, Hart departed sharply from their view of what law is. He agreed with them that for any law there are 'social sources' (his term, not theirs). But he disagrees about the nature of those sources. Hart's theory of law as a system of social rules, a 'union of primary and secondary rules', is radically different from Bentham's and Austin's accounts of law and laws.[1] For them, the rules of a legal system are (in the main) 'commands' issued by political superiors to subjects within political societies. 'Political superiors' are those whom others, for any reason whatsoever, *habitually* obey. And those superiors who do not themselves habitually obey any higher superior are sovereigns. Laws are commands issued directly or indirectly by sovereigns to subjects. The point about 'commands' is that (as distinct from requests, invitations, etc.) they imply the threat of a sanction to be enforced against those who do not comply.

Hart's theory of social rules is constructed on the basis of a critique of these notions. In particular, it turns on the inadequacy of the notion of 'habit', which relates to *external* regularities of behaviour, to capture the *internal* attitude essential to the full and proper elucidation of the idea of a rule. Thus, while agreeing that law always and necessarily derives from 'social sources', Hart disagrees profoundly with Bentham and Austin as to the proper characterization of those sources. His doctrine here also differentiates him from the greatest of the other legal positivists among his own near contemporaries, Hans Kelsen.[2] For Kelsen, as for Hart, law is intrinsically *normative*; that is, it determines what ought to be done relative to a certain form of social order, not what actually *is* done. As a follower of Kant, Kelsen takes this to mean that there is a separate category of human thought, the category of the *ought*, which is radically distinct from the *is* and from that principle of causality, which is presupposed in all our thought about natural processes. Hart disagrees. To understand the normativity of legal, moral, or other social rules, we need only reflect on human *attitudes* to human action. This we shall see in chapter 4.

Kelsen's 'Pure Theory of Law' aims to establish what makes possible knowledge of the law as an objective normative order. His answer is that whoever interprets law normatively as a jurist necessarily presupposes a non-positive 'basic norm', according to which the human act of creating the historically first constitution of a given legal order is valid and ought to be obeyed. Such a presupposition has a rational foundation if the legal norms that the constitution itself validates are effectively in force in the territory to which the constitution belongs. He thus considers that the task of the jurist is concerned with 'pure' legal cognition, having no concern with descriptive sociology, psychology, politics, economics, or ethics. The juristic task is to produce a rationally structured representation of all the norms of law that are valid according to the presupposed basic norm. Kelsen's theory in effect sets out the framework for such a rationally structured representation of a legal order. This has to take into account also his further assumption that an identifying characteristic of law is the way in which it authorizes particular legal 'organs' to apply coercive sanctions to persons in the event of their acting in certain ways. Hart several times acknowledged his debt to Kelsen's analysis of legal order as he established it on the above premises. His own hermeneutic concerns, however, led him to give an account of rules, duties, and authority that relates these concepts both to particular social contexts and to individual or group attitudes. In doing so, he rejected Kelsen's programme for a 'pure' theory of law; his own debt here being, ultimately, to Hume, while Kelsen's is to Kant.

A final and necessary point to make about Hart's legal positivism concerns the relative indeterminacy of social rules and thus also of legal rules. As against the 'rule-scepticism' of leading twentieth-century American proponents of 'realistic' jurisprudence, Hart does indeed affirm that law essentially comprises *rules*. He further affirms that a great part of legal business consists in the straightforward and uncontroversial application, observance, and enforcement of rules. But he accepts, in partial agreement with the realists, that rules cannot settle everything. Being framed in language, rules are 'open-textured' and often vague. What they prescribe or prohibit or enable can be totally unclear in problem cases. Yet decisions must be reached, and by the hypothesis, the rules can be no more than one inconclusive factor in making and justifying the decision.

So Hart concludes that within the framework of rules whose meaning is clear enough for some purposes, there is and must be a considerable range of *discretion* left open to judges and other officials. And in exercising this discretion, they necessarily and properly have regard to *nonlegal* factors such as moral and political opinion, expediency, and *raison d'état*, as well as reflecting on the general background of legal rules and principles for such guidance as they can give. 'The law' is not an entire, complete, and closed normative system that can, even in principle, determine for all purposes everyone's rights. A suitable metaphor might compare law in action to a musical performance that is only partly covered by the musical score. The performers have to do a certain amount of improvisation, and while they should try to follow the general spirit of the melody as gathered from the incomplete score—a matter in which some performers show greater virtuosity than others—it is a delusion to suppose that there is just one way of filling in the gaps so as to achieve a uniquely proper fit with the parts that the score does completely state.

In thus trying to meet the realist critique of the formalism that may appear to be implicit in any theory that says law is a system of rules, Hart has laid himself open to attack on the opposite flank from those who deny his doctrine of judicial discretion. Most prominent in this line of attack is Ronald Dworkin, his successor as Professor of Jurisprudence at Oxford. In its mature forms, says Dworkin, the law completely determines everyone's rights.[3] The judges have no business to do other than render to every person his or her rights. This is not, in the Hartian sense, a discretionary task, though it is a difficult and inescapably controversial question *what* rights exactly the law does grant in what contexts to what persons. That question calls for an anxious exercise of the adjudicator's best judgement, and this can be said to involve discretion in a 'weak sense'; but it is weak precisely because it is only an interpretative discretion. There is just one improvisation on the scored melody which is uniquely right and fitting, can we but find it.

The grounding of Dworkin's thesis lies in what we might call 'social rule scepticism'. Law is not just a social practice which spawns social rules. The legal order stems from a background morality some of whose principles are embodied in political institutions. That background morality is the morality of the political community to which the law belongs. The rules made by institutional office holders are a partial and incomplete embodying of the principles of the community's morality, understood as the set of principles that best justifies the historical record of the institutional decisions accumulated over time. The rights of legal persons are founded in these institutional principles and are only partly concretized via explicit rules. Hence silence or ambiguity in the rules merely obliges us to have direct recourse to the principles that are the true and ultimate ground of legal rights, anyway.

Not merely does Hart's theory significantly fail to embark on any substantial discussion of principles to parallel his discussion of rules. Thereby it is also seen to fall into such error as always befalls theories which mistake the part for the whole. Hence Dworkin's critique of the Hartian positivist doctrine of discretion leads him back to a radical critique of the doctrine of the social sources of law in Hart's version. In his final contribution, the *Postscript* to *The Concept of Law*, Hart doggedly reaffirmed his positivist position, though acknowledging that he ought to have attended more closely to the elements of legal reasoning in problem cases. He acknowledged the importance of argument from principles in such cases but denied that there was any basis on which to contend that these can always, or even often, point to a single correct answer such that the judge exercises only weak discretion in finding it. A later chapter will discuss whether the Hartian theory of social rules can indeed be extended to give a fully coherent theory of principles and other practical standards of conduct and of their role in legal reasoning.

At this point, one can deem complete the preliminary sketch of Hart's analytical philosophy of law. This sketch highlights three main points: (i) the social sources of law and the theory of legal rules as a special kind of social rules; (ii) the absence of a necessary conceptual link between morality and positive law, despite the manifest overlap of content and function between these; and (iii) the necessary incompleteness or open-ended quality of positive law, implying the existence of judicial discretion. The second of these, as was noted, may itself express a moral commitment. The moral commitment is to the freedom and responsibility of every individual, and especially of the analytical theorist, to remain open to moral criticism of positive law. Whatever is, is not necessarily right. In every advanced society there are existing legal rules and dominant moral opinions, these naturally intertwining and overlapping. What it is really right to do remains a question for the sovereign individual who dares not surrender her judgment to that of the lawful government or of the moral majority. She must indeed have regard to the actual law and the positive morality of her community as relevant to what is right; but only relevant to it, not determinant of the issue.

This claim for the sovereignty of individual conscience belongs to the heart of the liberal tradition and bridges the gulf between classical market liberalism and the liberal and social democratic philosophy, of which Hart's work as critical moralist presents an important instance. It is not clear whether socialists or Marxists can adhere to it without loss of self-consistency at the more fundamental points, though some believe that they can. If indeed they can, Hart's jurisprudential analysis has that ideological neutrality across the three main ideological positions of his times, which analytical work, by its nature, claims for itself (whether or not it is also *correct*). Otherwise, it is indeed a legal theory open for acceptance, if otherwise convincing, only to one or the other variety of liberal. That might itself be a ground for opposing ideological positions that are incompatible with the analytical approach.

ELEMENTS FOR CLOSER SCRUTINY

The foregoing résumé was offered as a sketch-map of Hart's jurisprudence. It may be helpful now to present an account of the areas to be investigated further and the order of proceeding. The first task is a discussion of Hart's theory of social rules (which will be presented as incomplete but improvable in its own terms) and the 'hermeneutic method' he brings to their elucidation (chapter 4). The questions there raised about standards of conduct, which are not rules, lead at once into consideration of his moral theory in chapter 5, and there one can find the germs of a theory of principles and values as standards. This facilitates a discussion in chapter 6 of 'obligation' and related ideas that fall within, but extend considerably beyond, Hart's notion of a primary rule. Following that comes a review of the notion of 'legal power', tied up as it is with Hart's conception of secondary rules (chapter 7)—the eighth chapter being no more that a brief note on Hart's analysis of the concept of a 'right'.

Throughout these chapters, the argument is that the Hartian *method* of analysis is a good one, and that its more rigorous application removes certain difficulties in the conclusions he himself drew. The same goes for chapters 9 and 10, which review the primary elements of law and the 'union of primary and secondary rules', which as Hart presented it in *The Concept of Law* seemed to lead into a logical circle. Chapter 11 is devoted to the judicial role and judicial discretion, covering Dworkin's criticisms. Chapter 12 relates Hart's analysis of sanctions to his philosophy of punishment, and chapter 13 appraises Hart's critical moral philosophy as the background to his legal positivism. Chapter 14 is an epilogue that surveys Hart's latest methodological concerns, especially as he developed these in his own *Postscript*.

CHAPTER FOUR

Social Rules

PRELIMINARY

The sketch of Hart's legal theory offered in the preceding chapter shows it to be a theory of legal order as an order of rules. These rules are a particular variety of social rules. As such they derive from social sources and exist in virtue of social practices. They do not exist in some ideal order or extra-terrestrial universe independent of what men and women living together socially do, say, and think. They are, on the contrary, an element in the doings, sayings, and thinkings of the men and women who live together in human social groupings. As will be seen, Hart represents them as dependent on, or expressions of, the attitudes of human beings toward their own and other humans' conduct and their ways of acting and interacting with each other as conscious agents.

It will be argued that the most distinctive and valuable element in Hart's work as a jurist lies in the way in which he addressed the explanation of laws as social rules and the explanation of social rules. He rejected the idea that rules are some kind of command or imperative. He rejected the ideas that they can be represented as simple behavioural generalizations about outwardly observable regularities in human behaviour and that description of social 'habits' can yield conclusions about social rules. He rejected the related idea that they are only predictive propositions or grounds for predicting how people will act in certain circumstances. He rejected the idea that they are merely expressions of human emotion or feeling.

He maps out a new route to the explanation of social rules dependent on what may be called a 'hermeneutic'[1] approach. This approach owes much to his appreciation and use of the linguistic analysis practised by his friend and contemporary, J. L. Austin,[2] and to themes advanced in Peter Winch's *Idea of a Social Science*.[3] Through Winch's work, Hart connects with the 'linguistic' philosophy put forward by Ludwig Wittgenstein[4] in his later years and also with Max Weber's insistence as a sociologist on the need for interpretive understanding (*verstehen*) as well as outward behavioural description of social actions and social institutions.[5]

There has been some speculation as to the extent to which Hart himself paid close attention to the work of Max Weber. Nicola Lacey draws attention to the fact that John Finnis found in Hart's library an annotated copy of *Max Weber on Law in Economy and Society*.[6] I can perhaps shed a little light on this. In the spring of 1968 when I was a recently elected fellow of Balliol College, Hart visited me at lunch to welcome me as one of the jurisprudence group in the Law Faculty of Oxford University. He was at that time full of enthusiasm for Weber's work, which he was currently reading and thought would be more accessible to law undergraduates than some more philosophical writings. My impression was that up till that time his acquaintance with Weber had been somewhat superficial and even indirect. When Hart ascribes to sociologists the job of *external* description of legal orders, he is presumably referring to Weber's view that the sociologist is not directly concerned with a normative interpretation of law, but with the probability that people in society will respond in certain ways to *their own* normative interpretation of the law. In relation to Weber's attempts to produce a typology of different forms of legal domination and different modes of legal thought or 'rationality' and to relate these to historical developments and changes in society at large, Hart has nothing to say. Indeed, as chapter 10 of the present work indicates, Hart's own account is deficient in its lack of any historical perspective on the development of the modern type of legal institutions covered by his 'secondary rules'. In this respect, his view resembles Kelsen's in so far as he holds that the task of analytical jurisprudence (compare 'the pure theory of law') is to analyse legal concepts for what they are, leaving to sociology the task of establishing the social content of *law* thus elucidated.[7]

However that may be, there is, one way or another, no doubt that Hart owes considerable intellectual debts to various predecessors. Nevertheless, as will be argued in this and following chapters, his practice theory of social rules—and thus of legal rules as a special type of social rules—makes a distinctive, original, and extremely fruitful contribution to jurisprudence.

SOCIAL RULES IN GENERAL

[I]f a social rule is to exist, some [members of the social grouping in question] at least must look on the behaviour in question as a general standard to be followed by the group as a whole. A social rule has an 'internal' aspect in addition to the external aspect which it shares with a social habit and which consists in the regular uniform behaviour which an observer could record. (C.L. p. 56)

That quotation puts squarely before us Hart's basic idea about *rules*. By contrast with those who stress the importance of 'habits', he is denying the possibility of explaining *rules* solely by reference to external regularities of behaviour.[8] To draw on an example of his: observation of the movements of motor vehicles at certain crossroads may reveal a significant statistical regularity whereby an extremely high proportion of the vehicles is observed to stop when a red light shines in their direction. But no such observed or described regularity is or entails a statement of the existence of a *social rule* about vehicle driving. To observe or to state that the pattern 'vehicles stopping when facing a red light' occurs in 99 percent of cases is neither to see nor to say that there is a rule. The same would hold if it were observed that 99 percent of drivers play car radios when stopped at traffic lights.

As the quotation says, however, externally observable regularity or patterning of behaviour is necessary to the explanation of a rule—necessary, but not sufficient. The further necessary element is an element of *attitude* among members of a group whose behaviour does reveal such patterning. 'Drivers stop their vehicles when facing a red traffic light' is (statistically) a descriptive truth about patterns in behaviour. If it is also true that among some members of some group we find 'a critical reflective attitude to [that] pattern of behaviour as a common standard' (*C.L.* p. 57), then the addition of that 'internal' attitude to the 'external' regularity of behaviour is sufficient for the existence of a rule. The rule can be stated in such terms as: 'Drivers ought to stop their vehicles when facing a red traffic light'. Given that *attitude*, the group in question has more than merely a shared 'habit' of stopping when facing a red traffic light, as perhaps its members have a 'habit' of playing car radios when stopped at traffic lights; it has a *rule*.

As points of distinction between 'habit' and *rule*, Hart mentions also two other matters. First, in the case of a *rule* about doing something, deviation from the normal pattern of behaviour is treated as a fault or lapse open to criticism; but failing to act in the way in which there is a general habit of acting 'need not be a matter for any form of criticism'. To carry on our example: people do get criticized for 'jumping the lights', quite apart from any legal enforcement or sanctioning procedures; they don't get criticized for not playing their radios when stopped at the lights. It is quite possible both that there *is* a general habit of playing car radios then and that *no one* gets criticized for not doing so.

Second, in the case of a *rule*, the criticism made when people do deviate from the pattern is regarded as justified or legitimate—their deviating constitutes of itself a good reason for criticism by others, or indeed for self-criticism. This means that those who criticize another's action—jumping the lights, say—are not in turn open to justified criticism for criticizing the original actor. That other himself, or at least other members of the social group, hold such criticism to be proper.

Both of these points Hart makes before he introduces the concept of the 'internal attitude' or 'point of view'. They are, he says, included within it or at any rate fully understandable only with reference to it. Especially with regard to the second, this is obviously the case; the concept of a 'justified' or 'legitimate' criticism itself presupposes social standards, norms, or perhaps even *rules* about how people should deal with each other. And even as to the first, the question of what sorts of reactions by one person to another's doings constitute criticism requires for its answer reference to *attitudes*. We have, therefore, to look more closely at what Hart says about this attitude.

> What is necessary is that there should be a critical reflective attitude to certain patterns of behaviour as a common standard, and that this should display itself in criticism (including self-criticism), demands for conformity, and in acknowledgements that such criticism and demands are justified, all of which find their characteristic expression in the normative terminology of 'ought', 'must', and 'should', 'right' and 'wrong'. (*C.L.* p. 57)

A further feature or element of this *attitude*, providing a further contrast with merely habitual behaviour, is that adults in relation to children or the otherwise uninitiated "strive to teach [and] intend to maintain [the pattern of behaviour as a pattern]" (*C.L.* p. 56). Also, as this seems to imply, people (when acting in relevant circumstances) display or evince their intention to maintain the pattern by actually shaping what they do in accordance with the pattern, at least whenever they become conscious of the eligibility of some alternative. Playing chess, one might be tempted to make an illicit move of one's knight in the hope of getting away with it; but one decides not to because one's *attitude* is one of 'critically reflective' commitment to 'playing the game'; at least, if caught, one acknowledges oneself to be in the wrong. Otherwise, one is not merely 'not playing the game', one is actually failing to play it.

Hart's theory as so far sketched is open to a serious objection. The notions of 'criticism' and 'justified criticism' were said to depend for their explanation on an identification of the postulated attitude; but the attitude appears to be explained centrally by reference to criticism and its justification. It is a 'critical reflective attitude'. This difficulty is not surmounted by his reference to the 'characteristic expression' of the attitude 'in the normative[9] terminology of "ought", "must" and "should", "right" and "wrong".' Such expressions are equally available and equally used (characteristically) in situations where the speaker is not invoking any kind of a social rule. To take a commonplace counterexample to Hart's theory, vegetarians who say that it is wrong to eat the flesh of other animals may be quite well aware that there is no social rule condemning carnivorousness in their community. Yet (whatever the value of their moral opinions) they would make no linguistic error in calling eating flesh 'wrong'. And if they taught their children that it is wrong to eat animal flesh, neither would they be teaching the children an existing social rule, nor would the existence of a social rule be necessarily the outcome of this teaching, however successful.

Despite these problems, Hart's attempt to highlight and focus on an 'internal aspect' of social rules as against mere habits and external regularities of behaviour can legitimately be considered correct in its essentials. Let us first consider the force of the objection to taking the use of normative terminology as a sufficient identifier of the *attitude* Hart is trying to elucidate. What that objection shows is that attitudes matter, but that Hart has been insufficiently subtle in differentiating between relevant attitudes. What is the difference between somebody holding that meat eating is wrong and that same person holding that crossing a red light is wrong or that smoking before the Loyal Toast at formal dinners is wrong?

If there were no differences, the objection laid against Hart would lose force. If there are differences, and there are, how are we to capture them save by trying to understand the differences of judgment expressed in the three given instances of calling something 'wrong'? To capture that, we must grasp what we would be doing if we were the person making these judgments and making them seriously. That is to say that the explanation we seek must be sought not at the level of outward observation, experimentation, etc., but rather at the level of 'hermeneutic' inquiry. We have to interpret the meaning of such judgments from the point of view of being the person who passes judgment rather than from the point of view of one who scrutinizes behaviour from the outside. Hart's introduction of the idea of an 'internal aspect' into the discussion of rules was on this very account a decisive advance for analytical jurisprudence; as P. M. S. Hacker has said, it involved the introduction of the *hermeneutic method* to British jurisprudence.[10] And that method, as will be argued, is the essentially appropriate one to the subject matter.

These considerations suggest that Hart's elucidation of *rules* is not radically mistaken, but is only incomplete. What it rightly does is direct us to the question: what are the *attitudes* to patterns of social acting which, together with some regularity in action (or 'behaviour'), must exist or be held by human beings for it to be true that for some group of human beings a *rule* exists? To answer that crucial question we must start from, but cannot finish with, the materials which Hart has furnished.

THE INTERNAL ASPECT OF RULES RECONSIDERED[11]

A 'critical reflective attitude' can best be understood as comprehending an element of cognition, caught by the term 'reflective', and an element of or relating to volition or will, caught by the term 'critical'. The cognitive element covers the very notion of a 'pattern' of behaviour—a capacity to conceive in general terms some such abstract correlation of a certain act with certain circumstances as 'drivers stopping their cars when facing a red light', 'human beings refraining from eating animal flesh'. It further covers a capacity to appraise actual doings or contemplated doings against that abstract and general pattern and to register instances conforming to, not conforming to, or irrelevant to the pattern. Since the pattern is a generalized one of act-in-circumstances, whenever the circumstances exist, an act is either a conforming or non-conforming one, and when they do not exist, the pattern is irrelevant.

The element of volition or will comprehends some wish or *preference* that the act, or abstention from acting, be done when the envisaged circumstances obtain. Such wish or preference need not be unconditional; commonly, such a preference may be conditional upon the pattern in question being one for which there is and continues to be a shared preference among an at least broadly identifiable group of people. The preference depends on a network of mutual beliefs and expectations.[12] This would apply in the case of a person's preference or wish that those who drive cars in the United Kingdom drive on the left-hand side of the road. This would be pointless if it ceased to be a mutual preference shared by all or most such drivers. Further, as the last example indicates, such a preference or wish need not be conceived as an ultimate wish, a wish for something as an end in itself. I have an ulterior reason for preferring that drivers keep left, namely that adherence to some conventional arrangement (either 'keep left' or 'keep right') will enhance my own and others' safety on the roads, and hence will conduce to the protection of life and limb.[13]

(What distinguishes our imagined vegetarians is that they make no assumption that the pattern of behaviour they favour, not eating meat, is a conventional one or one common to members of the groups in which they move. They hold it to be a preferable pattern to the common one, and their volitional commitment to it is a commitment on a point of principle and hence not in any way conditional upon common or shared observance in a group. This explanation depends upon the account of principles and other standards [as distinct from rules] developed in the later parts of this, and in the next, chapter.)

In so far as it is possible to distinguish between emotional elements and volitional elements in human attitudes, it seems correct to view the 'internal aspect of' or 'internal attitude to' rules as comprehending the volitional rather than the emotional. Hart stresses that the latter is not necessary to what he envisages:

> The internal aspect of rules is often misrepresented as a mere matter of 'feelings' in contrast to externally observable physical behaviour. No doubt, where rules are generally accepted by a social group and generally supported by social criticism and pressure for conformity, individuals may have psychological experiences analogous to those of restriction or compulsion. When they say they 'feel bound' to behave in certain ways they may indeed refer to these experiences. But such feelings are neither necessary nor sufficient for the existence of 'binding' rules. There is no contradiction in saying that people accept certain rules but experience no such feelings of compulsion. What is necessary is that there should be a critical reflective attitude to certain patterns of behaviour as a common standard . . . . (*C.L.* p. 57)

This seems correct in what it says. But it is a deficiency of Hart's account in *The Concept of Law* that he fails to elucidate what is denoted by rules being generally *accepted, supported* by criticism, supported by *pressure* for conformity, and so on. As I have suggested,[14] an elucidation of these features must be by reference to a volitional element: a wish or will that the pattern be upheld, a preference for conforming or non-conforming conduct in relevant circumstances. Such wishes or preferences may be, probably are normally, wishes or preferences for states of affairs which themselves are or conduce to some ultimate ends or values, as John Finnis has argued.[15] But people do have affective or emotional attitudes to whatever they do hold as ultimate ends or values. So we ought not to make the mistake of supposing any entire disjunction between the volitional and the emotional, even while agreeing with Hart that 'feeling bound' in particular is not necessary to the 'internal aspect' of any rule.

SOME KEY TERMS REVIEWED

The foregoing account extends, but is consistent with, the theory expounded in *The Concept of Law*. It enables us to assign clearer meanings to some crucial terms and ideas in Hart's discourse about rules. The notion of an 'internal point of view' or 'internal attitude' is to be understood by reference to those who have and act upon a wish or preference for conduct in accordance with a given pattern. This applies both to their own conduct and to that of those others to whom they deem it applicable, as indicated *inter alia* by the criticisms they make and the pressures they exert.

'Acceptance' of a rule seems to cover two distinguishable attitudes. The stronger case, that of 'willing acceptance', is the same as the above with an elaboration upon it. Not merely has one a preference for observance of the 'pattern', but one prefers it as constituting a rule that one supposes to be sustained by a shared or common preference among those to whom it is deemed applicable. The latter feature, for reasons which will appear, is essential to acceptance of a *rule* as such.

When some people have that attitude of acceptance—*willing acceptance*—a weaker case may also exist. This is found in the case of those who are aware that there are some such willing accepters, who are aware that the rule is held as applicable to themselves, and who therefore have reason (a) to conform to it and so avoid justified criticism of themselves and (b) to prefer that it be generally applied to all others to whom it is held applicable rather than that their own unenthusiastic conformity be taken advantage of. People in this position may be said 'merely to accept' or 'unenthusiastically or reluctantly to accept' or to 'accept without fully endorsing' the rules.

This in turn would enable us to give some sense to the concept of a 'group' of people, which is a key term for but not explained by Hart.[16] From the standpoint of all those who accept (either willingly or reluctantly) a rule, that rule has some more or less determinate range of application to human beings. From that standpoint, all those to whom the rule is applicable constitute a *group*. Often, but not always, the ground for applying the rule is that the persons in question have some common characteristic (apart from the applicability of the rule) that is held to be a reason for the rule's applicability. Often there is more than one rule, even a coherent set of rules, which is held to be applicable to whoever has the relevant characteristic. These are common cases, whether or not the characteristics relate to voluntary choices made by individuals (club membership, agreeing to take part in a certain game), are consequent on voluntary choices (taking a job that requires membership of a trade union because of a closed shop arrangement), or are considerations independent of a person's choice (membership of a family, baptism into a religious faith in childhood, for most people citizenship or nationality, membership in some racial or ethnic grouping). Even brief reflection on these distinctions between criteria of group membership would seem to indicate an interesting typology of differences between rules relative to the groups and types of groups to which they are attached.

What may be noted is the fact that some groups, including the group of citizens of a state (particularly important in a discussion of positive law), are not or are not mainly comprised of volunteers. Hence arises the possibility that people can be judged to be bound to conform to rules that they do not accept even in the weak sense. But, where that is so, such people may find themselves to have strong and purely prudential reasons for avoiding being detected in breach of rules, which once accepted are accepted as applicable to all group members. The strength of these prudential reasons is, obviously enough, proportionate to the numbers, power, and influence of those who do accept the rules and the weight of preference they have for conformity to this or that rule. Hart himself drew attention to this fact, although without explaining all that is necessary to clarify it:

> The external point of view may very nearly reproduce the way in which the rules function in the lives of certain members of the group, namely those who reject its rules and are only concerned with them when and because they judge that unpleasant consequences are likely to follow violation. (*C.L.* p. 90)

The foregoing suggestions aim at clarifying the central ideas of *group*, *member*, *acceptance*, *nonacceptance*, and hence *rejection*, which I would take to imply not merely a possibly passive absence of any wish or preference for conformity to a relevant 'pattern of behaviour', but an active preference for nonconformity, subject only to prudential avoidance of detected nonconformity.

There is a related difficulty about how we are to understand the 'external point of view'. What Hart calls the 'extreme external point of view' is the case of a person who, as an observer of human behaviour, restricts himself to viewing it 'purely in terms of observable regularities of conduct, predictions, probabilities, and signs' (*C.L.* p. 89). Notice that there could be two cases in which one might hold this point of view. First, one might fail to understand or realize that some regularity in human behaviour is ascribable to rule-acceptance-and-observance as explained by Hart. For example, Kafka's novels abound with characters who observe others' behaviour but wholly fail to understand it as being oriented to social rules and conventions. Second, one might adopt the standpoint of a natural scientist or behavioural scientist concerned to establish regularities of human behaviour. Such a scientist might restrict his/her view solely to bodily conditions or movements without regard to supposed subjective grounds for acting held by the population subject to scrutiny. In this second case, the party may be one who, *acting as a scientist*, 'keeps austerely to this extreme external point of view' or may be one who, *acting as a citizen*, accepts the rules of the relevant community. Such a person's scientific observation is not necessarily a pointless enterprise. There are dimensions of understanding other than the hermeneutic, and the methods of natural science, while not relevant to interpreting the orientation of actions to rules, may help us to amend, partly at least, some of our understanding of and attitudes to behaviour and, hence, our readiness to subject it to rules. A case to which Hart drew attention (*L.L.M.* p. 68) was the contribution scientists made during the twentieth century to revolutionizing social attitudes to sexual behaviour.

In a sense this 'extreme external point of view' is a chief or primary target for Hart's criticisms. His argument in the earlier chapters of *The Concept of Law* is aimed at showing why John Austin's mode of theorizing about law is necessarily inadequate. Austin's[17] (and Bentham's[18]) starting point is that of a 'habit of obedience' by a population to an individual or collectivity (the *sovereign*), who issues general commands to the members of that population and has the power and the purpose to inflict some evil by way of sanction upon those who disobey. But to speak only of 'habit' in such a context is, in effect, to confine oneself to viewing conduct 'purely in terms of observable regularities of conduct, predictions, probabilities, and signs'. It is to confine oneself, in short, to the 'extreme external point of view' and thus to commit oneself to a scheme of description or understanding which precludes an adequate representation of rules, including legal rules, as they function within the consciousness of people in society.[19]

So the prime point of attention in relation to the 'extreme external point of view' is a methodological one. The method of observation of conduct from that point of view, however useful it might be for certain scientific purposes, including at least some varieties of sociological inquiry, is inadequate to capture those concepts of lawyers and of laymen that are bound up with rules and standards of conduct. We must have a different point of view. But what point of view?

It is an unsatisfactory feature of Hart's account that he passes too lightly over the other variant—the nonextreme variant, presumably—of the 'external point of view'.

> Statements made from the external point of view may themselves be of different kinds. For the observer may, without accepting the rules himself, assert that the group accepts the rules, and thus may from outside refer to the way in which *they* are concerned with them from the internal point of view. [Alternatively], we can if we choose occupy the position of an observer who does not even refer in this way to the internal point of view of the group. (*C.L.* p. 89)

If there is any point of view which seems to capture that which the Hartian legal theorist as such must hold, it is surely this 'nonextreme external point of view' depicted by Hart. He does, after all, describe himself as a legal positivist, taking as his ground for that the proposition that understanding a law or a legal system in its character as such is a matter quite independent of one's own moral or other commitment to upholding that law or legal system and of one's view as to the moral quality of the law or legal system in question. Hence, precisely what the legal theorist of Hart's school must do is take as his standpoint that of a person who understands and seeks to describe legal rules as they are held from the 'internal point of view' regardless of any commitment he himself has for or against these rules in their internal aspect.

To be an 'outsider' in this sense is neither necessarily to be a member nor necessarily to be a nonmember of the group governed by those legal rules (or, *mutatis mutandis*, some other set or system of social rules). It is simply to hold apart questions of one's own commitments, critical morality, group membership or nonmembership, in order to attend strictly to the task of the descriptive legal or social theorist concerned to portray the rules for what they are in the eyes of those whose rules they are.[20] This is no doubt easier to do if one is, for other purposes, an 'insider'. But that is contingent. This, surely, is the central methodological insight of Hart's analytical jurisprudence. It is what justifies our styling his approach a 'hermeneutic' one.[21]

Further to elucidate this 'nonextreme external point of view', we must refer back to the clarification given earlier of what the 'internal point of view' requires. We saw that it has two elements: cognitive and volitional. Now we may notice two points. The 'nonextreme external point of view' requires (a) full sharing in the *cognitive element* of the 'internal point of view'—the understanding of the pattern or patterns of behaviour as such— and (b) full appreciation of, but not necessarily sharing in, the *volitional element*—the will or preference for conformity to the pattern as a standard. Take a case: I, who am not a practising Christian but who has had much exposure in particular to the Scottish Presbyterian mode of Christian observance, can give an account of the rules and articles of faith by which Presbyterians conduct themselves. I could doubtless do it better if I were or had for some time been a fully committed member of the Church. But my giving a fully adequate descriptive account of the rules and articles of faith would require understanding and appreciation of these as committed members understand them, not volitional commitment by me to them. Here, of course, one touches on a range of subject matter, focal to one strand in the hermeneutic tradition, that is concerned with explanation and interpretation of religious texts and traditions. But there are, as here indicated, other strands. And for that reason, and to avoid the awkwardness of continuing to talk of a 'nonextreme external point of view', I shall henceforward dub that position the 'hermeneutic point of view', and foist this upon Hart in the hope of making clearer an essential but not fully elucidated fulcrum of his theory and methodology. His theory stands or falls upon the truth of the propositions that social rules can only be understood, analysed, and described from this 'hermeneutic point of view' and that legal systems can only be understood, analysed, and described as specialized systems of social rules.

A part of the grounding Hart gives for these propositions is the evidence of linguistic usage, in particular the use of the 'normative terminology of "ought", "must", "should", "right", and "wrong".' What Hart has to tell us here is concerned with the presuppositions implicit in our use of such terminology. Those who speak of what one *ought* to or *must* do or not do, who discourse about what is *right* or *wrong*, reveal themselves as presupposing some standard of rightness or wrongness. That is, they disclose that their point of view is an internal one with respect to such standards. Hence Hart chooses to call statements of the right and the wrong and such like 'internal statements'. That we are familiar with and regularly make or hear such statements is one way of drawing our attention to that very 'internal point of view' that, upon consideration, we see them to presuppose. This, Hart claims, is the real payoff of the linguistic approach to philosophy.

. . . [T]he suggestion that inquiries into the meanings of words merely throw light on words is false. Many important distinctions which are not immediately obvious, between types of social situation or relationships may best be brought to light by an examination of the standard uses of the relevant expressions and of the way in which these depend on a social context, itself often left unstated. In this field of study it is particularly true that we may use, as Professor J. L. Austin said, 'a sharpened awareness of words to sharpen our awareness of phenomena'. (*C.L.* p. v)

The words just quoted are drawn from the point in the preface to *The Concept of Law* where Hart made a claim (since hotly disputed[22]) to be engaging in 'descriptive sociology' as well as conceptual analysis. The words and the claim were uttered with reference to the asserted importance of the distinction between 'internal' and 'external' statements.

There is, it is submitted, an important point and a sound claim to be made here. But the point and the claim are vitiated by the ambiguity earlier discovered in Hart's talk of the 'external point of view'. We distinguished an 'internal', a 'hermeneutic' or 'nonextreme external', and an 'extreme external' point of view. If there are *three* distinct points of view, not a simple internal/external dichotomy, what is to become of the internal/external distinction in relation to statements?

The answer is that it is simply not true that all statements of *ought, must, should, right, wrong, obligation, liability*, or whatever do presuppose an assumption *on the speaker's part* of the 'internal point of view' or of committed acceptance of rules or other standards. Such statements do certainly presuppose some rule or standard to which reference is made. But it need not be a standard that the speaker accepts or adheres to from the 'internal point of view'. Consider the difference between 'As a good Catholic, you ought to go to Mass today' (i) uttered by a parish priest to a member of his flock and (ii) uttered by a nonbeliever to a friend whom she supposes to be one of the faithful. There is a difference indeed, but the truth of the statement *conceived as a statement* (not an exhortation, an implied reproach or criticism, or whatever) is quite independent of the character, or standing, or viewpoint of the person who utters it.

Any such normative statement may be made *either* from the 'internal point of view' *or* from the 'hermeneutic point of view', and the mere act of making such a statement is entirely ambiguous in its presuppositions between the two. What is the case, however, is that the 'hermeneutic point of view' is possible only if an actual or hypothetical 'internal point of view' is postulated or presupposed. In this way, it is true that what Hart perhaps misleadingly calls 'internal statements'[23] do presuppose and thus draw attention to the actual or hypothetical existence of an 'internal point of view'. My ability to state, explain, and interpret rules and other standards and their applicability to given cases (my ability to take on the 'hermeneutic point of view') does indeed depend upon the supposition that somebody or some people accept(s) such rules or standards. But I need not be one of those people; nor does my making such a statement of itself disclose any volitional commitment of my own.

Hart's view of this matter is different. At pages 102–3 of *C.L.*, he characterizes an *internal statement* as one that 'manifests the internal point of view and is naturally used by one who, accepting the rule . . . applies [it]'. The *external statement* by contrast is 'the natural language of an external observer . . . who, without accepting [the] rule . . . states the fact that others accept it'. But the error here is in supposing that those who are outsiders to a particular rule or rule system are restricted to stating facts *that* . . . or facts *about* the rule. Not so. In the first edition of this book a contemporary example of this was given:

> As a non-citizen of the USSR, and one who has little liking for its political and legal principles, I can nevertheless make true statements *of*, as well as true statements *about*, Soviet Law. 'Soviet citizens may not hold or deal in foreign currencies' is a true statement of a rule of law which obtains within the USSR. It is not a statement *about* that rule. Here is a statement *about* it: 'It is unlikely to be repealed in the coming decade'. Neither statement *itself* says that anyone accepts the rule, though they both presuppose that someone does.

It is a pleasant irony that repeal of such Soviet laws did come just outside the decade in question.

Hart (*C.L.* p. 101) certainly did make the point that the student of Roman law may make the study of that subject more 'vivid' by speaking 'as if the system were still efficacious', discussing 'the validity of particular rules', and solving problems 'in their terms'. That implicitly recognizes the difference between what is involved in stating a rule and in making statements about it. To that extent, it demonstrates rather than alleviates the unsatisfactory quality of his earlier distinction between internal and external statements.

RULES AND OTHER STANDARDS

A further difficulty that was raised but not resolved earlier can be raised again in this connection. Not all of the statements (or utterances of other kinds) that people make using normative terms do in truth presuppose the existence of a *rule* as such. Certainly, they all presuppose *some* standard (rightness, or wrongness, etc.). But are all such standards *rules*, let alone *social* rules? Or are rules (or social rules) merely one group among the standards of judgment of conduct that people may hold, appeal to, or apply? Hart reveals himself as assuming an affirmative answer to this question when, for example, he sets out his starting point for clarifying the nature of morality:

> It is . . . necessary to characterize, in general terms, those *principles, rules and standards* relating to the conduct of individuals which belong to morality and make conduct morally obligatory. (*C.L.* p. 168; italics added)

Later, in the same passage (on the following page), he uses *standards* in a way that suggests it is in fact a general term embracing the whole group of 'rules, principles, and standards'.

Surely he is right in this. The vegetarian whom we thought about earlier presumably holds it as a principle that one ought not to eat the flesh of animals. But is there from his or anyone's viewpoint a *rule* against doing so? Being noisily drunk on a public bus offends a widely held conception of decency, propriety, or good behaviour, and this may be manifested in criticism, pressure to be quiet and behave oneself, and so on. (An incident involving noisy drunkenness occurred in the Edinburgh bus on which I travelled home on the evening I originally wrote this.) But such incidents can occur without its being true that there is a *social rule* against being noisily drunk on buses (in Edinburgh or anywhere else). Shared standards of propriety, decency, and good behaviour are not necessarily *rules*. The trouble is not that Hart fails to see and give some allowance for the fact that not all *standards* are *rules*, nor that *principles* are distinct from *rules* (a key point in Ronald Dworkin's criticism[24] of Hart's theory). The trouble is that Hart has not himself clarified what the assumed distinction is.

What follows is no more than a brief sketch of the outlines of a possible Hartian clarification of that point, one that he might have moved toward accepting in his own later thought.[25] *Principles* are, both in the legal[26] and the moral[27] case according to Hart, characterized as being *rational* grounds of conduct and as being *general* in their scope. *Rules*, it would seem by contrast, are essentially *conventional* and thus may be (in a sense) *arbitrary* in the specific form they take, as with the British 'keep left' rule in driving—why not 'keep right' as elsewhere? The point or *principle* involved is clear—to provide safe driving conditions. The *principle* is eminently rational, but that does not make 'keep left' more rational than 'keep right' or vice versa. An arbitrary choice having been made or an arbitrary practice having developed, one would be irrational not to adhere to it, so long as it is indeed a *shared* standard rather obviously shared by almost all of one's fellow drivers. So in relation to *standards* that are *rules*, it would seem important to note the point made earlier—that the element of *preference* involved in the 'internal point of view' tends to be *conditional*. One has a *preference* that a given pattern be adhered to by all, and this *preference* is in some degree *conditional* upon the pattern's being and continuing to be supported by common or convergent *preferences* among all (or nearly all) the parties to the activity contemplated.

This may in turn remind us of another feature of *rules*—that we think of them as relatively 'cut and dried', often even as captured in writing. The way in which we sometimes talk of 'unwritten rules' conveys a hint that these are considered relatively unusual. An 'unwritten rule' is an instance of a conventional *standard of conduct* that is well understood and clear-cut in its provisions, as is usual with rules which are enshrined in a particular verbal formula.[28] This expresses better the point about arbitrariness, and points to a difference between *rules* and broader or vaguer *standards* of rectitude, propriety, decency, or whatever. The difference simply arises from the degree to which people share in conceiving a reasonably cut-and-dried 'pattern of behaviour' as the standard or something altogether vaguer.

These reflections are not unimportant for those whose focus of concern is law, in particular *positive law* or *state law*. It is (certainly in Hart's view) a particular feature of governance under law that state legal orders are characterized by the existence of institutions and procedures for formulating in relatively clear, precise and authoritative ways those governing *standards of conduct* that are legal. If the reflections of a moment ago were correct, then it would be a noticeable and distinctive feature of legal order that it does, through its institutions and procedures, convert vaguer standards of conduct into *rules* as such. And indeed these reflections are significant outside the sphere of *positive law*. The other walks of life in which *rules* as such apply tend to be those where there exist institutions and procedures that likewise give some precision to standards and conventions. This is the case in organized games, voluntary associations, families (to some degree), companies, trades unions, schools, universities, and the like. In some of these cases, moreover, the rules are actually given the name of 'laws', 'statutes', or 'bylaws', as in the instance of the 'Laws of Golf', the 'Laws of Association Football', the 'Statutes of the University', or the like.

To the extent that my sketched differentiating features of *rules* as against *standards of conduct* in general are acceptable, they do then give ground for supposing that *rule* may be a concept particularly apposite and relevant to/ in jurisprudence. What would be less convincing would be to suppose that *rules* as such would have any great prominence in morality, which (aside from some forms of religious ethics) is not in any large degree institutionalized.[29] Indeed, according to the powerful Kantian school of ethical thought, which insists on the autonomy[30] of moral agents as such, morality cannot be authoritatively institutionalized through social agencies. The heteronomous moral development of the child may be mediated through the inculcation of rules laid down by parental authority, but eventually the adult agent is his or her own final moral authority.

Hart's own recognition of this is somewhat muted by the prominence that he gives to the concept of a *rule* and by his failure to expound the distinction that he implicitly observes as holding between *principles, rules*, and other *standards*. It is, however, significant that it is within those chapters of *The Concept of Law* dealing with "Justice and Morality" (ch. 8) and "Morals and Laws" (ch. 9) that he most stresses the important part played by *principles* and other kinds of standards alongside of *rules* as such. Of the relative standing and relative importance of rules and other standards in morality there is a good deal more to be said; but it will be said in the next chapter.

SUMMATION

We have considered here the central and distinctive element of Hart's contribution to descriptive jurisprudence—his elucidation of the idea of a *social rule* and the methodology he applies in that elucidation. His idea that *rules* have an 'internal aspect' has been endorsed but has not been found sufficient to distinguish *rules* from the other kinds of standards whose existence he acknowledges. The 'internal aspect' and its associated *attitude* (the 'internal point of view') have been found to be well-grounded but insufficiently analysed; a fuller analysis discloses both cognitive and volitional elements in the attitude. *Willing acceptance* of rules involves the full volitional commitment that the 'internal point of view' entails, while there is a weaker case of mere reluctant or unenthusiastic acceptance parasitic on the former. Where there is common acceptance of certain standards envisaged as being shared or conventional standards, those who accept them belong to a *group*. But (from the 'internal point of view' *of these accepters*) so do all to whose conduct the standards are deemed applicable, and that in turn commonly depends on the possession of some characteristic that is not necessarily a voluntarily acquired one. Hence, Hart's crucial conception of a *group* appears not to have been prior to or definable independently of his conception of a *rule*.

The 'external point of view' is not necessarily that of an outsider to the group. In its 'extreme' form it comprehends the point of view of all those who, whether from ignorance of the agents' subjective meanings or from scientific commitment, are restricted or restrict themselves to observation of human behavioural regularity. This viewpoint is distinct from Hart's 'non-extreme external point of view'. I called that the 'hermeneutic point of view' because it is the viewpoint of one who, without (or in scientific abstraction from) any volitional commitment of his own, seeks to understand, portray, or describe human activity as it is meaningful 'from the internal point of view'. Such a one shares in the cognitive element of that latter point of view and gives full cognitive recognition to and appreciation of the latter's volitional element. Thus she can understand *rules* and *standards* for what they are, but does not endorse them for her part in stating or describing them or discussing their correct application. This 'hermeneutic point of view' is in fact the viewpoint implicitly ascribed to and used by the legal theorist, scholar, or writer who follows Hart's method; this is why Hart ought to have sharpened his distinguishing of it better than he did.

That being so, Hart's definition of 'internal statements' of legal and other rules has to be rejected. 'Normative statements' as I call them, following Joseph Raz,[31] do indeed presuppose an actual or hypothetical 'internal point of view' held by someone, but not necessarily the statement maker. The making of such statements is compatible either with the 'internal point of view' or with the 'hermeneutic point of view'. And, we may add, the understanding of them is essential to the prudentially calculated survival or comfort of the group member who does not accept the *rules* but wants to avoid the reactions of those who do. It may be a bit highfalutin to ascribe to train robbers a 'hermeneutic point of view', but to the extent that they use legal understanding to avoid detection or conviction, that is what they have.

Finally, reflection on the presuppositions of such statements led us back to recognition that Hart insufficiently defines the differentiating features of rules as against principles and other standards; although, certainly, he has made his case for distinguishing all these from concepts such as 'habit' conceived in external terms.

CHAPTER FIVE

Morality, Positive and Critical

PRELIMINARY

In the previous chapter, it was observed that it is particularly appropriate to use the term *rules* for certain standards of conduct. This term well suits those standards that contain some tinge or element of the purely conventional or arbitrary and perhaps for that reason have achieved some canonical or authoritative formulation. Such formulation may take place through established institutions or procedures, not necessarily those of the state and its organs or institutions. On the one hand these can be distinguished from principles, on the other from standards *simpliciter* or 'norms in a general sense'. These distinctions must be held in play in any consideration of Hart's work. Before we proceed to a study of Hart's specifically legal analysis, there are points here to be probed. Even though this involves an inversion of Hart's order of proceeding in *The Concept of Law*, it seems best to come at them first through a consideration of the descriptive and analytical part of his moral philosophy.

POSITIVE MORALITY

In a relatively early essay on "Legal and Moral Obligation", Hart gave vent to a criticism of what he took to be excessively 'protestant' in R. M. Hare's ethics.[1] His criticism was directed against theories that base the whole of morality on the autonomous self-legislating choice of the moral agent. For such theories, moral obligation depends on such an agent's laying down his or her own universal prescriptions of conduct for himself or herself and (so far as concerns that agent's judgment and treatment of them) all other moral agents. Why does Hart see this as 'too protestant'? The answer is that in Hart's vision of them, morality and moral obligation are at base social conceptions.

Morality stands alongside law (and above manners, etiquette, tradition, convention and usage, even linguistic usage, scholarly discipline, rules of games, etc.) as a great social regulator. Religion seems to belong in this scheme of things as a source of morality, or perhaps for believers a form of morality, at least 'positive morality' in the sense explained later. The observance of shared or common rules and standards of conduct is what enables human beings to live together—and survive together—in tolerably peaceful and thriving societies.

Perhaps there exist or have existed very primitive societies that lack established organs of rule making and rule enforcement. In such societies, shared or common rules and standards, practised as a matter of custom, tradition, and usage, are all that humans have in the way of social regulation. The common rules and standards are backed only by more or less vague and diffuse forms of social pressure, or by highly problematic ones such as the feud or vendetta. Hart, as we shall see, ties the development of specifically differentiated 'law' to the emergence of rule-enforcing and rule-making organs, institutions, or authorities. But even where, in 'developed' societies, law has clearly emerged as a distinct and institutionalized system, social coexistence or collaboration remains in a high degree dependent on people's observance of shared rules and standards by no means fully coextensive with the ones enforced as law.

Of such shared rules and standards, some have a particular *importance* in furthering social coexistence and survival, in that they determine the wrongfulness of interpersonal violence, interpersonal dishonesty and unfaithfulness to undertakings, taking of or intermeddling with valued objects in others' possession, failures in familial responsibilities, and the like. Others concerning such matters as sexual or religious taboos have at least as much felt importance, though Hart as social critic takes leave to doubt their actual importance.

This first characteristic of (i) *importance* goes along with three others. Rules and standards of this kind enjoy (ii) 'immunity from deliberate change' since no one can or does establish or abrogate them by any act of or akin to legislation. The kinds of conduct that they stigmatize as 'offences' are only and essentially (iii) voluntary or wilful conduct, as distinct from accidents, mistakes, reflex actions, or whatever. They are (iv) backed or supported by particular forms of pressure, such as appeals to moral norms as good in themselves and appeals to the conscience of the 'wrongdoer', as well as by cruder threats of punishment or social ostracism.

Hart's suggestion is that any rules or standards that are shared or common standards of a group and that couple the characteristic of perceived importance with the other three are properly deemed to be moral standards. Taken together, they constitute a 'morality', that is, the morality of the group in question (the *group* being itself, observe again, in a sense constituted by or by reference to the standards and their application). Manifestly a 'morality' in this sense does not rest solely or sufficiently on the autonomous universal prescription of each and every moral agent acting for his own part. Much of it is learned, much from anyone's point of view a matter of imitation and going along with the herd, perhaps because one desires that there be a herd along with which to go. To get to know such rules and standards requires adoption of the hermeneutic point of view. Yet morality in this sense is therefore as much a matter of fact as is football, and the fact that some acts are morally wrong is as much a fact as the fact that Muhammad Ali was at one time World Boxing Champion. That however does not make it independent of human volitions and commitments (and, as we shall see, values); for these we saw to be required elements of the internal point of view, itself presupposed in the hermeneutic point of view.

A morality as so characterized is social rather than individualistic, and it is the morality of a group of people who live together and interact socially. Subsequently to the publication of *The Concept of Law*, in his also celebrated *Law, Liberty and Morality* (1963), Hart revived a usage established by John Austin and other nineteenth-century utilitarians when he chose to call such a morality a 'positive morality'. He did so in order to sharpen a distinction previously foreshadowed in *The Concept of Law*. To quote from *Law, Liberty and Morality*:

> I would revive the terminology much favoured by the Utilitarians of the last century, which distinguished 'positive morality', the morality actually accepted and shared by a given social group, from the general moral principles used in the criticism of actual social institutions including positive morality. We may call such general principles 'critical morality' . . . (*L.L.M.* p. 20)

CRITICAL MORALITY DISTINGUISHED FROM POSITIVE MORALITY: PRINCIPLES AND VALUES

Chapters 12 and 13 of this book contain a discussion of Hart's own critical moral principles in their substance. The present aim is only to note and to understand his distinction between 'positive' and 'critical' morality, his idea that there is a moral position from which a morality may be criticized. Here is what he said about that in *The Concept of Law*:

The further reaches of morality take us in different ways beyond the confines of the obligations and ideals recognized in particular social groups to the principles and ideals used in the moral criticism of society itself; yet even here important connexions remain with the primordial social form of morality. It is always possible, when we come to examine the accepted morality either of our own or some other society, that we shall find much to criticize; it may, in the light of currently available knowledge, appear unnecessarily repressive, cruel, superstitious, or unenlightened. It may cramp human liberty, especially in the discussion and practice of religion or in experimentation with different forms of human life, even when only negligible benefits are thereby secured for others. Above all, a given society's morality may extend its protections from harm to its own members only, or even only to certain classes, leaving a slave or helot class at the mercy of their masters' whims. Implicit in this type of criticism which (even though it might be rejected) would certainly be accorded recognition as 'moral' criticism, is the assumption that the arrangements of society, including its accepted morality, must satisfy two formal conditions, one of rationality and the other of generality. (*C.L.* p. 183)

As appears, the possibility of critical morality depends on the possibility of framing principles that are both rational and general (Kantians would no doubt prefer to say 'universal'[2] or to add 'universal' to 'general'). But in what sense rational? Hart himself does not subscribe to the 'rationalist' mode of Natural Law thought, which portrays certain principles as direct insights of or deliverances of 'reason', our calculating faculty.

'Rationality', it appears, relates back to ideals and values. Values and disvalues, according to Hart in the closing pages of *Law, Liberty and Morality*, are not susceptible of proof. Whether repression, cruelty, and superstition are evils (negations of value), whether enlightenment and human liberty are goods—these are not matters we can prove. Nor even can we prove that life or survival is a good, though indeed 'an overwhelming majority of men do wish to live, even at the cost of hideous misery' (*C.L.* p. 192). We can, however, take note that a whole range of our everyday concepts like 'danger and safety, harm and benefit, need and function, disease and cure' (*ibid.*) would become empty if we do not postulate a deep-seated human disposition to ascribe value to life and its enhancement.

A vast philosophical literature exists concerning the nature and foundations of such values and our awareness of them. Are they in some sense objective features of our world or our human nature, which we apprehend by some special mode of cognition or intuition,[3] or which we perceive by some 'moral sense'?[4] Or are they projections of and from our own affective and emotional makeup, resting on those more enduring, persistent, and steady sentiments, which Hume called the 'calm passions'?[5] From such debate Hart expressly holds back, though one may catch more than a passing hint that his sympathies lie toward the Humean view. What most concerns him is to register the points that values neither possess the simple rational demonstrability of mathematical propositions nor derive from some arbitrary volition or existential choice. Whatever the ultimate account of them, we cannot but recognize them as inextricably interwoven with a whole range of concepts like those listed above (danger and safety, etc.) and hence attested in infinitely various ways in common everyday talk. Here again it is worth remarking that common everyday talk is *common*—common to all who speak the language, common because of the shared semantic and other conventions without which talk would be mere noise.

This suggests that values are whatever human beings hold to as the underpinning reasons[6] behind more immediate reasons for acting, for approving action, and for preferring certain ways of acting and states of affairs to others. They are as such not necessarily themselves backed by further or ulterior reasons. This we express rather than explain in saying that, for us, something or other is 'good in itself'; whatever is good in itself is, for that person, an ultimate as distinct from a merely instrumental or derivative value. Hence arguments concerning what is of ultimate value cannot proceed by way of demonstration or proof. That people do 'have values' in this sense seems plain. It remains plain even if, like Hart, we leave open the questions in what sense values might be said to 'exist', by what means we may know of them, and by what biological, psychological, or sociological processes we come to hold whatever values we hold.

What, then, has rationality to do with these values? Hart's answer would seem to be that rational human beings cannot but give their minds to clarifying, rendering explicit, and forming a coherent view of what would otherwise be no more than a set of inarticulate implicit ideas of what is good. Being built into the traditions and practices of our communities, these would be perennially at risk of ossification with the passage of time. Essential to this process is the attempt to frame articulate general principles about conduct. The principles we seek are ones that tend to advance or promote the realization of our values in a coherent way. This requires reflecting about and making explicit the initially inarticulate value assumptions that are inevitably implicit in the choices we make as active social beings. Rationality of principles, in addition to their formal properties of universality and generality, requires that they be geared to some coherent scheme of values. Principles that seem attractive but on careful consideration turn out to be inimical to our real values ought to be rejected by any rational person.

That this is Hart's view is perhaps better borne out by studying how he himself argues a moral case in his own right than by resting solely on his own descriptive analyses. To that end, the powerful eloquence of his per-oration in *Law, Liberty and Morality* is fine evidence:

> I have . . . assumed from the beginning that anyone who regards [the present] question as open to discussion accepts the critical principle, central to all moral-ity, that human misery and the restriction of freedom are evils: for that is why the legal enforcement of morality calls for justification. I then endeavoured to extricate, and to free from ambiguity of statement, the general principles under-lying several varieties of the more extreme thesis that the enforcement of [posi-tive] morality or its preservation from change were valuable apart from their beneficial consequences in preserving society. These principles in fact invite us to consider as values, for the sake of which we should restrict human freedom and inflict the misery of punishment on human beings, things which seem to belong to the pre-history of morality and to be quite hostile to its general spirit. They include mere outward conformity to moral rules induced simply by fear; the gratification of feelings of hatred for the wrongdoer or his 'retributory' punishment, even where there has been no victim to be avenged or to call for justice; the infliction of punishment as a symbol or expression of moral con-demnation; the mere insulation from change of any social morality however re-pressive or barbarous. No doubt I have not *proved* these things not to be values worth their price in human suffering and loss of freedom; it may be enough to have shown what it is that is offered for the price. (*L.L.M.* p. 83)

One reason for looking at this eloquent and heartfelt piece of argumen-tation is to remind ourselves again about the 'internal point of view', this time as regards critical morality. Hart's position revealed in that passage is no mere posture of hermeneutic appreciation of the view that human mis-ery is evil. It is a deeply committed one. He is rejecting and inviting us to reject certain principles because, as he reflects on them and invites us to re-flect on them, they are geared not to the realization of coherent values, but to 'things which seem to belong to the prehistory of morality'. We for our part may have or make a like commitment after due reflection on what we hold to be acceptable and rationally coherent values; or we may disagree. But in either event we can at least understand what he is arguing, since oth-erwise the question of agreement or disagreement *could not* arise.

That in turn must further our understanding of 'positive morality'. It is not after all a mere pun on the word 'morality' that allows Hart to speak both of 'positive' and of 'critical' morality. Not merely do both sorts of morality have a common reference to and concern with how we are to live together socially. They are both in the same way dependent on the attitudes people bring to bear on social conduct judged against standards for that conduct. Positive morality itself is said to require a 'critical reflective attitude to certain patterns of behaviour as a common standard' (*C.L.* p. 57). Critical morality is a refinement, a further development from that. It brings under critical reflection our ways of passing judgment on behaviour and the—perhaps merely traditional—standards we use in doing so. Critical morality seeks to exhibit and lay bare the value assumptions implicit in positive morality, to reassess these and render them coherent, and thus to develop critical principles by reference to which we can reappraise and re-orient our ordinary day-to-day judgments and standards of judgment. If we do not reorient them, that will show that we have merely entertained and understood, but not accepted, the critical principles in question.

STANDARDS OF DIFFERENT KINDS

We are now in a position to make progress in capturing the difference between various types of standard-for-conduct and their place within positive morality. That there is a positive morality of a group depends on some people fully accepting some standard patterns of behaviour for the critical appraisal of conduct. The volitional commitment involved in this presup-poses an engagement to some values, possibly inexplicit ones. These values must be subject to some kind of implicit ranking, for without that, Hart's criterion of *importance*, the first feature of moral rules and standards, would be empty.

These presupposed values however are themselves also 'standards' in the sense that judgments of conduct can have direct reference to them. The man who gets drunk on the bus and creates a disturbance with cursing and swearing and pouring out his private woes to perfect strangers is acting badly. His behaviour gives offence whether or not it is technically in law 'an offence'. Decency and modesty of behaviour and considerateness for the sensibilities of others are values to be promoted and observed. There is, ac-cording to what I understand to be the prevailing standards of middle-class Edinburgh, virtue in developing and showing these qualities. By simple reference to those considerations, accepted by all or some of the bus riders, the drunk is misbehaving. He generates hostility toward himself, and some courageous lady passenger may in due course tell him to get off the bus, in terms sufficiently resolute to bring this about. (That is what happened on the bus I was riding.)

To act indecently, to act immodestly, to act inconsiderately—these are moral misdemeanours. Not because there are *rules* in our morality defin-ing these qualities. There is not even any clear-cut *rule* against being noisily drunk or quietly drunk on the bus. We have conventional understandings about obscene and nonobscene registers of speech. We have conventional understandings about engaging strangers in conversation or letting them alone. We have expectations, albeit somewhat inexact, about the level and pitch of voice that is right in public-service vehicles, such that all who want to talk to a neighbour can do so others being neither shouted down nor distracted from the evening newspaper as the case may be. The general values of decency and modesty come to have particular applicability in a given case only through reference to such understandings. The value of considerateness has then a second-level applicability since it involves not infringing expectations, which conventional understandings lead us to have. This interaction of general values with 'conventions'[7] and 'understandings' is essential in a morality. Without the latter, it would not even be unconventional to shout 'Bugger all bishops!' on a bus; but it is in fact highly unconventional, as it would also be unconventional for a professor to shoot dead a troublesome student. In each case, however, it is grossly misleading *merely* to call the action an 'unconventional' one. In different degrees of gravity, the actions are *offences*. That is because they flout seriously held values.

(My running story about the drunk on the bus might raise for lawyers a seemingly obvious objection. The criminal law *does* have a rule against such doings—that against breaches of the peace. It may also be the case that the bus company has bylaws regulating misconduct on buses and authorizing its employees to eject miscreants from buses. But these objections are beside my point. Here, there are positive moral standards in operation quite apart from the legal ones, and they are not rules. What is more, 'breach of the peace' as a criminal offence presupposes and, in application, refers to these standards. What the drunk does is not a breach of the peace unless he does create a disturbance, which he does only if and so far as he does flout understood social standards.)

In at least the ways I have suggested, reflection on Hart's work leads us beyond it to a better understanding of those positive moral standards that are not rules, depending rather some interaction of social conventions and seriously held (even if not very well articulated) values. The degree of seriousness with which we hold to them is in fact the measure of that 'importance', which Hart rightly puts in the forefront of his explanation of what it is to have a morality at all. It also goes some way to explaining his fourth feature—appeals to conscience as a form of moral pressure.

Are there then no moral rules? There could be none, if Hart were entirely correct about the immunity of 'morality' from legislative or quasi-legislative change. As was said earlier, the point about a rule is that it is a relatively cut-and-dried formulation of how to act, and it is thus apt to have some arbitrary element in it. Were it true that there are no moral analogues of legislation, it would follow that there are no moral rules. But it is not true.

Many of the most important parts of everyone's life depend on successfully coordinating with other people. Most of us live at home with family, friends, flatmates, fellow residents in a hostel, or whatever. Most of us work not as solitaries but alongside of workmates. Often this necessitates more than simple broad understandings and loose conventions as to how we will rub along together, though it is well to observe that these can never be either dispensed with or wholly supplanted. There are at least three ways in which we can get something more explicit than mere convention.

First, a practice or usage may arise by regular repetition of some pattern. Here is an example: The children finish school at four o'clock and come home hungry. Their parents finish work around five o'clock and come home hungry. One or the other parent prepares a family meal for half past six. The origin of the practice is simply to meet a common need in a co-ordinated way. The more it goes on, the more securely each of the parties comes to expect that it will be that way. Nobody ever gets round to saying or writing 'Supper in this house is and shall be at six thirty in the evening'. Nevertheless, that is taken for granted and in all sorts of ways alluded to. Here we have a good example of an unwritten or even unspoken rule which everyone understands, acts by, and uses in passing critical remarks (*'You're late today'*). It has relative precision and a certain arbitrariness (6:30 precisely; why not 6:15, or 6.45, or 7:00? Just because this, not those, is the time we happened to fetch up with).

The second possibility is that some such rule could be fixed on by explicit agreement of the parties to it. The family *agrees* that 6:30 will be a convenient time for everyone, subject to variation on high days or holidays or specially for someone who has inconsistent commitments. The university department agrees that recurring tasks shall be shared among the members *this* way rather than that. Agreements like this can be changed by later agreements or tacitly varied in practice to suit what turns out more convenient. The agreement originates but does not fully constitute the conventional rule which operates in practice. Practices can be further varied by agreements. And so on.

The third possibility is some interposition of authority. The head of the house (a position determined, as Bryce sagaciously observed,[8] inversely by the relative indolence of the cohabitants) says what time is to be suppertime. The foreman or head of department lays down an assignment of regularly recurring tasks. *Not necessarily* because anyone accepts that this is an exercise of a preestablished authority, which ought to be obeyed in itself, the arrangement laid down can be accepted as a rule in practice.

In all these ways, rules covering parts of our social interactions can come into being, develop, and be changed. But what, it may be asked, has this to do with morality? Even in the simple cases I have mentioned, the rules have much to do with morality because in these cases the crucial value of considerateness to others enters in. To fail to turn up at the right time for a meal someone has taken trouble to get ready at that time is to show an inconsiderateness, which is not excusable except when attributable to genuinely unforeseeable and unplanned diversions—as distinct from wilful pursuit of mere diversions. To fail without warning to carry out one's particular allotted tasks shows at least inconsiderateness to one's workmates and perhaps imperils the good working of an enterprise on whose success yet others depend. The values at stake cannot be promoted except by adherence to *some* rules or conventions. The rules serve particular conveniences or even needs for all those whom they cover, and without some rule or convention these conveniences or needs would be unsatisfied. Considerateness for others involves as a minimum that one refrain from inconveniencing them or obstructing the satisfaction of their need. Over a whole range of matters, it can in fact at this minimal level only be satisfied by attending to and fulfilling what the relevant rule requires or giving fair notice that, exceptionally, one cannot.

We spoke above about authority. There is another relevant sense in which reference to authority can occur. Saintliness, great moral wisdom, and supposed divine inspiration are all qualities that can endow an individual with one variety of moral authority. Such a person may sum up for us the requirements of a moral life. To such a person's summation may be ascribed authoritative status, authoritative clarification of what our values require in important and recurring cases. The Ten Commandments leap to mind as the grand example of this, certainly with regard to the way in which they have been received and conceived among people other than the wandering Israelites to whom Moses first revealed them as the commands of their God to them. Not merely do we deplore failures in respect for life, which we value. We hold that there is a rule: Thou shalt not kill. Not merely do we deplore lack of respect for one's own and others' familial commitments. Thou shalt not commit adultery is a rule—albeit a rather frequently violated one.

Nor is it an insignificant fact that certain of the more basic legal prescriptions, in societies that have achieved a specialized development of positive law, may be taken as canonical formulations of moral requirements. 'Due process of law' for Americans and 'Hear both sides of a case before deciding' among British people are instances of moral rules. We can call them *rules* because they are rather clear formulations of what would otherwise have been vaguer ideas of the right way to do things instancing a value of fairness and they have been received from technical law into popular consciousness.

So of course a morality includes rules, and they can come into being, change, achieve canonical formulations, and so forth. In that sense, Hart is wrong about 'immunity from change', and if he were not wrong about that, he would be wrong in thinking there can be moral rules. But we have now seen that what makes them *moral* rules is their intrinsic involvement with values people hold seriously. It is not the rules but the *values* that are immune from deliberate or quasi-legislative change. To say this is to make again the Hartian point that values do not 'derive from some arbitrary volition or existential choice'.

CRITICAL AND POSITIVE MORALITY IN INTERACTION

Now we must reconsider the interaction of critical morality with positive morality. Some individuals more than others are apt to reflect on the moralities of the groups they belong to and of other groups. By working over conceptions of values and trying to gain a coherent view of them, one can formulate or sketch critical principles. Conventions and rules that, for example, concretize requirements of considerateness to others or of decency or modesty may seem in that light to have degenerated into an excessively uptight and hidebound ritualistic observance of convention, rule, and punctilio for its own sake, serving no need or convenience and so on. 'Ruliness' (as distinct from unruliness) may have come to be treated as valuable in itself. Here there is room for a revision in values and an abandonment or adjustment of some of our conventions or rules. If the critical moralists do their work well and persuade their fellows of the greater rationality of their view, the effect over time must be a change in the positive morality. This, however, can be a risky job. Of critical moralists, the two most notable in Western history were executed, one by hemlock and the other by crucifixion.

If change does occur and the commonly held moral positions of groups and communities adjust themselves to the critical critique, we will then have ground to ascribe to the adjusted positive morality the principles (perhaps in turn adjusted) that the critical moralist propounded. This ascription will be justified whether one thinks that principles of critical morality and people's adherence to them are causes of change in social organization or are merely ideological responses to changes of some more fundamental kind. All the more will this be so if one supposes both the idealist and the materialist view to be exaggerations of half-truths. Accordingly, from the viewpoint of those who seek a hermeneutic understanding of that morality, the critical principles will have explanatory power. It is just as likely that from the internal point of view—the viewpoint of those whose morality this morality is—the principles will be held as justifying grounds for lower order conventions, rules, and judgments. So in addition to understandings, conventions, rules, and values, there will be principles of positive morality as well.

Thus may we re-work the materials Hart has given us in order to capture a clearer, more satisfactory and unified view of the two aspects of morality, positive and critical, and of the varieties of standards for conduct therein embraced.

CHAPTER SIX

Obligation, Duty, Wrongdoing

'RULES OF OBLIGATION'

The *obligatory* character of morality and of law is their distinguishing feature according to Hart. Though morality and law are different from each other in ways yet to be seen, together they distinguish themselves upon this point of obligatoriness from the great range of other rule-governed areas of social behaviour—for example, games, etiquette, grammar, good manners. Law and morality have the special feature that they give rise to *obligations*; they make conduct nonoptional. (Some might wonder how Hart's account might allow for religion and custom, which commonly are thought of as giving rise to 'religious obligations' or 'social obligations'. The answer is that religious codes of behaviour and social customs are both instances of what he calls 'positive morality'.)

How then are we to understand this use of the concept 'obligation' as a concept common to, and special to, law and morality? Hart's earlier[1] and most persuasive answer to this question is given through his theory of social rules (though it reflects the partial deficiences of that theory). There is, he says, a special class of rules whose special characteristics separate them out from other rules as 'rules of obligation' or 'obligation imposing rules'. He claims that 'though the line separating rules of obligation from others is at points a vague one, yet the main rationale of the distinction is fairly clear' (*C.L.* p. 86). Once we understand this rationale, we can see why it is the case that, for example, the grammatical rule against saying 'you was' cannot be expressed in terms of an 'obligation' not to say 'you was'. By contrast, such moral rules as the promise-keeping rule or such legal rules as that against theft can quite properly be expressed in terms of obligations—obligations to keep promises, not to steal.

Not all moral rules or legal rules are of this kind, but all the others interrelate with these basic rules of obligation. Of such rules, explains Hart, there are three distinctive features. The *first* is *seriousness of social pressure*:

> Rules are conceived and spoken of as imposing obligations when the general demand for conformity is insistent and the social pressure brought to bear on those who deviate or threaten to deviate is great. (*C.L.* p. 86)

The social pressure he has in view has two main forms. On the one hand, it can consist of appeals to a person's conscience and to her feelings of shame, remorse, or guilt about what she has done or proposes to do. On the other hand, it may take the form of external pressures such as overt hostility towards one's acts, perhaps even going the length of physical sanctions or punishments. Consistent with his view about the nature of social or positive morality, Hart suggests that where pressure of the former kind is prominent, the rule and the obligation it prescribes are normally considered moral in character. But where the pressure prominently involves physical santions or punishments, 'we shall be inclined to characterize the rules as a . . . form of law' (*C.L.* p. 86).

The *second* (and a subsidiary) feature of obligation-imposing rules is the *importance* of the values promoted by their observance.

> The rules supported by this serious pressure are thought important because they are believed to be necessary to the maintenance of social life or some highly prized feature of it. (*C.L.* p. 87)

Hence, characteristic cases of obligations are those arising under rules against violence to the person, deceit, and breach of promise. So also rules which 'specify what is to be done by one who performs a distinctive role or function in the social group'—though in this case 'duty' may be a commoner locution.

The *third* (also subsidiary) feature is *possible conflict between obligation and desire*:

> [I]t is generally recognized that the conduct required by these rules may, while benefiting others, conflict with what the person who owes the duty may wish to do. Hence obligations or duties are thought of as characteristically involving sacrifice or renunciation, and [there is a] standing possibility of conflict between obligation or duty and [self-]interest . . . (*C.L.* p. 87)

These three features do not of themselves fully explain what it is for somebody to have, or to be under, an obligation. Suppose, however, that members of a group accept a certain rule. The pressure they bring to bear for conformity to it is great. It is held by them to be geared to promoting some important value, though quite often individuals find observance of it to conflict with doing as they would like. This situation, says Hart, is the one in which the term 'obligation' has meaning. A statement such as 'you have an obligation to do *x*' is a prime example of what he calls an 'internal statement' expressing the judgement of one who adheres to the rule from the internal point of view. The judgement is that you must do *x* since the rule is supposed applicable to your case.

'Having an obligation' is a very different matter from either 'being obliged' or 'feeling obliged' to do *x*. One is obliged to do *x* in any case where doing *x* is a necessary condition for avoiding some threatened evil substantial in character. 'The gunman's threat obliged the teller to hand over the cash', 'the swift approach of the bus obliged me to make a leap for the pavement' – these are characteristic instances of 'being obliged'. But such statements are not Hartian 'internal statements', nor are they normative statements at all. They apply notions of the causation and motivation of acts, not of the normative quality of acts. That I am very likely to be punished for not doing *x* does not of itself mean the same as that I have an obligation to do *x*.

Likewise, since 'obligation' statements are 'internal' ones, they are not to be confused with statements about feelings of psychological compulsion experienced by agents (as some of the earlier 'Scandinavian realist' writings[2] suggested):

> there is no contradiction in saying of some hardened swindler . . . that he had an obligation to pay the rent but felt no pressure to pay when he made off without doing so. To *feel* obliged and to have an obligation are different though frequently concomitant things. To identify them would be one way of misinterpreting, in terms of psychological feelings, the important internal aspect of rules. . . . (*C.L.* p. 88)

Hart's rationale for obligation-imposing rules carries a heavy freight and has a lot of work to do. For obligation and duty are more or less equivalent terms, in his opinion, and they tie up with a range of others.

> The criminal law is something which we either obey or disobey and what its rules require is spoken of as 'a duty'. If we disobey we are said to 'break' the law and what we have done is legally 'wrong' a 'breach of duty' or an 'offence'. . . . [In the law of torts] too, the rules which determine what types of conduct constitute actionable wrongs are spoken of as imposing on persons, irrespective of their wishes, 'duties' (or more rarely 'obligations') to abstain from such conduct. (*C.L.* p. 27)

It is clear from this that Hart is making a large and important claim, namely, the claim to have found a new way of establishing an underlying unity among all these notions such as 'duty', 'breaking' the law, 'wrong', 'breach of duty', 'offence', and 'obligation'. To all such notions, he is applying his hermeneutic method of exhibiting the context to which somebody who seriously employs the notions is necessarily alluding, albeit tacitly. The central use of such notions is in the making of 'internal statements', which appeal to or apply a rule without necessarily or usually proceeding to an explicit statement of the rule. The rule to which tacit appeal is made in any such case, claims Hart, is one exhibiting his three special features: *seriousness* of social pressure behind the rule, *importance* of the values its observance promotes, and *possible conflict* between an agent's wishes and what the rule prescribes.

The hermeneutic element in Hart's account differentiates it from previous elucidations of the same notions, which focused also on sanctions (seriousness of pressure, in Hart's formulation) but from an external point of view. John Austin[3] conceived of duties as being those acts that one is commanded to do under the threat of some sanction for disobedience; hence having a duty is simply being exposed to the likelihood of a sanction. O. W. Holmes[4] similarly suggested that the notion of 'duty' has an essentially predictive function, the predictions in question being as to the likelihood of courts imposing sanctions in given cases.

Even Hans Kelsen,[5] to whose 'normative science' of jurisprudence Hart owes so obvious a debt, eschews reference to 'internal attitudes' as foreign to his 'pure' theory of law. Hence his conception of duty is merely a logical derivative from his theory that all laws are norms authorizing the imposition of a sanction, as in the simplified formula: *if anyone commits murder, let him be imprisoned for life*. If such a norm is valid, it entails two propositions: committing murder is a 'delict'; not committing murder is a 'duty'. Kelsen considers the use of such terms as 'delict' or 'duty' to be only for the purpose of secondary or derivative formulations of norms whose pure and primary form simply authorizes sanctions when certain acts take place.

Kelsen's view, Hart suggests, inverts the proper order of things. The primary point of law or of morality is to settle what it is obligatory for people to do. Although obligations, duties, etc. presuppose rules backed by serious pressure, or indeed sanctions, the idea that such rules primarily authorize sanction imposition by legal officials and only secondarily require other people to *do* things misrepresents the social reality of the matter. Austin and Holmes, on the other hand, in effect adhere simply to the external point of view from which 'obligation' is falsely conflated with 'being obliged'.

OBJECTIONS

Despite its claimed and indeed its genuine superiority over prior theories, Hart's theory can itself be shown to be defective. First, it ties the relevant concepts solely to *rules*; but earlier chapters of the present book have shown that 'rule' is too restrictive a category to comprehend all that needs to be said about moral values, standards, and principles. Nor is there better reason to suppose that law is an affair of rules *only*. Why suppose that it is always a 'rule' that is being appealed to when claims about obligations, duties, offences, etc. are being made? This seems quite implausible. Second, it seems to tie the concepts of 'moral obligation', 'moral duty', and the like exclusively to *positive* morality because of the insistence on 'serious *social* pressure.' May the critical moralist not claim, for example, that by her principles the members of parliament are duty bound to repeal a certain law, even while she readily accepts that the most serious social pressure is against its repeal? Surely she may.

The proper course for resolving such difficulties is not to abandon the hermeneutic method but rather to press it further forward. I shall do so in the first place by urging a point passed over very lightly by Hart in *The Concept of Law*, though previously pressed more strongly by him in his earlier papers "Are There Any Natural Rights" (1955) and "Legal and Moral Obligation" (1958). The point is that terms such as 'obligation', 'duty', 'offence', and 'wrongdoing', though interrelated, are not identical in use. Of such terms 'wrong' or 'wrongdoing' are the most fundamental, given the concern of both morality and law to draw a line (by no means always the *same* line) between right and wrong conduct. Some, but not all, wrongful acts are breaches of obligation. Some, but not all, wrongful acts are breaches of duty.[6] Some, but not all, wrongful acts are offences, crimes, sins, etc.

If the hermeneutic method is a sound one, it ought not to have the effect of lumping all these categories and concepts together under so potentially misleading a title as 'rules of obligation'. (The title is misleading because it generates confusion as between rules that themselves determine obligations and rules that for some reason one has an obligation to obey. This confusion has been exploited by critics such as Rodger Beehler[7] and Roscoe Hill.[8]) Rather than lumping the different notions together as Hart does, we should explicate their differences. We should then show how they severally relate to the central idea that in morals, in law, and perhaps in other spheres we have to do with what I shall call 'requirements' of right conduct, marking the line drawn between what is wrong and what is, at least, acceptable. An approach to this can helpfully be made via some brief words about differentiating features of 'obligation', 'duty', and 'offence'.

Obligation. One common specialized use of the term 'obligation' concerns relationships between persons that have some normative import. For example, there are parental obligations, contractual obligations, promissory obligations, obligations of gratitude, obligations to make reparation or other amends for wrong done, and so forth. To have such obligations implies (*a*) that one stands in a certain relationship with another, as parent, contractor, promisor, beneficiary, or harm doer; and (*b*) that because of that relationship one is *required* to act in certain ways towards the other. What one is required to do depends, of course, on some understood moral or legal standard, according to which the existence of that relationship has the consequence that one is required to do certain actions, which, in the absence of the special relationship, one would be free to do or not to do as one chose.

This usage of the term 'obligation' has etymological roots which go back to the Latin legal term *obligatio*, which the Roman lawyers indeed defined as a *vinculum iuris*, a 'binding legal tie' between persons 'whereby we are held to a requirement of rendering some performance according to our civil law'.[9] Of course, the relational usage is not the only usage of the term in modern times, especially not since its appropriation by moral philosophers. Yet it seems that almost always the idea of 'being under an obligation' carries a rebuttable contextual implication that there is someone *to whom* one is obligated.

Duty is a term that also has a specialized as well as a generalized use. Consider phrases like 'the duties of the Minister', 'the duties of foreman', 'the duties of a professor', 'parental duties', and 'a manufacturer's duty of care in the preparation and packaging of products'. In these, the reference is to (*a*) a person's holding of a special position, office, or role and (*b*) the things which that person is required to do in virtue of holding that special position, office, or role. *Because* one has such and such a position, one must do *x*; to do *x* is one of one's duties in that position. Again, this presupposes some understood standard, moral, legal, or other—for example, the rule book of one's place of employment—whereby holding *that* position requires one to do *these* things. Again, though 'duty' has a wider and more indiscriminate use, there is perhaps always some weak contextual implication that any duty owed is owed because of some position held. At its weakest in the case of pure 'moral duties' one has to do *x* simply because one is a moral agent—and almost everyone has that role, so the idea of a special position here reaches a vanishing point.

Another very common application of the concept of 'duty' is where someone is held to *owe* a certain duty *to* someone else, as when we say that an occupier of premises owes to those who foreseeably come on the premises a duty to take reasonable care for their safety. In such cases, it seems natural to hold that those to whom the duty is owed have a 'correlative right', as the point is commonly put. Such duty–right relationships are obviously analogous to 'obligations' or, in some cases, identical with them. But not all duties are relevantly 'owed to' determinate other individuals. It seems that even in the case of duties 'owed to' someone, the person owing the duty normally owes it in virtue of some special role or position.

Of course it is the case that in their vague and general use, 'obligation' and 'duty' have come to be more or less interchangeable; but each retains also its historically earlier special sense and specialized usage, and this to some extent infects the general use. Hence, neither is a suitable term for the function Hart assigned to 'obligation' in his attempt to erect 'rules of obligation' into a master class of fundamental legal or moral rules.

Offence. It should not now surprise us to come across the further point made by A. M. Honoré in his essay on 'Real Laws',[10] namely that legislative formulations of the criminal law never, or scarcely ever, prescribe 'obligations' or 'duties'. Legislatures in this field use as their standard formulae such phrases as: 'If any person knowingly and wilfully does x, he shall be guilty of an offence and shall be liable upon conviction to punishment p'. Criminal law is a calendar of 'offences', 'crimes', felonies', 'misdemeanours', etc., and 'offence' is nowadays the generic term. As Honoré says, there is only one duty in criminal law, the duty to commit no offence. As I would add, that might be called the most basic 'duty of a citizen'—the role of citizen requires one to respect the law, even if higher moral loyalties sometimes do and should override the duty.

Let us notice again that our various specialized terms are not readily interchangeable. Breaking a contractual obligation is not committing an offence, nor is committing an offence necessarily a breach of any obligation. For lawyers' purposes the commission of an offence may also amount to breach of a statutory duty, and this in turn may result in an obligation to compensate an injured person. But 'offence', 'duty', and 'obligation' here express different legal perspectives on the same event or chain of events. They ought not to be conflated in too cavalier a fashion.

All these terms do, however, have a point in common. To break an obligation, to break a duty, or to commit an offence is to do wrong. There are different kinds of legal and moral wrongdoing, and the mistake is to treat the species 'obligation' as though it were the genus. There are, we may say, various kinds of legal or moral requirements about behaviour. I shall argue in the next two sections that all forms of wrongdoing are breaches of requirements about conduct which are properly viewed as 'categorical' requirements. In so doing, I shall distinguish all such categorical requirements from other social rules and standards that function as purely 'hypothetical' requirements, in a sense to be explained. This will further enable us, in a later section, to see why it is the case that categorical requirements tend to become crystallized in the form of social and legal rules, even though not all of them are necessarily crystallized in this form.

REQUIREMENTS AND WRONGDOING

At first sight, the reference to the notion of a 'requirement' may seem to involve explaining the obscure by reference to the more obscure (What is a 'requirement'?); even if not that, it certainly brings in the risk of inexactitude by excessive generality. Keeping one's contract and refraining from breaches of the peace may be legal or moral requirements; but making one's will in writing is also a requirement of the law, a requirement for validity of the will. A main aim of Hart's inquiry is, and of ours ought to be, to capture the *difference* between these types of requirements, hence the notion of 'requirement' is not alone sufficient to our task.

A 'requirement' is a necessary condition, a *sine qua non*, a 'without which not' of something or other. But of what? In the case of a will, of a contract for the sale of land in most jurisdictions, or of incorporating a company writing is a requirement—there must be some written instrument. But such a requirement is, in a Kantian sense, hypothetical. It has to be envisaged that someone wants to make a legally valid will, a legally enforceable contract for the sale of land, or a legally incorporated company before it can be true that the law's requirements are requirements for her/ him. They are, if she/he does want to achieve such legal effects, requirements for fulfilling that wish, simply because they are necessary conditions of fulfilling it. By contrast the requirements that we keep our contracts and refrain from breaches of the peace seem not to be directed towards fulfilling any wish.

This recalls Hart's third distinguishing mark for 'rules of obligation', the possibility that in such a case there can be conflict between what an agent desires and what the rule requires. We are tempted, perhaps, to conclude that some legal or moral requirements are 'categorical' because not envisaged merely as necessary conditions for fulfilling some presumed specific desire or aim of the party concerned. This seems to make a clear contrast with the 'hypothetical' requirements for making an enforceable contract or whatever, assuming that that's what at the moment you want. In fact, although this tempting suggestion points us in the right direction, it is still insufficient.[11]

The 'duties of the foreman' are indeed those very functions which a fore-man *qua* foreman is required to fulfil, and that they are so is independent of the particular wishes or desires the present foreman happens to have. But nobody has to be a foreman just as nobody has to make a will. If you want the foreman's job, *this* is what you have to do; and if you want to make a will, *that* is what you have to do. What's the difference? Is one set of requirements somehow *more* 'hypothetical'? It may seem only a fine distinction to point out that having the foreman's duties is a *consequence* of becoming a foreman, while executing a written instrument is a condition of making what is deemed a valid will. Yet we shall see in due course that the distinction, though fine, is all-important.

Anyway, do not all 'obligation-imposing rules' constitute self-seeking reasons for doing required acts? Hart says that such rules are backed by 'serious social pressure'. If that is so, then it is always true of anyone who wants to avoid this 'serious pressure', that fulfilling one's obligation is a requirement for satisfying that wish. No doubt one may incur the cost of sacrificing, on occasion, some other desire. But often people engaged in complicated legal transactions have likewise a heartfelt desire to cut corners on the legal formalities and expenses, and this desire conflicts with their other desire to get a result that is watertight in law.

To this objection, the Hartian reply would be that people may find themselves 'obliged' to act in certain ways in order to avoid (as they want to avoid) legal sanctions and moral reproaches or indeed in order to secure legal validity for their transactions. For Hart, this 'hypothetical' aspect of the situation is distinct from that other aspect which we evoke 'from the internal point of view'. From that point of view we say that, as well as being obliged to do x for fear of adverse reactions or for fear of the miscarriage of a transaction, someone has also an obligation to do x.

Now certainly from that internal point of view we deploy the concept of 'wrongdoing' without any reference to a particular agent's wishes. Mac-beth, say, makes it known as clearly as possible (*a*) that he is indifferent to our moral reproaches and our attempts to punish him; and (*b*) that he no longer has any concern to act decently. Everything said in chapters 4 and

5 about 'the internal point of view', 'acceptance' of rules and other standards, and about the nature of 'groups' indicates that we are in no way debarred from condemning Macbeth's actings as wrongdoings. Nor are we debarred from trying to *do* something to put a stop to them, even although his wishes and desires no longer function for him as any sort of obliging motive to observe our standards. These are the standards of the group he has contemptuously rejected, but to which we say he still belongs by our standards.

It is not an accident that in exploring the somewhat elusive but tempting notion of categorical requirements, we have arrived at discussion of 'wrongdoing'; for this concept is precisely adapted to explaining why some requirements can be relevantly deemed categorical. The whole Hartian project of establishing a hermeneutic understanding of moral 'principles, rules, and standards' was shown in the previous chapter to postulate that people hold seriously certain values which they consider important. Certain sorts of conduct, seen in the light of existing conventions and rules, may flout or go directly against such values. Taking these values as standards of judgement, such conduct is in itself and of its own quality wrong. We are concerned in such judgements with 'conduct' not mere 'behaviour'. Therefore we need to know or have reasonable beliefs about an agent's intentions and motives in order to have a view of what she or he is *doing* (over and above mere bodily motion). But once we have made an appreciation of what s/he is doing, the question whether s/he is going against some value (e.g., acting cruelly, inconsiderately, dishonestly, or indecently) does not depend on whether or not s/he wants to avoid cruelty, inconsiderateness, dishonesty, indecency, or whatever. It depends on whether we who pass judgement do really deem these evils or disvalues. Nor does this depend on *our* casual wishes, for, as was said, values in Hart's scheme of things do not 'derive from some arbitrary volition or existential choice' (p. 71 above).

Here arises, however, a problem. Are not values as much standards for judgements of excellence or goodness, and degrees of goodness, as standards for judgements about wrongdoing?[12] To this question the answer must be affirmative. A quotation from *The Concept of Law* may help both to illustrate the problem and to guide in solving it:

> It is . . . both true and important that morality includes much more than the *obligations* and *duties* which are recognized in the actual practice of social groups. Obligation and duty are only the bedrock of morality, even of social ['positive'] morality. . . . [E]ven within the morality of a particular society, there exist side by side with the structure of mandatory moral obligations and duties and the

relatively clear rules that define them, certain moral *ideals*. The realization of these is not taken, as duty is, as a matter of course, but as an achievement deserving praise. The hero and the saint are extreme types of those who do more than their duty. What they do is not like obligation or duty, something which can be demanded of them, and failure to do it is not regarded as wrong or a matter for censure. On a humbler scale than the saint or hero, are those who are recognized in a society as deserving praise for the moral virtues which they manifest in daily life such as bravery, charity, benevolence, patience or chastity. The connexion between such socially recognized ideals and virtues and the primary mandatory forms of social obligation and duty is fairly clear. Many moral virtues are qualities consisting in the ability and disposition to carry forward, beyond the limited extent which duty demands, the kind of concern for others' interests or sacrifice of personal interest which it does demand. Benevolence or charity are examples of this. Other moral virtues like temperance, patience, bravery, or conscientiousness are in a sense ancillary; they are qualities of character shown in exceptional devotion to duty or in the pursuit of substantive moral ideals in the face of special temptation or danger. (*C.L.* pp. 182–3)

It is upon Hart's suggested 'connection between such socially recognized ideals and virtues and the primary mandatory forms of social obligation and duty' that I shall focus attention. Hart's whole theory can be seen as oriented towards the thesis that people in societies and people as critical individuals do attach themselves to certain values which are both fundamental standards of judgement and the basis for all other less fundamental standards. It has to be conceded that this is not an interpretation of his position that he favoured, and as chapter 14 will show, it is an aspect of his earlier thought that he played down in his latest writing. Nevertheless the grounds of this interpretation are clearly laid down in his writing when he was at the peak of his creative powers, and they have a greatly persuasive character.

That we set value on, for example, considerateness for others implies that we can rank or grade different ways of acting as more or less considerate. Some acts and some individuals' whole style of living may show exceptional excellence (or 'virtue') on that scale. Others, without showing excellence, nevertheless do not go against this value; without being particularly considerate, they are not actually *inconsiderate*. Others again positively go against this value or even flout it—they are decidedly inconsiderate, or even grossly so, perhaps to the point of vindictiveness or even cruelty. What this shows is that we are dealing with a scale against which acts or, in respect of their dispositions, people can manifest different degrees of goodness or badness accordingly as they more or less advance or go against the value in question. But there is a 'cutoff point' where, for want of considerateness, an act would be 'wrong'. Below that point there are, of course, varying degrees of wrongness and of seriousness of reproach. Not all wrongs are equally wrong, although all are alike in that they fall below a cutoff point.

We may compare (for this purpose only) the somewhat formalized analogy of an examination marked on a hundred-point scale. Every performance that achieves a mark less than 50 percent is a failure—but of course there are marginal failures, clear failures, disastrous failures, and total failures. Likewise, among all those that pass, some show such special excellence as to tend towards the 100 percent mark while others are bare passes and so forth.

In matters of morality at least, it seems that our judgements as between what conduct is 'right' or 'all right' and what is 'wrong' presuppose some such more or less understood cutoff point. To act wrongly is to fail to come up to scratch in relation to some seriously held and important value; 'wrongness' is wrongness from the point of view of one who seriously holds that value and interprets the cutoff point so. Even if the cutoff point is only a vague one, we could be sure that some act went sufficiently far below any reasonably interpreted cutoff point to be clearly wrong. We 'draw the line somewhere' –and wherever we might draw it, *this* falls short.

THE HARTIAN CRITERIA REEXAMINED

These reflections enable us to reconsider Hart's first criterion as to 'rules of obligation'. 'Seriousness of social pressure', especially in the moral case, is a difficult notion to tie down. 'It may be limited to verbal manifestations of disapproval or of appeals to the individual's respect for the rule violated: it may depend heavily on the operation of feelings of shame, remorse, and guilt' (*C.L.* p. 86). That is all very well and good. But how *can* you appeal to my reasonable feelings, as distinct from my perhaps pathological feelings of shame, remorse, or guilt? You can do so only by showing that I am failing to control those dispositions of mine that are pulling me towards a substantial shortfall in some important value such as considerateness, justice, steadfastness, honesty, self-command, decency, modesty, or whatever ('shame'). You might also do so by showing that some past act of mine has exhibited some such falling short ('remorse'); or by showing that some past, present, or contemplated act exhibits such ('guilt'). What makes a reproach a *serious* reproach is that it is reproof of that sort. Hence it is different from the reproach or reproof addressed to one whose acts are self-defeating. That is the difference between acting wrongly (e.g., exhibiting neglect for the bodily safety of others by driving too fast in icy conditions) and acting merely stupidly (e.g., in failing to execute a written contract when I do want to achieve a legally enforceable agreement to sell my house).

It is in just this sense that the considerations we are reviewing amount to 'requirements'; a requirement is a minimally necessary condition of something or other.[13] From the internal point of view as oriented towards moral values, there are 'requirements', which are, precisely, the requirements constituted by what are accepted as the 'cutoff points' on the scales set by those values whose 'importance' qualifies them as 'moral'. (This should lead us to doubt Hart's view that the 'importance' attached to certain rules is only a subsidiary ground for distinguishing those rules that are 'obligation-imposing'.) There are requirements of being acceptably considerate, just, steadfast, honest, self-controlled, decent, modest, or whatever. They are requirements for morally acceptable conduct, the minimum necessary for that as distinct from the higher reaches of excellence, praiseworthiness, saintliness, or heroism.

It seems no less clear that from the internal point of view as oriented towards legal standards there is a concern to discriminate between conduct, which in its substance as conduct falls short of relevant minima. Indeed, for the most part, legal concern focuses exclusively on the *requirements* of law-abiding behaviour as distinct from any possible excellence achieved on relevant scales. The line dividing right from wrong conduct is *the* crucial line with which lawyers and judges are primarily concerned; which is not, however, to say that once the wrongfulness of an act is established, no one cares about the degree of wrongness or badness involved. When it comes to the imposition of penalties, the difference between a mere infringement and a grave offence is all-important. Less frequently does law-in-courts concern itself with gradations of goodness above the cutoff line; the law as such is not much concerned about saintliness and heroism. But in such cases as the so-called rescue cases[14] this is a factor. For the rescuer's act of reasonable courage, although voluntary, does not debar him from recovering compensation from a person whose wrongful negligence created the danger to which the rescuer responded by bravely saving the primary victim of that negligence. Technically, that act of rescuing is held not to 'break the chain of causation' between the harm suffered and the negligent act. But the deeper reason for that holding is that it is not thought right that those who reasonably go beyond the call of duty should suffer for doing so, someone else having been at fault in setting up the danger to which they responded.

As Hart notes, even to *say* 'you are doing wrong' or 'you have done wrong' is to express a more or less serious reproach. In the case of a sensitive addressee who respects the opinion of this critic, the very saying of it may powerfully motivate the addressee both to make amends for what s/he has done and to avoid repetition of the wrong. It is, however, possible to hold that for some wrongs mere *saying* is not enough. Something must be *done*. If voluntary amends are not forthcoming, the wrongdoer must be compelled to make compensation. Against actual or apprehended insensitivity to mildly expressed but seriously meant criticism, it may be thought necessary to bring home the gravity of one's reproof of wrongdoing by some distinct act of punishment. This alone, it may be thought, will actually awaken the wrongdoer to the error of her or his ways, at the same time alerting to their potential error others similarly tempted.

Not merely is it possible to hold such thoughts. Legal systems, school and university disciplinary systems, codes of factory discipline, laws of games, and rules of clubs all provide in their different ways illustrations of actual social practices institutionalizing such punitive *doings* rather than mere reproachful *sayings* about the various relevant species of wrongdoing. But now we see precisely why resort to penalties (whether in football, in school, in the family, in the factory, or in law) is an index to the concept 'wrongdoing'. *Penalizing* someone may be considered to be necessary and justified as expressing forcefully and seriously an adverse judgement on conduct which falls below the line of requirement and as discouraging repetition of that conduct. Thus the act of imposing a penalty for some conduct is analytically the act of treating that conduct as wrongdoing—or, in cases of insincerity, purporting so to treat it. The hermeneutic theorist should be as interested in the 'internal aspect' of the concept 'penalty' as of the concept 'wrongdoing'. When one looks at it that way, one finds an interesting fact. It is possible for someone to think that doing x is wrong but no penalty need be exacted. But it is not possible for anyone to accept from the internal point of view that doing x ought to be penalized unless they already accept that doing x is on some ground and in some degree wrong.

The hermeneutic theorist should be equally aware that not all wrongs are offences subject to penalties. There are wrongs that are breaches of duty owed by persons in particular roles or ways of life to whoever else may be affected. This kind of wrongdoing, a 'tort' or 'delict', is a wrong as against any person harmed, at least if it was foreseeable that the person in question was likely to suffer such harm. There are wrongs by way of breach of obligation, so far as this is differentiated from 'breach of duty'—for example, promise breaking or breach of contract. As the very use of 'duty' or 'obligation' in such contexts suggests, the wrong is a wrong *to* someone. And accordingly, the focus of concern is rather with securing a remedy to the injured party, not with punishing the injurer.

RULES OF OBLIGATION?

Earlier, an objection was made to Hart's account of obligation and of wrongdoing, namely, that it is couched expressly and exclusively in terms of 'rules' as such, and that it seems to apply only to *positive* morality and to law. Such an objection could not be laid at the door of the alternative explanation developed in this chapter, by way of a more thoroughgoing application of Hart's hermeneutic method to the problem in hand.

The alternative explanation can accommodate various rather obvious truths, which subsequent work, for example, by Ronald Dworkin,[15] by Joseph Raz,[16] by Roscoe Hill[17] and by Rodger Beehler,[18] had shown to slip out from under the net of Hart's analysis. Our friend the vegetarian does not necessarily think that there is a rule against eating meat. But she does think it *wrong* in principle, and as a consequence, she may make it a rule for herself only to visit restaurants with a suitable cuisine when she eats out. While others may hold that regulations as to the keeping and humane slaughtering of sheep, cattle, etc. satisfy the minimum requirements of humanity and free us of the charge of cruelty to animals, she sets *her* cutoff point higher on that scale. Or again, legislators who had been convinced by Hart's writings on critical morality might rightly have conceived themselves to be under a duty as legislators to work for repeal of laws inhibiting freedom in sexual behaviour. But, if they did think that, they did not have to suppose that any rule required them so to act. Indeed, it would have been absurd if they had. Finally, while most moralities allow that there are obligations of gratitude as between beneficiaries and benefactors, the very point of view from which such obligations are recognized is one that excludes tying down the appropriate expression of gratitude to mere rules. Admittedly, there may be some such rules, as under the once widely observed rule that guests should write 'bread and butter' letters thanking their hostess for her hospitality— nowadays a phone call or an e-mail will usually suffice.

It can be claimed as a distinctive merit of the present interpretation of Hart's theory that, by its reconsideration of his exposition at certain crucial points, it sets up a framework for explaining otherwise inexplicable aspects of the subject matter. Yet there remain powerful points in the simpler reading of Hart's theory which must not be passed over. While it is true that judgements about 'obligation', 'duty', 'offence', and 'wrongdoing' do not always and necessarily rest upon *rules* of conduct, there are in fact strong reasons why they regularly and frequently do.

The idea of a 'requirement' in the relevant sense was seen to relate to minimal satisfaction of some important value and thus to rest on some perhaps vague and implicit rather than explicit cutoff point. But this very vagueness is a matter of concern in social intercourse. People have reason to want to be clear about where the line is drawn. Employees want their duties clearly stated. Students want the university to lay down clear lines as to minimum disciplinary requirements (as well as minimum academic requirements). Members of a family want some clarity as to when they should turn up for meals, avoiding the reproach of inconsiderateness to whoever does the cooking. In general social relations within the various circles in which we move, we like to know what are the minimum moral requirements we are expected to live up to.

For this very reason, it is the case that in all the various ways described in the previous chapter, conventions and rules arise, whether by mere practice, by express agreement, by social authority, or by 'moral authority'. And so it is that, quite apart from law, there exist conventions about conduct on buses, rulings that settle employees' duties, rules of university or college discipline, and rules as to mealtimes. There are also grand moral rules or maxims or commandments like 'Thou shalt not kill', 'Thou shalt not commit adultery', 'Thou shalt not steal', 'Thou shalt not break thy promises', 'Thou shalt not tell lies', and so forth.

These are not independent of the values people hold and hold to be important. (Both in his account of morality and in his account of obligation-imposing rules, Hart stresses the criterion of 'importance'.) Rather, they are ways of settling relatively clearly where in relation to these values the minimal line is drawn. This makes clear why, as has already been stated, 'rules' are both in a sense arbitrary and also to an extent precise, 'cut-and-dried'. The arbitrariness in question does not conflict with the proposition that rules settle requirements rationally related to important values. But, as every examiner and examinee knows, where *exactly* one draws the line is, within a range of a few points, arbitrary. It is sometimes better to get things clear than to get things absolutely 'right'—sometimes indeed the only rightness is clarity, and that is when it is right to have rules.

So far, I have abstained from referring within this section to positive law. But it must be obvious that everything said so far about the reasons for seeking clarity about minimal moral requirements applies with yet more force to legal requirements. For here the polity brings to bear its organized coercive power to enforce the making of amends for breaches of obligation or of duty and to enforce penalties for wrongdoing.

Once the Roman *plebs*, the disenfranchised body of the common people, seceded from the city and decamped to the nearby mountain (the Mons Aventinus). The first demand of the *plebs* was for *laws, leges*, clear statutory rulings settling the minimum requirements, in place of appeals to a not clearly understood traditional conception of *jus*, rightfulness. That was locked in the bosoms of the patrician pontiffs, the priest-magistrates who then governed in questions of right and of wrong. The *plebs* did indeed get what they had demanded. The Commission of Ten was set up to reduce the laws to writing, and in due course the Statute of the Twelve Tables was promulgated, enunciating all the laws.[19]

This demand of the *plebs* is a recurring demand of all those who live under civil government. It is a principle of the critical morality which Hart applies in criticizing *Shaw* v. *DPP*,[20] namely the principle that there ought to be no criminal charges or criminal penalties save for breach of clear and pre-announced laws (*Nullum crimen sine lege, nulla poena sine crimine*). Hart argued that the reinvention of 'conspiracy to corrupt public morals' to all intents and purposes infringed that principle. Nor could originality be claimed by or for Hart in this matter. At least since Beccaria's and Bentham's time,[21] it has been a widely held principle in modern societies that offences require clearly enunciated laws, and indeed nowadays it is written into all contemporary declarations or conventions on human rights.

Hence it is true, at least of modern legal systems, that the *legal* forms of wrongdoing everywhere tend to be expressed and expressible in rules properly so called, rules which set the minimum standard of law-abiding behaviour. But, even in law, rules need not be conceived as the *only* grounds of wrongdoing, of obligation, or of duty. When it comes to disputed questions of interpretation or of analogical development of rules, the underlying grounds—principles and other standards—come again to the fore. This should not, however, be thought to deprive of its real force and merit Hart's insistence on the existence of 'primary rules of obligation' as a ground-floor element of law. And even though one ought not to accept a conflation of all

forms of wrongdoing with the specific case of breach of obligation, there
are powerful grounds for accepting the main lines of the thesis which Hart
propounded in those terms.

A CONCLUSION ON THE HARTIAN CRITERIA

A final word may be said about Hart's three criteria for distinguishing
rules of obligation, as he calls them.

As to 'seriousness' of reaction, we may assent. But we note that in the
moral sphere, reaction is serious precisely in that it stigmatizes certain
conduct as 'wrongdoing', as a falling short of the minimum requirement
of fulfilling some important value whose importance is independent of
the agent's present particular desires. Very often, but not invariably, this
'falling short' involves breach of a more or less clear convention or rule
that clarifies where the line is drawn with respect to that value. In law especially, one common mark of such seriousness of reaction is the imposition
of what is viewed 'from the internal point of view' as a 'penalty'. Hence,
conversely, whenever legislators resort to the device of imposing what they
call 'penalties' for those who engage in certain sorts of conduct, they at
least are estopped from claiming that they do not take a serious view of the
undesirability on some ground of such conduct. In cases of breach of obligation and breach of duty, a different form of 'sanction' is commonly employed (viz., the imposition of an enforced requirement to make amends
for nonperformance of what one has an obligation or duty to do or of some
directly enforced order for compliance). In the legal even more than in the
moral sphere, this involves the articulation of rules that clarify the requirements in question.

As to 'importance', it needs only to be repeated again that this implies
values and some ranking of values. And, as Hart says, in social contexts,
one prominent dimension of importance is, precisely, the securing of the
conditions for continuing social coexistence and cooperation. But this cuts
both ways. Whatever requirements of conduct are for any reason deemed
important, those who break them may indeed be thought to endanger the
conditions of social coexistence and cooperation. No one who had reflected
on Durkheim's sociological scrutiny of law[22] could doubt the significance
of the observation that the perceived 'dangerousness' of conduct is at least
as likely to stem from the fact that it trenches upon values and requirements considered important as to stem from its 'harming' people or society

according to rationalistic utilitarian criteria of harmfulness. Since one condition of social coexistence and cooperation is a sharing of views on what is important, this is not too surprising.

As for the possibility of conflict between obligation and desire, this indeed fits in with the idea that in some sense the relevant minimum requirements of moral rectitude and legal propriety are 'categorical'. Certainly, people are in some cases free to 'opt in' to some regime of obligation or duty, for example, by accepting appointment to some job. It can therefore be the case that their being called on to meet certain requirements is a consequence of fulfilling the desire that led them to 'opt in'. To this extent, there is a similarity with formal requirements in the case of wills, of certain contracts, of constituting trusts, of incorporating companies, and so forth. But the point is that once one has 'opted in', one faces certain requirements of substance in relation to one's conduct, out of which one cannot unconditionally opt. The act of opting in engages one with the minimum requirements of important values, likely enough prescribed in rules. These are requirements one must fulfil even against one's wishes.

Hence, although our inquiry leads us to doubt that 'obligation', 'duty', 'offence', and 'wrongdoing' relate *only* to rules as Hart claims, and although it leads us to reject his conflation of these related ideas, it does not lead us to a radical rejection of Hart's proposed criteria. It leads us to a reinterpretation of them.

CODA: HART ON PEREMPTORY REASONS

This chapter so far accounts for Hart's view of the relevant matters as stated in *The Concept of Law* and sundry earlier writings on the same theme, and it suggests one way of taking forward the ideas there by reinterpreting them. Subsequent to the writing of the first edition of this book, Hart returned to the theme and reinterpreted his own ideas in somewhat different terms, in a way that shows the high respect he had for the work of Joseph Raz. Essentially, the trajectory of his thought was to consider the 'internal aspect' of conduct in terms of the reasons people can have for acting, that is, the different kinds of reasons they can have for doing whatever they do.[23] In this context, to consider that conduct of a certain kind is obligatory is to consider that there is a particularly strong reason for so conducting oneself. The strength of such a reason is not just a matter of its relative weight in a competition among reasons. It is strength in the sense of what

Hart calls a 'peremptory' character. It both sets a reason to do *this* and excludes one's admitting into current practical consideration other normally acceptable reasons that point to doing something, indeed anything, other than *this*. Here, it seems, we are brought back to the idea that obligations may conflict with desires. The point is that desires, however strong and however weighty they normally are as reasons for pursuing the conduct that helps us fulfil them, simply have to be set aside and disregarded whenever the fulfilment of some obligation proves incompatible with the pursuit of this or that desire.

Hart's way of reinterpreting obligations and the like owes much to the ideas that Joseph Raz developed in his account of what he initially called 'exclusionary reasons'[24] and subsequently developed further under the name of 'protected reasons'.[25] These are both reasons for engaging in certain conduct and reasons that exclude giving attention to other rival reasons that might otherwise have a bearing on a certain course of action.

It is undoubtedly true that a hermeneutic approach to understanding rules, principles, and other standards of conduct, and concepts like 'right' and 'wrong', or 'obligation' and 'duty', requires attention to how we use these in our processes of reasoning. When we reason or reflect on what to do in a practical way, how do such standards or concepts figure in our reasoning? Hart's answer is that we must regard them as 'peremptory reasons' in the sense indicated—or, as it might be, we deem them 'exclusionary' or 'protected' reasons in the Razian terminology. This insight is important. It captures in a clear way the notion of a 'requirement' as was developed earlier in the present chapter.

From a legal point of view, there is indeed here and now a reason for me not to take and drive away my neighbour's car. This is so, however urgently I wish to and however easy it may be to do so, since she happens to have left the key in the ignition. This is a peremptory reason, cutting off reference to my other possible reasons for simply taking the car. The reason is not solely that there is a rule of the criminal law that prohibits taking and driving away the vehicle of another without that other's consent. The exact reason not to take this car is that it is a wrong, an offence, for me to do so on this occasion in these circumstances in which I have not obtained the express or implied consent of my neighbour. To justify the proposition that this act is in this way wrong, I do indeed refer to the general legal prohibition expressed in a rule of currently valid criminal law. But I also, and necessarily, refer to the existing facts and circumstances in virtue of which that rule applies to me now in respect of this very car belonging to this particular neighbour.

Morally speaking, I may consider the act wrong just because it violates due respect for my neighbour's expectation of peaceful enjoyment of her property. It is interesting to consider what further reasons enter into that moral deliberation. It certainly need not involve reflecting on any particular moral rules, though it will include as a background fact that the car belongs in law to my neighbour, or at least is in his or her lawful possession at the time in question. It may also include reflection on reciprocity and good neighbourly relations. From the moral point of view, a similar peremptory character obtains. It seems possible, after all, to accommodate the later idea about peremptory reasons into the interpretation of the earlier writings that occupies most of this chapter.

CHAPTER SEVEN

Powers and Power-Conferring Rules

THE CONCEPT OF NORMATIVE POWER

> To promise is to say something which creates an obligation for the promisor: in order that words should have this kind of effect, rules must exist providing that if words are used by appropriate persons on appropriate occasions (i.e., by sane persons understanding their position and free from various sorts of pressure) those who use these words shall be bound to do the things designated by them. So, when we promise, we make use of specified procedures to change our own moral situation by imposing obligations on ourselves and conferring rights on others; in lawyers' parlance we exercise 'a power' conferred by rules to do this. (*C.L.* pp. 43)

Assuming that the preceding account of 'obligation' and related concepts was satisfactory, it is relatively easy to develop and account for a concept of 'power'. Let us take a phrase out of the above quotation, varying it slightly.

> If the words 'I promise you that I will do *this* act' are used by an appropriate person to an appropriate person on an appropriate occasion, then the person uttering them shall be bound to do the designated act in favour of the person addressed.

That is at once more formalized than anything we would expect to find in popular moral consciousness, and yet at the same time vague at key points. What persons and occasions are 'appropriate'? The tacit supposition is presumably that one is not insane, not joking, not playacting, not constructing philosophical examples, not under duress, not drunk, not promising to commit some crime, or something like that. Let us suppose, from the standpoint of a given social or positive morality, that the vague points can be clarified in terms of well understood, even if not commonly articulated, exempting or vitiating conditions. Then it seems reasonable enough to treat Hart's formulation, or my variation of it, as giving a somewhat precise and formal definition to the widely held moral rule that 'people should keep their promises'.

It is interesting to note that, both as Hart formulates it and as I reformulated it, the rule in question belongs to Hart's class of 'obligation-imposing rules'. It tells us what one 'is bound' to do. The obligation in question is, however, conditional. It is a condition of my coming under *that* obligation to you that I have said the appropriate words in the appropriate circumstances, both of us being appropriate persons. In fact, we can justifiably impute to the person who uses the words 'I promise to do *x*' the intention that his addressee should take him to intend incurring such an obligation. Because of the meaning of the word 'promise' anyone who uses it is normally *estopped* from denying such an intention. So we can reasonably impute it to him. (Sometimes we make false representations, whether expressly or implicitly in what we say or do, and those to whom we make them take them for true. Then it is unfair to those others if we afterwards make against them claims based on the true state of affairs. Hence the useful legal concept of 'estoppel'—we are *estopped* from making any claim which involves 'giving the lie' to our earlier false representation.)

Given that such is the intention, or the justifiably imputed intention, of one who says 'I promise', the case we have here is one of a kind noted in the concluding section of the preceding chapter. To promise is to 'opt in' to a particular obligation. He who promises intends to become obligated, whatever his ulterior intentions or motives. I can promise you something to please you, to placate your wrath, to enable you to plan some important venture that I hope you will undertake, or indeed in order to set you up for some fiendishly clever fraud. In all events, achieving these ulterior ends depends on my undertaking the obligation and on your seriously believing that I have undertaken it and can be trusted to act accordingly. It is to *this* feature of the situation that Hart draws attention in calling the making of a promise the exercise of 'a power'. The rule is such that one can voluntarily opt in to the conditional obligation it stipulates—for that is the condition on the obligation, one's voluntarily opting in.

Hart in various places stressed the notion that powers give us 'facilities'. But we ought to be careful about that in such a case as promising. You are assuring me that you will be going to Switzerland on holiday. I want to go only on condition that you go. I ask you, 'Is that a promise?' You say, 'Yes'. From whose point of view is the power of undertaking a promissory obligation a 'facility'? Yours or mine? Should we say that because A has a power to obligate himself in favour of B, it follows that B has in the same sense a power to invite A to exercise the first-order power of obligating himself? Or is it just the case that in the natural way of things he *can* do that? So it seems.

Suppose we envisage a morality in which the previously stated rule is further elaborated in the following way:

> If the words 'I promise you that I will do this act' are used by an appropriate person to an appropriate person on an appropriate occasion, *then provided the addressee accepts the promise*, the person uttering the promise shall be bound to do the designated act in favour of the person addressed, *unless the latter subsequently releases the former from this obligation*.

This is a very recognizable view of the conditions upon which promises become binding, and of a condition on which the promisor can be released from his or her obligation to perform. Sometimes philosophers are tempted to suppose that such conditions are necessary to the very idea of 'promising'. But that is silly. Legal systems vary (in these and other matters) as to the conditions of obligation and of release therefrom; so may moralities. There can be no more than a family of promising conventions and rules, all having generic resemblances to each other as between differing communities just as there is a family of contract laws differing in detail as between different jurisdictions.

Suppose anyway a morality which contains a proviso for acceptance and a provision for voluntary release by the promisee, as in the italicized words above. Because of the proviso, there are two conditions upon one's becoming obligated by a promise. First, one must (intentionally) 'opt in' by 'making a promise'; but secondly, the other party must (intentionally) accept that opting in. So A's power is only a power to undertake a conditional obligation, the condition being that B accept the promise. This means that by A's act of making a promise, B acquires a power—the power to put A under obligation by accepting. A's initial act thus changes B's position precisely in the sense that B now has power by accepting to 'bind' A, or, by rejecting, to leave him or her quite free of obligation under this title. In a case in which A has made and B has accepted a promise, A has an obligation to B to do whatever was promised. But under the rule contemplated, B has a certain continuing power, the power to release A from that obligation. If she exercises that power, A will not after all do wrong in failing to perform as promised.

On inspection, this examination of two versions of a fairly simple 'obligation-imposing rule' shows us several types of power. First, under the simpler version, there is the power unconditionally to incur an obligation—by promising. Second, under the more elaborated version, there is the power, by promising, to incur a conditional obligation. But here the exercise of this power involves conferring a power on the promisee—the power, by accepting, to make A's obligation unconditional; we might even say 'the power to impose an obligation on A'. Third, there is the power exercisable by the promisee, under the more elaborated version of the rule, to release or liberate the promisor from his or her obligation.

So in any classification of these 'normative powers', in this case 'moral powers' since the norm in question is a moral rule, we must include at least power to incur obligation, power to impose obligation, power to confer power, and power to release from obligation. But what do we mean in calling all these powers 'normative powers',[1] as distinct from things people just *can* do, like speak English? The key point here is that all the acts that are acts of exercising the so-called power are acts which necessarily and intrinsically *invoke* the rule in some way.

When I say that I 'invoke' a rule I mean something rather complex. Not only do I intend my act as an act fulfilling a condition set in the rule. I intend that the other party recognize that I intend my act as an act fulfilling a condition set in the rule.[2] So when a rule sets a condition which can be put in operation only when someone intends his or her act as fulfilling that condition, and intends that he/she be recognized as so intending, the rule confers a power. Where one so acts with reference to a conditional obligation, the power one exercises is power to incur or to perfect an obligation. Where a condition is set allowing release from obligation, the power one exercises with reference to that condition is power to release from obligation. Where a condition is set enabling the actor to put someone else in the position of having a 'power' under this definition, the actor's power is one of conferring that further power.

What if somebody who does not mean to 'invoke' a rule in this way nevertheless acts in such a way as to lead someone else to believe reasonably that he/she has the intention? I say, 'I promise to come to your party' meaning it as a joke and unreasonably supposing you will take it so. But in the circumstances you quite reasonably take it as a serious promise, as I only afterwards discover. Since the only way we can gather people's intentions is by their outward and visible or audible acts, there is a practically universal understanding that people must be deemed to intend their acts to be interpreted as a reasonable addressee would interpret them. Whatever actual intentions people had or *say* they had when they did so-and-so, we justifiably impute to them the intention disclosed by that reasonable and probable interpretation. Therefore my references to intention above must be taken as including justifiably imputed intentions, what lawyers sometimes call 'objective' intentions.[3]

This elaboration of what is meant by 'invoking' a rule is essential to the definition of 'a power'. Power is conferred by a rule when the rule contains a condition that is satisfied only by an act performed with the (actual or imputed) intention of invoking the rule.

It could perhaps be said that this notion is implicit in what Hart says about powers and power-conferring rules. But it is only a somewhat shadowy and implicit idea, and accordingly it needs to be brought out and made explicit. For otherwise we should be forced into the odd conclusion that among the powers conferred by morality and by law are powers to commit wrongs and so to make oneself liable to reproaches and punishments. But this is not so. True it is that he who commits murder does wrong. True it is that only those who take human life with certain (actual or imputed) intentions commit murder. But the relevant intentions required by the moral or the legal definition of murder do *not* include an intention that one's act be recognized as one intended to satisfy the conditions for being 'murder'. Hence, although it is true that only the intentional commission of certain acts can make me guilty of murder and liable to punishment therefor, it is not true that I have 'power' in our technical sense to incur that liability.

On just this ground, we should not suppose that the mere fact that some regimes of duty are such that we can become subject to them only by 'opting in' of itself implies a legally or morally conferred power to opt in. A passing allusion was made earlier to the duties to which every manufacturer as such is subjected in favour of those who consume its goods. If you manufacture consumer goods, you are subject to a certain 'duty of care'. People who manufacture goods commonly do so intentionally and of their own free will. Wise and conscientious people no doubt take care to discover the duties expected of them. Hence somebody who goes into manufacturing may well do so with the honest intention of incurring and fulfilling the duties of that calling. But it is obvious that such an intention is not in truth a condition of *having* those duties and being *required* to fulfil them. This becomes obvious upon scrutiny of the relevant rule in Scots and English law, which no doubt coincides with a widely held proposition of positive morality:

> [B]y Scots and English law alike a manufacturer of goods which he sells in such a form as to show that he intends them to reach the ultimate consumer in the form in which they left him, with no reasonable possibility of intermediate examination, and with the knowledge that absence of reasonable care in the preparation or putting up of the products will result in injury to the consumer's life or property, owes a duty to the consumer to take that reasonable care.[4]

The law sets conditions for a person's incurring that duty to take reasonable care, and the conditions include certain intentions (and knowledge) of the manufacturer. But the intentions do not include an intention to become bound by fulfilling the condition. The rule applies whether or not one 'invokes' it. This further clarifies the reason why such requirements as those falling upon a manufacturer towards consumers or on a parent towards his/her children must be regarded as categorical, not hypothetical, despite the fact that it is a matter of choice whether or not one steps into the relevant role in the first place.

Hence the particular definition given to 'normative power' is essential to clarity of thought. It enables us to discriminate, as we ought to discriminate, between two distinct things. (*a*) There are cases where obligations or duties are incurred only on condition that one acts with the actual or imputed intention of invoking the conditions for having the obligation or duty—or of imposing it on someone else, or of releasing someone else from it, or of creating conditions in which someone else has such a power. (*b*) There are cases where obligations, duties, etc. are conditional on free and intentional acts of individuals, but are not in the same sense within their power.

W. H. Davies's 'Super-Tramp'[5] always committed offences in early winter in a town with a tolerably comfortable jail. The point of doing so was to get convicted and imprisoned. The end that this served was his survival and reasonable comfort during the harsh North American winter. As he 'worked the system', the law provided him with a facility. This illustrates well the truth that not every way of acting in knowledge of the law and with a view to making the law's provisions serve one's ends can be viewed as an exercise of legal power.[6] There is doubtless an infinity of ways in which the law can be used as providing such 'facilities'. Not every such case is one of legal power.

These reflections indicate the need for a certain caution about certain claims made by Hart in relation to legal powers:

> Legal rules defining the ways in which valid contracts or wills or marriages are made do not require persons to act in certain ways whether they wish to or not. Such laws do not impose duties or obligations. Instead, they provide individuals with *facilities* for realizing their wishes, by conferring legal powers on them to create, by certain specified procedures, and subject to certain conditions, structures of rights and duties within the coercive framework of the law.
>
> The power thus conferred on individuals to mould their legal relations with others by contracts, wills, marriages, etc., is one of the great contributions of law to social life . . . (*C.L.* pp. 27–28)

This is certainly one of the most important points in Hart's legal philosophy, and an important basis of its continuing claim on our attention. What is needed, however, is a refinement upon the idea that law provides 'facilities for realizing . . . wishes, *by conferring legal powers*'. That is indeed true, but we must distinguish the facilities so provided by conferment of 'powers' from the more general ones. And that requires our earlier stated definition of 'normative power', of which legal power is a species.

POWERS AND RULES—AND OTHER STANDARDS

> Such laws [as those which confer power to make valid contracts or wills or marriages] do not impose duties or obligations. (*C.L.* p. 27)

> Such power-conferring rules are thought of, spoken of, and used in social life differently from rules which impose duties, and they are valued for different reasons. What other tests for difference in character could there be? (*C.L.* p. 41)

The above quotations indicate another basic proposition of Hart's in connexion with the concept of power. It is a fundamental proposition for him in his rejection of Austinian theories of law as 'command'. As he says, laws that simply define offences subject to penalties, or that otherwise impose obligations or duties, can (albeit imperfectly) be assimilated to the model of 'orders' of a 'sovereign' backed by 'threats' of a penalty. But one of the facts that Hart presents as fatal to acceptance of that model is the fact that not all laws *do* impose obligations. Some confer powers, and these really are a different kind of rule, because they are 'thought of, spoken of, and used in social life differently from rules which impose duties'. Fortunately, Hart has a better case against the Austinian model than this. The 'hermeneutic' analysis of rules and other standards is what shows that rules and obligations are conceptually quite different from the orders or even the general commands of an habitually obeyed 'sovereign' whose expressions of will count as 'commands' because and when they are backed by the explicit or implicit threat of a sanction (an 'evil') to be enforced in case of disobedience.

Given a proper and hermeneutic explanation of obligation and duty and, in general, 'categorical requirements' or 'peremptory reasons', it is in turn possible to explain the concept of normative power. But to do that, it is *not* necessary to postulate the *prior* existence of a separate class of rule whose sole function is the conferment of power. The very case which Hart uses as his simplest instance of a moral rule that confers power is the case of the promise-making rule discussed above. But even in its more elaborated form that rule was an 'obligation-imposing rule'; the 'powers' were conferred by the rule because of the conditions set for determining when a person *is* 'bound' in virtue of the rule, and how he can become released from being so bound, otherwise than by simply rendering performance. Let us recall the basic sentence of Hart's text:

> [I]f words are used by appropriate persons on appropriate occasions . . . those who use these words shall be bound to do the thing designated by them. (*C.L.* p. 43)

On *that* formulation, or on the variants of it which I suggested, the rule in question does not solely confer power nor solely impose obligation. It does both. By imposing an obligation which is conditional on the performance of a 'rule-invoking' act, it also confers a power. What is more, it proved easy to show how a slight elaboration on the conditions of the obligation resulted in a statement of an obligation-rule under which a plurality of powers exist as a result of the complex conditions to which the obligation of the promisor is made subject.

Hence the very way in which Hart introduces his idea of power seems to falsify his main thesis that *wherever* there are rule-conferred powers, there are necessarily distinct rules which operate *solely* to confer powers. The very attractive simplicity of his introductory statement shows how untrue it is that in ordinary un-theoretical speech we apply any very exact criteria as to the distinction which might be thought to exist between one relatively complex rule and two simpler but mutually interrelated rules.

We could, after all take Hart's formula and rephrase it this way:

> (i) If an appropriate person uses appropriate words on an appropriate occasion [with a certain actual or imputed intention], she or he makes a promise.
> (ii) A person who makes a promise must do as she or he has promised [unless the promisee releases her/him before performance] (i.e., she/he will be guilty of wrongdoing if she/he fails to do as promised).

Should this variant formulation be accounted a *better* or a more *authentic* formulation than Hart's own? It *says* the same thing, but says it in two propositions rather than in one.

The question just asked is an odd one. Promising is a feature of most, perhaps all, positive moralities, and one of those features in relation to which rules as such are likely to exist in various groups and communities, whether the rules are settled by custom, by agreement, or by authority. But there is not the least reason to suppose that every group has exactly the same rules as every other. It is a more than proper task for empirical sociology or social anthropology to produce a comparative study of the ways in which different groups and communities conceptualize promising and related rules. In some groups it might turn out that Hart's introductory formulation more or less hits the mark. In others it might turn out that the 'two rules' version works better. On such points we need something a great deal more rigorous than Hart's simple assertion about how (as he supposes) 'rules are thought of, spoken of, and used in social life'. On such points, Hart lays himself wide open to such charges as those of J. P. Gibbs[7] and others that he resorts to unjustified reliance on armchair sociology and treats empirical questions of sociology as though they were conceptual questions only.

Joseph Raz,[8] however, has shown that there is a task for legal and other normative theorizing which is not the same as the (equally important and interesting) empirical inquiries of sociology. One aim of theorizing is to produce a clear systematic understanding of the subject-matter. It is for the theorist to produce a typology of rules and to establish principles of individuation. To reflect on one's own everyday consciousness of social and moral rules and standards is to reveal the improbability that one has *any* exact criterion to settle where one rule stops and another begins. Let me offer my own introspection as an example. For my own practical purposes I am totally indifferent to the question whether there is *one* power-conferring and obligation-imposing rule about promises, as in Hart's introductory formulation, or *two* rules set out as in (i) and (ii) above. It comes to the same thing either way. As a practical moral agent, I don't care two pence whether you call it one rule or two rules, just so long as promises go on getting made and getting kept. In either event, they will.

If that view were a common one, it would be very improbable that within any community of people there would be any consensus or even opinion as to how much material goes to making *one* as distinct from *two* promising rules, to say nothing therefore of the likelihood of consensus of opinion across different groups with different detailed views about promises and the conditions of perfect promissory obligation.

Hence Raz is correct. Systematic clarification of such matters requires that the *theorist* settle grounds for classifying rules into different types, and for 'individuating' rules. Theorists are not asking a question to which 'positive moralities' (or even systems of positive law) necessarily have an answer in advance. As I, but perhaps not Raz, would say, theorists are in this way providing principles for mapping out the contents of positive morality and positive law, though they must do so in a way that makes it possible to remain faithful to a hermeneutic understanding of positive law and positive morality, one that does no violence to understanding their requirements as they appear 'from the internal point of view'. Conceptual work of this kind is not, as Gibbs suggests, alternative to or subordinate to empirical sociology. Until it is done, empirical sociology has no relevant questions to ask. Once it produces some answers, our conceptual formulations ought indeed to be adjusted in the light of findings achieved by the use of such formulations, and then more questions asked and so forth until a reflective equilibrium is achieved.

That view of the matter again indicates why Hart's approach is worthy of approval even when it is wrong in detail. His later essay on Bentham's theory of legal powers[9] shows him readier than he was in *The Concept of Law* to concede that there is a possible and interesting analysis of legal power which expounds it by way of an analysis of conditions upon obligation and on release from obligation. (Here one might inject a word of regret that his generous treatment of Bentham's contribution on this point was never paralleled in a similar reconsideration of the caricature in *C.L.* pp. 35–8 of Kelsen's theory on power and competence in law.) The concession to Bentham is justified since, as we have seen, a good method for explaining the concept of power is the method of elucidating the way in which it is possible for obligations to be conditioned on rule-invoking acts, whether or not we envisage power-conferring rules as separate rules-in-themselves for some or all purposes.

LEGAL INSTITUTIONS AND INDIVIDUATION OF RULES

Is there a theoretical purpose which can be served by individuating power-conferring elements as separate rules? There is at least a possible reason of simplicity, of reducing complexity. When we divided Hart's introductory formulation into two separate 'rules', (i) and (ii), we made the matter simpler. Sentences or rules containing a multiplicity of conditional clauses are relatively harder to understand than a series of manifestly interrelated but simpler sentences and rules. Secondly, in so far as rules give guidance about conduct, they may bear on different people's conduct and at different times. I act today with reference to the conditions for incurring an obligation when I make you a promise. But it may be a promise to pay £100 in a year's time. And in the interim you may decide to act so as to release me. If you don't, it is not until the end of the year that it falls to me to fulfil the 'categorical requirement' of paying. During the year, or until you release me, my position will be one of having a continuing conditional obligation.

Even stronger is the case where I make a will that is valid in law. Only after my death does it become incumbent on or open to anyone to do anything about implementing my will. And then there are several different classes of people affected. Named executors can seek or decline judicial confirmation; if the court confirms their appointment, they incur the duty of executing the provisions of the will. Tax officials have also duties and powers in respect of the estate. And so forth. A theory which suggests that all these people are variously engaged at different times in invoking or observing various conditions or requirements of *one single rule* would be open to the reproach of needless complexity. It will improve understanding if we aim for the simplicity of individuating the normative material available to us into a set of rules which are transparently interrelated, each focused on a particular transaction and each so framed as to show why the various transactions do connect logically together.

Just how is this useful objective achieved? The answer is revealing for the light which it casts on various concepts of great interest to legal and moral philosophy. Take the simple case of a promise by A to B today that she will pay £100 in a year's time. By today's transaction A incurs an obligation in favour of B. This day next year she must do the act she promised, pay £100. During that space of time a relationship set up by the act of promising subsists between them, except that B is able to terminate it. If A pays as promised, that also terminates the particular relationship. If A fails to pay without having been released, her omission is a wrong as against B and until something is done about it a new relationship holds.

What do we call the relationships in question? The answer is obvious and confirms what was said in chapter 6. The first is 'an obligation'. From the act of promising till the act of performing there is a 'subsisting obligation' between A and B, A is 'under an obligation' to pay B £100. Failure to pay is wrong and then a second relationship arises, since A is (during some stretch of time) 'in breach of obligation' to B. Before the due date, B has power to *release* A from obligation; after non-payment he has power to waive (or 'forgive') the breach, and to release A from any continuing obligation.

In short, 'obligation' is a concept whose use enables us to capture the relationship over time between the act of making and the date for keeping a promise. 'On 1 May 2006 A said something to B.' 'On 1 May 2007 A had to, and did, pay £100 to B.' But these two are linked together if in 2006 A made a promise and in 2007 it is that promise she has to keep. Between the two dates, there is, from the internal point of view within this morality, 'an obligation' on A in B's favour. This does not make it unconditionally true that A will do B wrong if she fails to pay; it is only conditionally so, since B has power to release A from the obligation, and there may be other cancelling conditions such as death of either party.

Thus the concept of 'obligation' can be (and surely it commonly is) used to span several rules. By one rule, certain acts count as incurring an obligation; by another, a person has a power to release from obligation. If the obligation remains uncancelled and not overridden by any superior requirement on the due date, then on that day it is wrongful for the promisor to fail in making performance. By resort to the idea of an obligation as something which endures over time we enable ourselves to do two things:

(i) We thus reduce to simpler components the various elements crushed together into such a formulation as

> If a person makes a promise, then if the promisee accepts his promise, and if he does not before the date of promised performance release the promisor from having to perform, and if no other ground cancelling or overriding the requirement to keep the promise has occurred by the due date, the promisor must act as he promised; otherwise he is guilty of wrongdoing.

(ii) We also locate the promising rules or practices in a general setting, since obligations may be of various sorts (promisory, familial, of reciprocity, of gratitude, arising from wrongdoing), all having the common characteristic that they subsist *through time*, and that, so long as they subsist uncancelled and not overridden, any act in breach of them is an act in breach of a categorical requirement, a wrongful act. Obligations exist through time; an act occurs at a point *in time*. This is why, although it is true that 'I have an obligation to do *x*' entails 'I must do *x*' or 'If I fail to do *x* I shall do wrong', the expressions are not identical. The obligation statement presupposes a subsisting relationship in whose context a certain act or certain acts are wrong. Even those who take the 'deontic' use of 'obligation' in sentences such as 'I/you/we/they have an obligation to do *x*', as simply an alternative formulation for 'It is wrong not to do *x*' or 'I/you/we/they must do *x*' or '. . . are morally/legally required to do *x*' must recognize there are those other non-deontic uses of the term in which we talk about 'incurring obligation', 'obligations subsisting', and 'obligations being cancelled'. The advantage of the account given between this and the preceding chapter is that it shows how these various uses hang together as rationally interrelated uses of the same concept.

Be that as it may, 'obligation' is certainly not the only term available to us in our task of showing the interrelations of separately individuated but closely interlocking rules. This is particularly obvious for such legal concepts as 'will', 'contract', 'marriage'—Hart's three favourites—and a host of others such as 'trust', 'mortgage', 'security', 'incorporated company', and so forth. All these are legal institutions, relationships set up under law and capable of existing through time.[10]

Under law, a person having certain qualifications (*capacity*) may in certain circumstances perform certain acts subject to certain procedural requirements, and thereby (provided he or she has the actual or imputed intention to invoke this provision) he or she (acting singly or interacting with one or more other persons) brings into being a will, a contract, a marriage, a trust, a mortgage, a security over this or that piece of property, or an incorporated company. Since in turn the existence of any one of these is a precondition for a whole variety of normative consequences at law, engaging duties or obligations or other powers of far more than one other person, covering far more than one type of action or transaction to be undertaken at a time possibly far removed from the original act of 'instituting' or bringing into being an instance of the institution in question, it is therefore obvious that the very use of these concepts 'contract', 'will', 'marriage', 'trust', etc. *inter alia* enables us to simplify our grasp of complex bodies of legal material. We treat as one rule the rule for making a will; we treat as separate rules those that say what is to be done with a valid will once its maker dies.[11] The postulated existence through time of 'a will' is what enables us to see the interrelations of these separate rules.

As with 'obligation', what exists through time may be brought to an end in time, whether by direct human intervention or otherwise. Hence for many such institutions there are terminative provisions—consider, for example, the rules as to termination of a contract by fundamental breach, by frustration, by supervening illegality, by performance, or by formal release or novation. The latter three cases involve *power* to terminate a contract; the former are cases where contracts are terminated otherwise than by anyone's exercise of power.

Moreover, as Hart points out, additional to these powers for making private arrangements there are provisions in some ways similar relating to public officials. For example, all developed legal systems make provision whereby certain individuals can try private litigation or can impose 'sentences' by way of penalties for offences. Such provisions commonly require that a person have certain permanent personal attributes (for example, citizenship, sex, having achieved a certain minimum age), have attained certain qualifications and undergone some form of training or acquired certain practical experience, and have been *appointed* to be a judge in a certain court. Only such an individual is *competent* to try and determine given classes of civil or criminal litigation. So only a lawfully appointed judge of a certain court has power to impose a sentence of imprisonment, or to make an order for damages in favour of the victim of a civil wrong, or to grant other such remedies as specific implement of an obligation, interdicts, injunctions, declarations, etc. And these powers are hedged round with conditions concerning the proper raising of an issue for trial or other judicial hearing, the proper conduct of the trial or hearing, the proper instruction of a jury (if there is one) and so forth.

Note that it is a precondition of the valid exercise of all these powers of a judge that the judge himself or herself have been validly appointed to be a judge of the court in question. But we do treat it as a *pre*-condition. The power of making judicial appointments is vested (say) in the head of state, acting upon certain ministerial advice. That somebody is a judge *is* (as may be said) a matter of fact or of 'institutional fact',[12] presupposing that a valid appointment was at some time made instituting him in judicial office.

There is good reason of clarity and of simplicity to follow a principle of individuation according to which the power to make judicial appointments is deemed to be covered by one distinct rule, or a set of rules for each class of judges, classified according to the range of *their* competence. What is more, as Hart rightly points out, these desiderata of theoretical and expositional clarity and simplicity are amply reinforced by the desideratum of achieving a good 'fit' with the generally understood implications and presuppositions revealed by elucidation of the concept of 'a judge' as that concept has meaning for those concerned from the internal point of view in the operations of courts and legal systems.

The point can be made with equal force in relation to the banal fact that judges day and daily pass sentences (e.g., sentences of imprisonment). The act of passing sentence is, like all acts, an act which occurs at a given point in time. The 'sentence' which results from that act, even more obviously than the 'obligation' which results from the act of promising, endures through time—through a 'stretch' of time, as popular parlance has it. If there is in respect of me a subsisting and valid sentence of imprisonment, that in turn has several implications in law. I lose my ordinary liberty of coming and going as I choose. Prison officials are in respect of me freed from the normal legal restrictions on inhibiting others' liberty of coming and going. The duties of their official role in respect of prisoners and their powers to regulate prisoners' behaviour become operative in respect of me. Parole board members and prison visitors have to exercise their various official powers and duties in respect of me. Electoral registration officers may in some circumstances be required to exercise their powers to prevent me using certain rights (to vote in elections) I would otherwise have. And so on.

The concept of 'a prison sentence' links together what (by its use) we can treat as a series of separate provisions governing sets of quite different people exercising quite distinct functions. In a not necessarily very exact way it makes possible an individuation of different transactions having a common focus. Thus there is merit in a theoretical approach to individuation of rules which treats the competence to pass sentences of imprisonment as deriving from a rule concerning judicial office of a certain rank, the competence being further regulated in particular cases by the penal provisions of particular Acts of Parliament or other rules governing particular offences. It is accordingly a merit of Hart's general approach to 'power-conferring rules' that it envisages such an individuation of rules.

PRIVATE POWERS AND PUBLIC INSTITUTIONS

To have reflected however briefly on the sorts of official powers exercised by judges is not unimportant for it refers back to those powers which according to Hart's theory may be envisaged as legal powers vested in individuals of appropriate *capacity* enabling them to arrange their own affairs within a large range of more or less free choice.

It might be objected that it does not take the law to enable people to make their own arrangements. Colin and Flora can set up house together and rear a family without regard to the law's formalities. On his deathbed Colin can tell Flora and the children what he wants done with his possessions, and they, full of conjugal or filial piety, may conceive themselves duty-bound to do as he has said, and do it. The law of the land, the positive law, does not *facilitate* such simple and natural transactions. It fetters and restricts them with burdensome requirements—and with costs.

This is true. What positive law, the 'law of the land', offers people is not the capability to arrange their own affairs. They have that anyway (and if they don't have it, the law cannot breathe it into them). What the institutions of positive law offer is not that capability, but the possibility of making enforceable arrangements. And that they offer conditionally. The characteristic conditions on the offer are as noted earlier. First, to whom is enforceability upon offer? There are apt to be general restrictions of *status* as well as particular requirements of *capacity* in relation to given transactions, and in bilateral transactions both parties must qualify (as the unfortunate businessman who thought he had made a contract for his company, but who found it was not yet incorporated, discovered to his cost in *Newborne* v. *Sensolid*[13]). Secondly, what acts must be performed subject to what other requirements of procedure (In writing? Under seal? In the presence of witnesses? Before a registrar or notary or other official? Subject to registration in official records? Subject to the payment of any fee, tax or stamp duty?) Thirdly, are there any required circumstances such as that some notice have been previously published, or, more commonly, is there simply a requirement that there be no vitiating circumstances such as duress, illicit ulterior purpose, material error, undue influence?

Such points as these Hart draws to our attention (*C.L.* p. 28), albeit subject to some vagueness on the 'individuation' of rules. Is there one rule as to testamentary capacity, another as to the acts, intentions, and procedures required for a valid will, another as to vitiating circumstances that justify setting aside an ostensibly valid will? Such vagueness is almost inevitably built into 'ordinary language' philosophizing, even where the 'ordinary language' in question has the relative precision of legal speech. So far as concerns Hart's contribution, the clarifying of these points and the drawing up of a 'full detailed taxonomy of the varieties of law comprised in a modern legal system' (*C.L.* p. 32) is a part of what belongs to the business of analytical jurisprudence beyond the original contribution by Hart.

If we look at the matter from the standpoint of those who (*a*) wish to secure the legal enforceability of their transactions and who therefore (*b*) seek guidance as to achieving that, then the concept of a power-conferring rule should perhaps be sketched as follows: Subject to prior conditions stipulating the required status and capacity in respect of the various parties to a transaction, in relation to subject matter within a specified range, one must carry out certain acts observing required procedural formalities (with the actual or imputed intention of performing the given act-in-law) in order to achieve a valid instance of the legal institution in question (contract of insurance, contract of sale of land, conveyance of property, trust, will, incorporation of company); all this subject to the proviso that no vitiating circumstance be present. What actually constitutes *guidance* to the party acting is the prescription of the acts he must perform in order to make the legally valid contract, will or whatever. Knowledge of the preconditions concerning status and capacity and subject matter, and of the proviso concerning what are vitiating circumstances is required for knowing whether one can in any case or in a given case achieve legal validity and hence functions as a qualification on the basic guidance given by the rule on *what to do*.

In so far, then, as the rule is prescriptive laying down *what to do* and *how to do it* (subject to preconditions and provisos), it is in a plain sense mentioned earlier a matter of 'hypothetical requirement': these are requirements of achieving an end one is presumed to intend and desire, the legal validity of *this* instance of this institution. Because such requirements, especially in matters of procedure, are generally to a considerable degree cut and dried and in the relevant sense arbitrary (one witness or two? a sealed instrument or not?), it is right and natural to conceive of the matter in terms of a *rule* as such.

This differentiates the case of formal legal power from other types of cases in which doings and sayings may lead us into enforceable obligations. We mentioned earlier the case of one who takes up manufacturing well knowing that those who manufacture are under a duty of care to potential consumers of their goods. Another case is that of 'estoppel' or 'personal bar'. For example, a person who regularly carries out dealings with tradesmen through a third party cannot simply stop honouring transactions made by that party, even if she has told him to stop acting as her agent. Unless she also informs the tradesmen, she is as against those tradesmen estopped from denying that the third party is her agent. This legal provision rests on the same broad principle of fair and honest dealing as do rules about contract. But it is wrong to say that one has 'power' to create an 'agent by estoppel'. There are no formalities to be observed in this case, no need for cut-and-dried arbitrary rules. The matter is one largely of principle, only partly tied down by case law rules. And these are not rules that have to be 'invoked' by people in order to confer the position of agent on the third party.

Unlike 'obligation' or 'duty' or 'wrongdoing', the concept of power is intrinsically bound up with that of 'rules' in the relatively strict sense ascribed to these both in this book and in ordinary usage. There is more than one way of acting which may have the effect of landing oneself with obligations or duties. But that way of doing so which counts as an exercise of power depends on rules, and on the invocation of rules.

Those private power-conferring rules which we have been considering are in their own nature purely hypothetical. They set requirements for achieving legal validity in a transaction; they do not require us to carry out such transactions, or even to carry them out validly; we *must* follow their provisions only if we *want* a legally valid and binding outcome. That is not to say that there cannot be present other grounds, even other rules, whereby on occasion we are required to exercise a relevant power. An obvious case in point is where A has made a contract to sell Blackacre to B. If *that* contract is valid and enforceable, then indeed A is under an obligation in due course to make a conveyance of Blackacre to B. The rule that requires fulfilment of such obligations in this case requires A to exercise his power to convey legal ownership of Blackacre to B. And of course sanctions are applicable against A if he breaks this contract. But the sanction is for breach of contract, not for breach of the rule as to conveyances of property in land.

It is one of Hart's strongest arguments against 'command' theories of law that they cannot give any adequate account of power-conferring rules. That there are certain requirements for validity of a will or of a conveyance or whatever, and that the consequence of ignoring them is the legal nullity of the transaction in question, does not show that 'nullity' is a sanction, a threatened evil as against whoever disobeys the order to make wills or conveyances thus and so.

Upon this point Hart is surely correct. As against Austin's[14] toying with the idea that nullity is a kind of sanction, Hart's argument stands. But Bentham[15] (with whom Austin disagreed on this point) suggested that rewards as well as punishments might be a kind of 'sanction'. It is a commonplace, however, that, as Erskine[16] put it, the stock of valuable goods to offer in reward is finite, so laws cannot practically be sanctioned to any great extent by the prospect of rewards.

When we consider the relationship of private powers with the public institutions of positive law, we may take leave to doubt Erskine's point. If we ask what reason anyone has for seeing to it that she executes this or that transaction with care for its legal validity, the answer is plain. Legally valid transactions are enforceable at law. There are courts and other official institutions which are both empowered and duty-bound to see to it that, at the instance of any aggrieved party, valid contracts, wills, trusts, conveyances, etc. are put into effect. The public functionaries in question, let us suppose, are astute and assiduous in using their powers in fulfilment of their duties. They do command, let us suppose, sufficient physical force to override any competition. The context, let us suppose, is one in which all uses of force otherwise than those authorized by general law or by particular official authorization constitute offences; and most such offences are successfully repressed in due course of law.

Given these suppositions, the substantial monopoly of force disposed by public officials in modern states makes it the case that a very significant reward is held out to those private persons who contemplate whether or not to make their transactions valid in law. The reward available is to have their transactions susceptible to being backed and enforced by those who have a substantial monopoly in the use of force. In a word, the *reward* for achieving legal validity, even at the price of burdensome formalities and heavy legal expenses, is a reasonably secure expectation that transactions will be honoured or sanctions exacted. So much is this so that (as Austin[17] did point out) substantive requirements of law are sometimes turned into additional requirements for validity of transactions, as in the case of the British law requiring payment of *ad valorem* stamp duty whenever transactions of certain kinds are effected. In this case, the legislature has resorted to the device of invalidating transactions on which stamp duty has not been paid, which is in fact a singularly effective sanction securing payment of a highly unpopular tax.

Colin and Flora in their rustic idyll were perhaps not much impressed by this reward at the prices exacted. But in the industrial and commercial world of relatively impersonal transactions conducted by relative strangers acting 'at arms' length' the matter may appear rather differently. It may be a relatively recent development whereby states have secured to themselves a centralised monopoly of force. (For example, in Scotland the abolition of heritable jurisdictions did not occur until 1748. Until then, justice and the control of armed force was not effectively centralised, but was subdivided locally on a territorial and clan basis. In France it took a revolution, followed by the Napoleonic reforms, to unify the state and its law.) But it has happened. In this world, Hart's power-conferring rules have vital importance. Whether we like it or not, that world is our world.

CHAPTER EIGHT

Rights

Although Hart wrote very extensively about rights,[1] space requires that this chapter be a short note. There are two reasons for this. First, his theory of rights was essentially an adjunct to and testing ground for his theory of obligations and powers. Second, his theory of rights belongs in part to his scholarly appreciation of other writers, particularly Bentham, which from considerations of space has mainly been excluded from the present book.

In his inaugural lecture "Definition and Theory in Jurisprudence" Hart gave early notice of his enthusiasm for Bentham's much earlier ventures into linguistic analysis. While rejecting Bentham's conclusion in detail, he accepted the Benthamite view that one should not define or explain terms like 'right' by proposing a definition *per genus et differentiam*. Such a definition would work by referring to the class of things for which the term stands and then by stating their special differentiating features within that class. Instead of that, one must consider their usage within complete phrases or sentences and elucidate the conventional conditions within which such phrases or sentences are properly used and are true. He readily embraced this view as a prefiguring of the programme of his own school's linguistic philosophy, which aimed at resolving philosophical problems by elucidating the use of problematic terms in their proper social and linguistic context.

As to the proper or standard usage of a sentence like '*x* has a legal right', Hart suggested that such a statement is standardly used for 'expressing a conclusion of law'. One may truly draw such a conclusion in respect of *x* in a given case if:

> (a) There is in existence a legal system.
> (b) Under a rule or rules of the system, some other person *y* is, in the events that have happened, obliged to do or abstain from some action. (Hart actually wrote 'is obliged' in 1953, but his later refinement of his account of 'obligation' makes it clear that 'is under an obligation' would be more appropriate here.)
> (c) This obligation is made by law dependent on the choice either of *x* or some person authorized to act on his behalf so that either *y* is bound to do or

abstain from some action only if x (or some authorized person) so chooses or alternatively only until x (or such person) chooses otherwise. (*D.T.J.* pp. 16–17)

At least in detail, this thesis is open to objections. The term 'right' is used properly and in a quite standard way in morality as well as in law. In either case, the term is properly used in other ways than to 'draw conclusions of law' (or morality) in particular cases falling under legal (or moral) rules. Sometimes it is even used expressly in setting *premises* for practical reasoning, as when legislative enactments expressly confer certain rights on generically or individually identified persons.[2]

Such a point is not fatal, however. For it would still be a question what is actually accomplished by rules which expressly confer 'rights', and the gist of the answer which Hart all along gave to that question is already found in his statement above. For in effect that statement locates rights at a junction point between duties and powers. Whoever has a right has a power exercisable by her or on her behalf. It is the power either to waive or to demand performance of some act which another person is duty-bound to perform. The other person's duty is thus conditional—it is a duty to act or abstain at x's demand, or unless x waives the requirement for it to be performed. Other powers may be added, and commonly are added. In the case of breach of such conditional duties, the law normally provides that x then has an option. She may either take legal action against the other person with a view to obtaining some civil remedy against that other, or may refrain from exercising that power to raise a legal action.

It is thus the case that when a legislature legislates expressly to grant a certain right, it effectively imposes a 'primary rule of obligation' on the community at large, while at the same time effectively granting all or some such powers as the ones mentioned above to qualified individuals. And all discussions of people's legal rights, even when not in the form of conclusion-drawing statements, refer to people's being in that position of having certain powers over the duties of others.

In a later essay on this theme (*B.L.R.*), Hart acknowledged that the simple power to waive or demand performance of a duty alluded to in 'Definition and Theory' is not essential to the existence of 'a right'. For example, a statute may impose certain duties on industrial employers to ensure safe working conditions for their employees and then may for policy reasons make any purported waiver of these by an employee void and of no effect. And still the employee is empowered to sue the employer for breach of this statutory duty when the employee has thereby suffered harm. Here only the power of legal action to remedy breaches of duty remains to the employee, not the power of waiving-or-demanding-performance. Yet still it is correct to say that such legislation confers rights—highly important rights—on employees; and so for other like cases.

Hence Hart's later account relates the existence of rights to the investment in individuals of certain powers of control over other people's duties. The fullest measure of control (making the individual 'a little sovereign' within a given sphere) covers power to waive performance, power to demand performance, and power to remedy breaches of duty by taking action at law, or to forego one's remedy as one chooses. When less than the full measure of control is given, but some exists, the legal situation in the case still belongs to the family of rights.

The family has yet other members, all of which have the common factor that the law leaves space for individual choice. Consider the right of free speech, the right to speak or be silent howsoever one chooses, subject to avoiding infringement of a variety of laws such as those concerning libel, breach of the peace, incitement to racial hatred, or the like. Here again the law leaves the individual in control—in control of what he himself says or does, rather than being in control over the duties of others. He is in control of himself because not duty bound to act in some given way.

Theorists such as W. N. Hohfeld[3] and others have tried to analyse the concept *right* into various distinct components. Hart goes along with them in agreeing to classify rights involving control over others' duties as 'claim-rights', rights involving control over one's own acts through freedom from imposed duties as 'liberty rights', and those powers that are exercisable at one's own free discretion as 'power rights'. His own particular point is that they all belong to the same family of rights because they share a common feature, namely, that they all involve legal protection, recognition, or respect of the individual person's *choice*.

This account, as Hart himself observed, fits less well certain kinds of 'immunity', where the point is not that the individual has choice or control over what she or other people do. Rather, the law *excludes* the exercise of powers, such as legislative powers, in a way that would divest the individual of previously enjoyed rights. For example, the Constitution of the United States forbids laws that abridge freedom of the press. As against the U.S. Congress in its legislative capacity, every U.S. citizen is immune from losing her or his right to a free press. Many of what political and constitutional theorists deem the most basic rights are or include such far-reaching immunities—the very thing that enables them to call some rights 'inalienable'.

Hart acknowledged that a different theory of rights might have to be constructed for these cases than his own 'choice' theory of legal rights. In this he apologized too much. He could have met the point by stressing that immunities go to the *protection* of freedoms of choice, not to their minimal establishment.

There may, as I have argued elsewhere,[4] be other objections to Hart's 'choice theory'; and these perhaps lead us back to a 'benefit' or 'interest' theory of rights, according to which the family of rights covers all cases of legal or moral protection of individual interests or goods. I do not canvass that question here. It is enough to have shown how, for Hart, a theory of duties and of powers is fully sufficient to the elucidation of rights. This is indeed one of the very strong arguments he can offer for his view that seeing law as a union of primary and secondary rules is a 'key to the science of jurisprudence' which unlocks hitherto impenetrable doors. Hence it is not surprising to find that from the time of his inaugural lecture, Hart always insisted that concepts such as 'legal right' presuppose the existence of a *'legal system'*, explanation of which is his fundamental aim.

The mainly legal analysis here discussed has for Hart a moral analogue. We shall see in chapter 12 how fundamental to his critical moral philosophy was this theory of moral rights based on the analogue of the legal theory about rights and about primary and secondary rules. But I am marching ahead of my theme. We have yet to explore the picture of law as containing these two sorts of rules.

CHAPTER NINE

The Legal Order I:
Primary Elements of Law

PRELIMINARY

The preceding chapters have examined the building blocks of Hart's theory of legal order. They have focused on rules and other standards in general, rather than making exclusive reference to law. They have considered Hart's vision of morality, particularly positive morality, as an order of rules bearing upon obligation, duty, and wrongdoing, and to some degree upon power. In relation to obligation, duty, and wrongdoing we found that Hart incorrectly conflates these three related but distinct concepts and that he reaches a false conclusion as to the necessity of 'rules' for defining these concepts.

In relation to power, however, we found that 'rules' are essential for its definition and that Hart is justified in claiming good grounds for differentiating power-conferring rules as a separate class of rules. At least in the case of developed legal systems, this makes clear the relationship that holds between private transactions and public functions of adjudication and enforcement. At this point, therefore, it becomes necessary to explore Hart's theory of the content and structure of a legal order.

THE PRIMARY ELEMENTS OF LAW

The primary elements of law according to Hart are certain basic rules of obligation. We have already reviewed Hart's idea that the 'importance' of certain kinds of restraint on conduct is a defining criterion for the concepts both of morality and of obligation. Certain kinds of restraint on killing, on violence, on dishonesty, deception and breach of faith, and on the free use of valued possessions are *important* for humans as social beings because they must have such restraints 'if they are to coexist in close proximity to each other' (*C.L.* p. 91).

Hart's conviction that such restraints are essential stems from his acceptance of certain elements in what is called the 'Natural Law' tradition[1] in

Western legal and political philosophy. Some branches of that tradition are founded on the belief that reflection on human nature—and perhaps also on the Divine wisdom—reveals to us various forms of good which must rationally be accepted as goals of human striving and endeavour. Those principles whose adoption and pursuance would promote the realization of these basic forms of good accordingly form a model or a set of basic prescriptions for human conventions, laws, and forms of government. Another branch of the tradition, giving yet greater primacy to the reasoning faculty, asserts that there simply are basic principles discoverable by reason (aided, perhaps, by Divine revelation) which have the status of moral axioms on which the right rules for social conduct are grounded. A third branch, associated particularly with the names of Thomas Hobbes[2] and David Hume,[3] rejects much of the 'rationalism' seemingly implicit in the former two. It is their view, more or less in the form suggested by Hume, which Hart adopts.

The story Hume and Hart have to tell runs broadly as follows. Human beings have a certain physical and emotional makeup, together with a certain rational capacity for planning and forethought and understanding of the causal sequences which they discover in the course of nature. They are also social beings whose survival depends on their cooperating successfully with others of their own kind. The world they inhabit does not guarantee them survival without effort, indeed cooperative effort. They have, as part of their emotional makeup, a powerful drive for survival of themselves individually and also for securing the survival at least of their own families and close associates. Examination of the actual mode of organization of human societies reveals certain standard or common features therein which we can infer to be essential conditions of individual and collective survival given our awareness of the qualities of human beings and the physical character of the planet they inhabit.

Let us review the qualities in question and the inferences they prompt. First comes 'human vulnerability': 'men are both occasionally prone to, and normally vulnerable to, bodily attack' (*C.L.* p. 194). We might add that, no doubt because of this vulnerability, humans are prone to retaliate bodily attacks, both in a spirit of revenge and in the hope of at least discouraging further attacks or even destroying the first attacker. But such a proceeding can easily generate a vicious circle of attack and counterattack. Hence, so long as human physical vulnerability continues, it is necessary that there be within communities (if not as between different ones) commonly understood and largely respected rules against interpersonal violence. These, says Hart, are summed up in 'the most characteristic provision of law and morals: *Thou shalt not kill*' (*C.L.* p. 195).

Second comes the fact of 'approximate equality' in physical and intellectual power among human beings. Since 'even the strongest must sleep at times', and is then surely vulnerable to others, the feature of rough equality reinforces that of vulnerability—everyone is at some time as vulnerable as anyone else.

> This fact of approximate equality, more than any other, makes obvious the necessity for a system of mutual forbearance and compromise which is the basis of both moral and legal obligation. Social life with its rules requiring such forbearances is irksome at times; but it is at any rate less nasty, less brutish, and less short than unrestrained aggression for beings thus approximately equal. (*C.L.* p. 195)

There are two startling omissions from Hart's treatment of this feature of approximate equality. First, it is only true of adults, and perhaps only of male adults. The relative subjection of women through many ages might of course be evidence for the theory that mutual forbearance and compromise are *necessities* only for those who *are* approximately equal in bodily strength and proneness to aggression. But the obvious extreme inequality and vulnerability of children as compared with adults is not mentioned by Hart. Second, as between *groups* or classes of men, extreme inequality is possible where one group has better organization and better access to useful resources than others. This is a fact for which Hart elsewhere makes proper allowance. But in any discussion of the approximate equality of men as naked individuals, the striking and often vast inequalities between different groups or classes of men *within and between organized societies* needs also to be mentioned. It is one of the effective outcomes of success in 'mutual forbearance and compromise' leading to organization of groups inside societies capable of dominating others.

The third of the basic human qualities discussed by Hart (and by Hume) is 'limited altruism'. All or most humans exhibit some degree of altruism, of 'disinterested interest in the survival and welfare of their fellows' (*C.L.* p. 196). But not unlimitedly so. Humans do not in general devote themselves wholly to the good of all humanity. If all or most of them did, there would be no need for social regulation and restraint. Humans as they are care most, as Hume pointed out, for the welfare of those closest to them, their children (again we find Hart remarkably lacking here in reference to parental responses to children), their remoter family, their friends, and their neighbours, perhaps even for some purposes their fellow countrymen.

They are strongly motivated also by sheer self-interest, but they are not 'devils, prepared to destroy reckless of the cost to themselves' (*C.L.* p. 196). If they were, they would be incapable of being restrained by any social regulations. But:

> As things are, human altruism is limited in range and intermittent, and the tendencies to aggression are frequent enough to be fatal to social life if not controlled. (*C.L.* p. 196)

The fourth basic fact has as much to do with the character of our planet as with our human qualities. It is a planet that supplies us only with 'limited resources' of the kind necessary for our survival, far less our commodious flourishing.

> The human organism might have been constructed like plants, capable of extracting food from air, or what it needs might have grown without cultivation in limitless abundance. (*C.L.* p. 196)

Things might have been so. But as a matter of ('merely contingent') fact they are not so. We need food, clothes and shelter (*C.L.* p. 196). We have to go about the business of winning them, whether by mere hunting and gathering (a case almost ignored by Hart, but supposedly the primeval human lot), or by cultivation of crops, or through some yet more sophisticated technology which exploits natural resources so as to increase the material comforts of life. The basic facts of the matter, setting aside any technological development and the modes of organization essential to it, 'make indispensable some minimum form of the institution of property (though not necessarily individual property)' (*C.L.* p. 196).

This thought can be given a Marxist form in the supposition that among humans there must always be some 'administration of things',[4] some way of regulating *who* has *what* access to *what* resources for survival and for comfort. And if there is that, there is always the possibility that someone will be at least tempted to take and consume or use that which has been allocated to someone else, so there must be some form of regulation against that. Thus we get the two sides of one coin: a notion of 'property' and a notion of 'stealing' or other prohibited taking or use of things, each of which implies and requires to be supplemented by the other.

There is a line of thought, which found early expression in Adam Smith's *Wealth of Nations*[5] and further development in Karl Marx's voluminous writings, according to which any idea of property presupposes some *permanence* of assets. Hence it would be absent from the simplest possible form of human life, that which Smith called a 'nation of hunters and fisher-men'. Those who live by the chase and by the wild fruits they can gather must indeed collaborate in the chase; but what they catch collectively they eat collectively, and quickly. Only with the domestication of beasts and the development of nomadic pastoralism, with its implicit possibilities of fortunate increase or disastrous destruction in a herd, does the question of *whose* herd it is and *who* has access to it arise. There arises a division between properties on a familial rather than individual basis, and a distinction between 'haves' and 'have-nots'. With that distinction arise relations of dependency (those who have no assets are dependent on those who do have them) and attitudes of jealousy or envy towards the fortunate. These in turn create a *motive* to interpersonal violence ('kill the herd owner and take the herd') and a need for organization and self-protection by those who have property against those who do not.

Hart is fairly open to criticism for taking a perhaps excessively static view of the relationship between human nature and the terrestrial environment in his sketch of the 'minimum content of natural law'. Yet it seems allowable that even a more dialectical view of the interaction between environmental problems and human responses, which responses in turn affect 'human nature' and the 'natural environment' generating new 'problems' for solution, would itself reveal 'truisms' about the need for human social regulation. These truisms would not be radically at variance with those suggested by Hume and Hart. At least, we must allow of that possibility for the moment in order to let the story continue.

Where it continues is with Hart's own recognition that any evolution of human society towards a division of labour requires the introduction of what (following Kelsen) he calls a *dynamic* element in social regulations. This contrasts with a purely *static* set of requirements against interpersonal violence, chicanery, deceit, and wrongful consumption or use of things. The further rules envisaged are

> *dynamic* in the sense that they enable individuals to create obligations and to vary their incidence. Among these are rules enabling individuals to transfer, exchange or sell their products; for these transactions involve the capacity to alter the incidence of those initial rights or obligations which define the simplest form of property. The same inescapable division of labour, and perennial need for cooperation, are also factors that make other forms of dynamic or obligation-creating rule necessary in social life. These secure the recognition of promises as a source of obligation. By this device individuals are enabled by words, spoken or written, to make themselves liable to blame or punishment for failure to act in certain stipulated ways. (*C.L.* p. 197)

We may accept that this doctrine allows not merely of a dynamic element in social regulation, but also of a dynamic element in social evolution; though this latter element is seriously understressed in Hart's writing.

One point against which chapter 7 of the present book has forewarned us is the supposition that the development of this dynamic feature in social rules itself implies the emergence of a specially differentiated set of 'power-conferring' rules. Where promissory obligation is recognized at all, it is of course true that people have 'power' to bind themselves to some performance, including the performance involved in sale or exchange. The performance involved in sale or exchange also (analytically) involves what a Hartian theorist recognizes as the exercise of 'power'.

We saw in chapter 7 how Hart in an unguarded moment himself treated 'promissory power' (to give it a name) as being implicit in a rule stipulating that people who say certain things are *bound* to do as they say. Here likewise we can suggest a 'primitive' formulation of the requirement to respect other people's property in which are implicit various powers of disposal of things:

> No one may partake of food caught in the hunt unless he was one of those who caught it, except if he has the permission of one who caught it, or has been given it by one who caught it, whether or not in return for some thing or service to be given back.

Here is another:

> Only a member of a family which has tilled a piece of land since time immemorial may enter on that land and use it, except by the permission of the head of the family, whether given freely or in return for goods or services.

I do not suggest these formulations by way of fictitious reconstructions of the rules of imaginary ancient communities. I present them as analytical models which prove the point that 'powers' to license access to things, to give them away or to exchange them can easily be conceived simply by reference to conditions on what Hart calls 'obligations'. There is no need for reference to a special class of rules regulating the validity of acts-in-law.

The fifth and last of the basic facts of human nature covered in Hart's minimum content of natural law is one which is advanced to account for the evolution of the public institutions whose interaction with private powers was discussed in chapter 7. It is what Hart calls the 'limited understanding and strength of will' possessed by humans.

The point here is that the previously noted facts making necessary certain sorts of social regulation are obvious facts. Hart indeed calls them 'truisms'.

It is open to everyone to understand the value and even the necessity of our having basic social rules and observing them. Even on occasions when we are tempted to make an exception in our own favour, we can sometimes restrain ourselves by an exercise of will power guided by an understanding of the social interest and of our own long-term self-interest. Understanding of the facts coupled with even limited altruism and a prudential regard for the disadvantage of detected wrongdoing, can restrain us against the pressure of immediate temptation; but it does not and cannot restrain all of the people all of the time.

> [N]either understanding of long-term interest, nor the strength or goodness of will, upon which the efficacy of these different motives to obedience depends, are shared by all men alike. All are tempted at times to prefer their own immediate interests and, in the absence of a special organization for their detection and punishment, many would succumb to the temptation. . . . .[E]xcept in very small closely-knit societies, submission to the system of restraints would be folly if there were no organization for the coercion of those who would try to obtain the advantages of the system without submitting to its obligations. . . . [Hence, all in all,] what reason demands is *voluntary* cooperation in a *coercive* system. (*C.L.* p. 198)

Of course, Hart is fully aware of an obviously possible blemish on this ostensibly rosy picture. Where there *is* a 'coercive system' there is *no* guarantee that there will be any equal or fair allocation of its advantages and benefits. Not everyone need have anything like equally good or strong reasons for voluntarily cooperating in the coercive system. Some may be rather its victims than its beneficiaries. For those victims—slaves, helots, unprivileged workers—the balance of the costs and benefits procured by evolution away from the 'small, closely knit society' may be weighted heavily on the 'cost' side of the account. The more that is so, the more coercive towards the underclass must be the organization of those who do have reason to cooperate voluntarily.

Hence Hart's 'minimum content of natural law' is in itself very far from being a guarantee of a just or good society, far less a set of principles settled by right reason for securing justice among human beings. That is not to say that he is himself indifferent to justice; he simply does not suppose that the mere existence of a legal order is itself a guarantee of justice.

Hart's fifth truism about human nature in any event allows him to account for the evolution of human societies away from 'small, closely knit' societies. Such societies might successfully sustain themselves simply by common observation of common 'static' standards outlawing violence, theft, and deception, and providing some rudimentary 'dynamic' element via the understood conditions implicit in some such standards. The more there is division of labour, however, the less closely knit society becomes. The less closely knit it is, the less effective are informal social pressures in guaranteeing compliance by most people most of the time. The more that is so, the stronger are the reasons for institutionalizing enforcement of common social standards through recognized public functionaries. The stage is set for mutually reinforcing developments of a kind which one does not have to be a Marxist to recognize as being in a sense 'dialectic'.

That takes us to a different point in our story. Suffice it at present to observe that Hart like Hume wholly rejects the fiction (found in Hobbes[6] and Locke[7] and others in the humanist tradition of natural law) of a contractual foundation for the institutions of political society. It is true that one can conjecture quite confidently what are the reasons that over time lead to the development by human beings of public agencies of civil government. Yet that development is spread over long tracts of time. Human beings did not at some point in history discover the inadequacy of an attempt to live by the basic 'static' rules for social cooperation as enforced by informal social pressure and individual self-help. They did not thereupon agree in solemn convocation to establish a common government for enforcing rights and repressing wrongs, the government deriving its legitimacy from the exchange of promises among the men who set it up. The development of public governmental institutions depends on evolution over time, the 'unintended outcome of intended actions' as Smith[8] and his associates argued. To that truth, Hart is wholly faithful. But before we proceed to reviewing the next stage of his argument, we must pause to consider a noticeable omission from the present stage.

WHAT ABOUT SEX?

Sex, in a word, is the remarkable omission from Hart's list of the basic features of human nature. Yet sex which is in almost all humans at times an urge whose promptings far transcend the limits of our strength of will guided even by a supremely rational understanding of long term, or even immediate, self-interest. Sex is a source of violent and ungovernable passion, leading men and women even to the launching of a thousand ships and the destruction of Troy, and other like extravagances. Societies are assuredly not 'suicide clubs' (*C.L.* p. 192), hence they do well to have some regulation of conduct that hedges in humans' responses to their sexual urges and instincts. Yet on the same ground, the régime for a whole society cannot be one of monastic chastity.[9]

Sex, after all, is not only for fun. It is the vehicle of propagating the species and procuring the continued vitality of families and societies. Hence it cannot be treated in isolation apart from the equally salient facts that (as noted earlier) the human young are not merely highly vulnerable but also incapable for many years of surviving without care and nurture by adults. Hence some social arrangements have to be made to allocate duties of care and nurture of the young. Any listing of 'primary rules of obligation' which omits reference to parental obligations and the reciprocal obligation of the young to care for the elderly is markedly deficient. It is as deficient as one that omits any reference to restraints upon the unfettered pursuit of sexual gratification when, where and with whom one pleases, just as the occasion suits.

Thou shalt not kill, says Hart, 'is the most characteristic provision of law and morals'. Be that as it may, it is in the original text flanked by: *Honour thy father and mother . . . that thy days may be prolonged, and that it may go well with thee, in the land which the Lord thy God hath given thee*, and *Neither shalt thou commit adultery*, itself followed by: *Thou shalt not covet thy neighbour's wife*. One popular conception of 'immorality' has at its heart concern over breaches of the last two mentioned.

It is all the more odd to find Hart passing over such matters in his discussion of the 'minimum content of natural law' when we note that Hume certainly devotes much space to consideration of sexual restrictions and to parental affections and duties.[10] A suspicion may be raised that Hart the critical moralist for whom many sexual taboos belong to the 'prehistory of morality' (*L.L.M.* p. 83) is reluctant to include rules about sexual conduct among those which human nature makes it necessary for thriving societies to have. This may also link up with some of his personal doubts and uncertainties as revealed in Nicola Lacey's biography.[11] Anyway, he does deliver himself of the opinion that 'a most prominent part of the morality of any society consists of rules concerning sexual behaviour' (*C.L.* p. 174–5). Yet he immediately adds that 'it is far from clear that the importance attached to them is connected with the belief that the conduct they forbid is harmful to others' (*ibid.*). He goes on to observe that 'sexual vetoes' are by no means 'immune from criticism or condemnation, where their maintenance is judged useless or purchased at the cost of great suffering' (*ibid.*), a point expressed with what is evidently deep feeling.

Whatever his personal anxieties, Hart's critical moral principles stand in their own right as principles that may command anyone's assent. It is indeed the case that some sexual restrictions are cruel and pointless. This, however, by no means falsifies the proposition that sexual unions and the related business of rearing and caring for and educating children in families are among the matters which it is important for *any* human society to regulate in *some* way. The case is akin to that of property; some regulation is needed, but there is no guarantee that the regulations that this or that society accepts will be either just or humane.

SOME FURTHER DOUBTS

To have found an omission in Hart's enterprise is not to have condemned it as misconceived. That it seems so natural to argue for the need of any society to have some requirements about sexual unions and the care of resultant children itself shows the force of Humean and Hartian arguments about basic elements which any social order can reasonably be expected to exhibit.

Hart indeed draws attention to anthropological evidence showing that known primitive communities do have social norms on just such matters as he deals with. Such communities can and do get by (being 'small and closely knit societies', and relatively static ones) without 'a legislature, courts or officials of any kind' (*C.L.* p. 91). Perhaps such a society may exhibit the tension, already described, between those who accept the rules and those who reject the rules except where fear of social pressure induces them to conform. But it is plain that the latter cannot be more than a minority, if so loosely organized a society of persons, approximately equal in physical strength, is to endure. (*C.L.* p. 91)

The structure of such a society, though it is certainly both customary and dependent heavily on tradition and usage, Hart prefers to call a 'social structure . . . of primary rules of obligation' (*ibid.*). To designate such rules, as either 'moral' or 'legal' would be anachronistic, because the contrast between these categories is one apposite only to a society which has developed specialized and differentiated institutions, so that *some* of its rules are specifically 'legal' ones. Nevertheless one might fairly reply that Hart's conception of a 'positive morality' being a theorist's term of art, it in fact covers and can properly be applied to this case of a régime of pure 'primary rules of obligation'.

The story so far suggests that what a society would have if it were lacking in formal institutions of civil government could be adequately comprehended solely by reference to primary '*rules*'. In view of our earlier review of the Hartian picture of moral 'principles, rules and standards' we are therefore entitled to make a fairly damaging objection to this. Surely shared values as common standards would be at least as prominent as those more detailed conventional cut and dried standards we rightly call 'rules'? Certainly there would likely enough be *some* rules, as the example of Moses's use of moral (and Divine) authority to reveal the ten commandments to his tribe suggests; but there would also be principles and other standards. Further, our scrutiny of the concept of 'obligation' has suggested that it is not applicable to the whole range of matters covered even within the story of the 'minimum content of natural law'. What that story suggests as necessary is a set of common understandings as to what constitutes wrongdoing, some relevant cases being indeed cases of breach of obligation. But 'thou shalt not kill' and 'thou shalt not steal' do not state or describe 'obligations'; they imply the simple propositions that killing is wrong and stealing is wrong. Moreover in so far as the social standards involved *are* rules and *do* relate to obligations, this should not be thought to preclude the applicability of the concept of normative power in the context of such a community.

While there is good ground to accept the point about 'minimum content of natural law', it is unfortunate that Hart chose the phrase 'primary rules of obligation' to describe the mode of self-regulation which even his ideal type of the most primitive community does and must achieve. It would have been better to call these primary or rudimentary elements of law by a different and less misleading name. 'Primary social standards' or even 'primary social requirements' would have been less misleading terms to have used.

As we shall see, one of the consequences of the development of formal legal institutions is the transformation of 'primary social standards' into that particular kind of standard which it is proper to call a 'rule'. To assume that 'rules' are a prominent feature of what Hart considers a pre-legal society is probably misleading. To assume that the *only* standards a pre-legal society could or would have are *rules* as such is pretty unconvincing. Moreover, it contradicts what Hart has to say about morality in relation to that very point (*importance* for social survival) at which his accounts of morality, of obligation and of the minimal elements of natural law overlap.

One further point: there is no reason to suppose that a 'pre-legal' society would necessarily lack the special kinds of formality associated with the exercise of 'legal powers'. Suppose it is against our primary social standards for anyone to use or eat a cow unless it is his own, it being understood that anyone who has had and openly used a cow for two years owns it and also its offspring, and that anyone who has been given a cow by its owner becomes in turn the owner of it. Especially where general social pressure and self-help are the only 'sanctions' behind such standards, there would be good reason for any 'giving' of a cow to be attended by public solemnities and formalities to let everyone know whose cow it now is. Otherwise the recipient may have fear of being subsequently accused of stealing it. Primitive legal ceremonies like the elaborate Roman procedure of *mancipatio*[12] which had to be performed to transfer ownership of domesticated animals have all the look of practices descended from remote antiquity and quite probably from a time when the Latins lived 'pre-legally'. There is no reason at all to suppose that such formal requirements cannot arise by simple custom and convention hallowed by tradition and usage.

Again, 'Thou shalt not covet thy neighbour's wife' makes perfect sense as a primary social standard (even a 'primary rule', if not strictly 'of obligation'), even though it presupposes some procedure whereby *this* woman becomes *that* man's *wife*. We cannot suppose that only with the development of formal law did such procedures arise (attended by more or less elaborate public celebration that all may know who is married to whom). Among the reasons for making no such supposition is the rather formidable one that in fact marriage is an institution in relation to the solemnization of which positive law is a relative latecomer. It was for long a non-legal institution of whose outcomes the law took cognizance. In Scotland, for example, it was not until well into the twentieth century that legislation abolished (or almost abolished) the old 'irregular marriages' based on immemorial custom, and only by a polite fiction creatures of positive law.[13]

None of this necessitates that as theorists we impute to societies that require either transfers of things or marriages to be 'formalized' in certain ways a specially individuated set of power-conferring rules. It remains possible to envisage such required formalities as mere conditions exempting men from prohibitions on wrongful taking of women or of chattels. But if the theorist chooses to fit such exempting conditions into *his* category of 'power-conferring rules', he will not necessarily err in doing so. If in the popular tradition of the tribe it is held that a marriage requires solemnization thus and so, or that transfer of a cow requires solemnization thus and so, theorists with hermeneutic concerns would misrepresent the case if they did not allow for that in their descriptions.

This point is of some importance for an appreciation of Hart's theory of legal order, and of what distinguishes that from pre-legal social order. His case is that all human societies whatsoever must (as a matter of 'natural necessity' *C.L.* p. 199) achieve some self-regulation by way of primary rules, as he calls them. It goes on to assert that the existence of legal order requires the presence of a further element, that of *secondary rules*. These *inter alia* provide for the existence of adjudicative and legislative organs and for some criteria settling *which* rules it is that the adjudicators are to apply and their enforcement officials enforce. But there is an ambiguity in Hart's way of putting his case. At some points he writes as though the difference between 'primary rules' and 'secondary rules' is identical with that between rules which, on his view of it, impose obligations and rules which confer powers. At other points, most fundamental to his theory, it is clear that some secondary rules may be duty-imposing.

The foregoing discussion has taken and read together Hart's thesis about pre-legal societies that have only 'primary rules' and his thesis about the 'minimum content of natural law'. It has shown on this basis that even a community whose social order Hart would account pre-legal need not be one in which powers to conduct certain simple transactions are absent. Indeed, it may even be sensible to treat some of these powers as regulated by special rules about formalities. Hence we ought not to accept any suggestion that 'power-conferring' rules are themselves a *sufficient* mark of 'legal order' as such. A fully developed legal order should be characterized not by the *existence* of powers but by the *kind* of powers it establishes. In turn, the existence of such a legal order may have an important bearing on the character of those powers whereby private individuals may carry out 'fully legal' transactions.

On that ground alone, we shall not follow the strand in Hart's thought which identifies 'secondary rules' with 'power-conferring rules'. How we shall identify the preferable strand is the question for the next chapter.

CHAPTER TEN

The Legal Order II: Secondary Rules

THE CONCEPT OF A SECONDARY RULE

The previous chapter showed clearly why Hart holds that 'rules of obligation' (in his terminology) are the primary or ground-floor element of legal order. Yet to elucidate primary social standards of that sort does not itself suffice to clarify the differentiation commonly drawn between the 'legal system' as such and positive morality, manners, religion, and the like in modern societies. In Hart's view, the essential differentiating feature of 'law' is in fact to be found in the very idea that laws as such belong to legal *systems*. The systemic quality of law is exhibited in the fact that primary rules of obligation can be and commonly are supplemented by 'secondary rules' which are logically interrelated with primary rules. Thus is established a network of interrelationships among various rules whereby the totality can be viewed as a single 'system of law'. Hence follows Hart's bold claim to have discerned anew the 'key to the science of jurisprudence'.

> [W]e have already seen . . . the need . . . to discriminate between two different though related types of rule. Under rules of the one type, which may well be considered the basic or primary type, human beings are required to do or abstain from certain actions, whether they wish to or not. Rules of the other type are in a sense parasitic upon or secondary to the first; for they provide that human beings may by doing or saying certain things introduce new rules of the primary type, extinguish or modify old ones, or in various ways determine their incidence or control their operations. Rules of the first type concern actions involving physical movement or changes; rules of the second type provide for operations which lead not merely to physical movement or change, but to the creation or variation of duties or obligations. . . . [I]n the combination of these two types of rule there lies what Austin wrongly claimed to have found in the notion of coercive orders, namely, 'the key to the science of jurisprudence'. (*C.L.* pp. 80–1)

Unfortunately, in this passage, central to Hart's whole theory of law, there are serious ambiguities, as Colin Tapper has pointed out.[1] One distinction drawn is that between rules laying down categorical requirements ('duties or obligations') and rules conferring power. Another is that between 'non-parasitic' rules and 'parasitic' rules—this is repeated at a later point where Hart remarks that secondary rules 'may all be said to be on a different level from the primary rules, for they are all *about* such rules' (*C.L.* p. 94). A third distinction is that between rules that concern 'actions involving physical movement or change' and those that lead 'to the creation or variation of duties or obligations'.

Of these distinctions, the first and the third have obviously something in common. In discussing powers, we discovered that analytically the simplest case of 'power' is the case such as that of promising, where a person is enabled to act in such a way as to incur an obligation to another. If we find it expedient, we can treat the conditions for making a promise as being provided for in a distinct rule, separate from the primary rule that one must do whatever one has promised. The act of making a promise is an act performed with reference to the conditions set in the rule which the promisor, as was said, 'invokes'. By contrast with that, a simple primary rule such as 'Thou shalt not kill' concerns only 'physical movement [and] change' (viz., the physical movements involved in the act of killing and the physical change between a living body and a dead one).

Since, by definition, acts that are exercises of normative power in general or legal power in particular involve the 'invocation' of rules (or conditions in rules), they do always involve what are sometimes called 'juristic acts' or 'acts-in-the-law'. They are acts whose point is that they produce not only or mainly physical consequences but also legal consequences. Hence there seems an obvious contrast with 'natural acts'—to give them a name—like killing or hitting. Even if legal consequences, such as liability to punishment, follow from committing such acts, the acts themselves are not essentially defined as rule-invoking acts or as acts whose point is to produce legal rather than physical consequences. Hence it may seem that the distinction between rules of obligation and power-conferring rules is identical with the distinction between rules regulating juristic acts and rules regulating natural acts.

The matter is not quite so simple, however. There are two complications: First, a difficulty arises from the very way in which power-conferring and obligation-imposing rules do interact. For example, a rule that enables people to make contracts (power-conferring) has a necessary relationship with what one might call the 'consequential rule'[2] that whoever has made a contract must fulfil her contractual obligations (obligation-imposing). But here the consequential 'primary rule' does not directly prescribe the performance of any particular natural act. To know *what* 'physical move-ment or change' one has to bring about in any given case, one must refer to the contract one made. Hence the *content* of one's obligation is deter-minable only by reference to the *content* of one's juristic act of making a contract.

Second, a difficulty arises because of the possibility that some duties and obligations may not merely depend for their content on reference to some juristic act, but may actually be duties or obligations respecting the exer-cise of some power and the performance of some juristic act. For example, people who have power to act as judges may also have duties in the role of judge concerning the way they are to exercise their powers. A simple ex-ample is the commonly acknowledged duty of those who exercise judicial powers to hear both sides of the case before deciding. A grander example lies at the very centre of Hart's legal theory. As we shall see shortly, Hart argues that the keystone of every legal system lies in its 'rule of recogni-tion'. This rule relates to the way in which judges have to exercise their powers—they have to do so by applying all such rules as are valid laws ac-cording to the rule of recognition. As Hart says:

> the ultimate rule of recognition . . . if it is to exist at all, must be regarded from the internal point of view as a public, common, standard of correct judicial decision. (*C.L.* p. 116)

The rule of recognition as a public, common standard of correct judicial decision is in an important sense a conventional rule; for not only is it founded on a common practice of judges and other officials, but also the (continuing) existence of the practice is 'part of the reasons [people] have for acceptance' of it (*Postscript* p. 255). It is a conventional rule that concerns duties incumbent on judges in the exercise of their judicial role. If a judge were to depart from the practice of applying in her decisions rules that satisfied the criteria of validity of law contained in the rule of recognition, she would act incorrectly—wrongly, indeed. She would be open to justified criticism from the internal point of view. Hence the common standard rec-ognized by judges is clearly enough a duty-imposing rule. They *must* act in accordance with the valid law of the land in exercising their power to decide cases, impose penalties, etc.

At this point, we naturally confront Hart's second suggested distinguish-ing feature as between primary and secondary rules, that between non-parasitic and parasitic rules. This idea is doubtless rather unhappily expressed in those particular terms. What is meant, as we saw, is a distinction between those rules that necessarily refer to other rules and rules whose content or point is not conditional on reference to yet other rules. Any rule that refers to other rules is 'secondary' by comparison with those other rules—the grandest case of all being the rule of recognition which, by definition, refers to all the other rules of a given legal system. The distinction between basic rules of obligation and all the other rules that are rules 'about' those basic rules of obligation seems in this light to be different from either of the other two distinctions Hart makes, and is perhaps the best of the three.

Here, however, the trouble is that we would wish to know which are the 'basic' rules of obligation and which are the other rules, whether power conferring or obligation-imposing, that enjoy secondary status because they are 'about' the basic ones. This may lead us back toward the view of basic obligations as those to do with natural acts—except that we have already found difficulties in that view.

A way to resolve these difficulties is as follows. Some standards of conduct are standards governing what I have called 'natural acts' purely and simply—acts like killing human beings or causing them bodily injury. These certainly must belong at the primary level in Hart's analysis. Other cases like the case of an obligation to keep one's contracts or to leave other people's property alone do indeed presuppose some structure of power-conferring rules. But although the exact bearing of such requirements in any given case does depend on understanding the legal effect of prior juristic acts performed by invoking other rules, the presently required act is not itself necessarily a juristic act. No invocation of any rule is necessarily involved in keeping one's contract or refraining from stealing.

This suggests an account of 'primary rules' which characterizes them as all those categorical requirements which govern natural acts and other acts that are not themselves always or necessarily rule-invoking acts (by contrast, for example, with requirements as to the right way to act in making a judicial decision). Such a suggestion conforms to Hart's basic idea of 'primary rules' as those which could in principle exist as meaningful social standards even in the absence of systemic interrelations with other rules. The 'secondary rules' on this view turn out to belong in something of a mixed bag. Certainly, all power-conferring rules separately individuated as such will count as secondary rules. But so will rules or other standards that impose duties on those who exercise powers, and so will rules that provide remedies or penalties for breach of primary rules, and so on. In general, secondary rules are the whole internally diverse class of rules that stand in some systemic interrelationship with other rules or standards of conduct comprehended by the above elucidation of the primary rules and standards of conduct. Not all secondary rules are power-conferring.

Given the centrality of this topic to Hart's theory of law, it is regrettable indeed that such vagueness and imprecision attends his distinction between the primary and the secondary in legal regulation. He is, however, rather more precise and explicit in his account of three main subgroups of the class of secondary rules — rules of recognition, rules of change, and rules of adjudication. As we shall see in the next section, his explanation of the systemic quality of mature legal systems depends very much on his elaboration of the interrelationship between secondary rules of those kinds and primary rules or standards of conduct. His concentration is not so much on the mere fact that there are some rules which confer powers as on the types of power that some centrally important rules confer. This is the real nub of his case concerning the way in which law is built up out of a union of primary and secondary rules.

BUILDING UP A LEGAL SYSTEM

Let us take as the primary standards of social order (avoiding the term 'primary rule' and with it the implication that *only* rules count) all those categorical minimum requirements of conduct that relate either to natural acts and abstentions or at least to acts and abstentions that can be done without any invocation of rules. These standards draw the line between wrongdoing and minimally acceptable conduct, some concerning the particular species 'breach of duty' and 'breach of obligation'. Some such standards societies must have, and only human ingenuity limits the number they can have. What reason could there be for going beyond the 'minimum content of natural law'? Or for elaborating 'secondary rules' on top of these primary standards?

Hart suggests that the social order of groups that lived solely by primary standards established by usage and sustained by diffuse social pressure and self-help would have three features which, from a certain standpoint (that of more developed societies), amount to 'defects'. There would be *uncertainty* as to where the line falls between wrong and acceptable conduct. The rules would be neither very exact nor very clear — so much so, I would think, as to make it misleading to insist on using the term 'rules' at all to cover the whole range of standards envisioned. There would be a *static* quality about the rules and other standards, rather on the same grounds as, for Hart, make 'immunity to deliberate change' a feature of moral requirements. What is established by long usage changes only by long usage. There will be critical problems for a society whose primary social standards are not readily adaptable to changing environmental circumstances affecting the common life, if for any reasons these circumstances start to change faster than new usages can develop. Finally, there would be *inefficiency*. 'Disputes as to whether an admitted rule has or has not been violated will always occur and will, in any but the smallest societies, continue interminably, if there is no agency specially empowered to ascertain finally, and authoritatively, the fact of violation' (*C.L.* p. 93). This third point dovetails with the message derived by Hart from his observations on the 'limited understanding and strength of will' possessed by humans (*C.L.* p. 198; discussed above, p. 122). The message was that some organized coercion of recalcitrant persons is necessary to ensure that those who do voluntarily observe the primary standards do not see themselves exploited by those who don't. It is inefficient or worse ('except in very small closely knit societies') to live without some system of authoritative dispute settlement and without enforcement agencies, the latter, however, being later in historical development than the former.

Each of these 'defects' has a possible 'remedy', each of which is in fact in operation in modern legal systems. *Uncertainty* is cured if there is a rule which provides authoritative identification of all the rules that are valid for a given society. Such a rule Hart dubs a 'rule of recognition'. The *static* quality of social standards is cured if there are rules that empower identified individuals or bodies to make changes in governing standards by the legislative enactment of new rules. Rules granting such powers Hart dubs 'rules of change'. *Inefficiency* is cured by rules empowering particular individuals or small groups to make authoritative determinations of disputed questions. For these rules, Hart's name is 'rules of adjudication'.

Rules of recognition, of change, and of adjudication are all, obviously enough, rules that fit the revised test for being 'secondary rules'. In addition, private powers of the kind reviewed in chapter 7 have the very point and purpose of enabling individuals to change their own legal position and that of others. Individuals can do so by incurring, imposing, or abrogating duties and obligations, granting or receiving permissions to do what would otherwise be wrong, conferring or transferring powers, and so forth. So rules that confer such private powers can be included within the class of 'rules of change', albeit in a subordinate position within the class.

Hart's treatment of the emergence of the 'remedies' to cure the 'defects' of the prelegal social order is thematic and schematic rather than historical. Elsewhere he duly allows for the evolutionary (as distinct from planned and chosen) character of most forms of social development. Even so, his talk of 'defects' and 'remedies' has more than a flavour of constructive rationalism about it, to use a phrase of F. A. Hayek's.[3] It is perhaps best seen as a kind of *ex post facto* argument. We now have criteria for 'valid law'; we now have legislatures; we now have courts and associated law-enforcement agencies. How would we fare without them? Badly indeed; for we would have to fall back on uncertain emanations of positive morality to ground our common life, our standards would freeze into a static pattern, and we would have less efficient methods of solving disputes of right, and no method of enforcing such conclusions as we reached.

While such an argument has an obvious and simple good sense as a broad justification for keeping institutions of the kind that contemporary states have, it should not be accepted as being any kind of an adequate historical account of the development of legal institutions. Hart indeed does not so present it, but it remains more than a pity that he did not take more account of the history of legal institutions in piecing together his story of the emergence of rules of recognition, change, and adjudication. No doubt he could have replied that, whatever the historical process, such rules have developed and do exist in modern communities. Once they have developed, what we have is a clear and central case of 'legal order' or 'legal system'. That is all that is needed to carry out the task in analytical jurisprudence that he set for himself. This is to explicate the structure of the mature legal order, showing how appreciation of that structure gives a framework for understanding many otherwise puzzling concepts in and features of legal thinking. It is what is needed to show how all that we recognize as 'law' contains some structural or functional similarity to the state legal order that Hart assumes to be the central instance of law.

PROBLEMS ABOUT THE RULE OF RECOGNITION

The defence offered for Hart's procedure is not to be rejected out of hand. Yet problems remain. Is it really true that adjudicative institutions are inconceivable without pure power-conferring secondary rules, as Hart contends in chapter 7 of *The Concept of Law*? In any event, is there not a problem of seeming circularity in the interrelationship of secondary rules of 'recognition, change, and adjudication', and is this not damaging to it even as an analytical model?[4]

Consider: the rule of recognition, as a 'common, public standard of correct judicial decision' (*C.L.* p. 116), is 'binding . . . if accepted' (*C.L.* p. 235) and it is essentially a conventional rule (*Postscript* p. 255). As was said, it states the duty of judges to apply all and only rules valid according to certain criteria of legal validity. If there is a 'rule of change', that rule empowers some legislature or legislator by the use of some procedure to make new rules, which count as 'valid laws' whether in addition to or in derogation from old ones. So the criteria of recognition for valid rules of law necessarily include, as a criterion of validity, valid enactment of rules by the legislature (or legislator) in exercise of the power conferred by the rule of change. But, in turn, the rule of recognition presupposes the existence of 'judges' whose official duties are regulated by the rule of recognition. And there are, *per* Hart, 'judges' only if there are people empowered by a rule (or rules) of adjudication to make authoritative determinations of legal disputes. Are we to say that the rule of adjudication is a 'valid' rule or not? It can be so only if it satisfies some criterion set in the rule of recognition. But the rule of recognition presupposes 'judges', and 'judges' presuppose a rule of adjudication. Which member of this logical circle of rules is the ultimate rule of a legal system?

Hart is perfectly clear that for every fully mature legal system there is an 'ultimate rule of recognition' which is 'ultimate' in this sense: it is not itself validated by any superior norm or rule, not even a juristically presupposed 'basic norm' of the kind Kelsen[5] contemplates. It is not itself meaningfully called 'valid' or 'invalid'. Its existence as a rule is constituted simply and solely by the fact that 'from the internal point of view' it is 'accepted' (*willingly* accepted) by at least the judges and other superior officials exercising powers within the system. It is a conventional rule in the sense that an existing pattern of conformity to it is part of the reason for individuals' acceptance of it. It 'exists' in the same sense as some 'rule' of 'positive morality' such as 'Lying is wrong', by the custom and usage of those bound by it. Such persons refer to it both as a guide to their own conduct and as a ground for critical appraisals of others' conduct, taking it for granted that others also adhere to it. In a just society, it could well be accepted and willingly endorsed by citizens in general, as well as officials in particular. But acceptance by the latter group is alone both necessary and sufficient to its existence. Not all societies endowed with legal systems are just.

Like the standard metre bar in Paris, the rule of recognition sets criteria against which other rules can be tested. One cannot ask whether the standard bar is *itself* really and exactly a metre in length, for there is no superior test of 'metricity'.[6] Likewise one cannot ask whether the rule of recognition itself is valid, since it sets the standard of validity of all other rules in *that* legal system (*C.L.* p. 109). And that is what the rule of recognition is: a standard for the validity of all rules other than itself. If there is one legal system in the United Kingdom, there is one rule of recognition. If there is one rule of recognition, it can be asked of every formulable rule whether it satisfies the criteria of recognition. The answer may be that *this* rule is, within the United Kingdom, valid for Scotland, *that* for England and Wales, *that* for Northern Ireland, *that* for the United Kingdom as a whole; *these* are not valid for this system at all. In this, says Hart, we find the very reason why there is a legal system at all.

The systemic aspect of law is constituted by the fact that all the members of a group of rules are validated under one set of more or less complex criteria of recognition, and in that light have complex interrelations with each other. We must contrast with such a system any mere 'set' of rules lacking in systematic interconnection with each other. A régime of pure primary rules is such a set, unified only in that they are all rules of and for one social grouping. Public international law Hart regards as likewise a set of rules, lacking in any rule of recognition, being simply the set of binding rules accepted by the states of the world in their dealings with each other (*C.L.* ch. 10).

The notion of 'complexity' in criteria of recognition can be illustrated as follows. Suppose a state with a written constitution. Its rule of recognition might run like this:

The judicial duty is to apply as 'valid law' all and only the following:

> (i) Every provision contained in the Constitution of 1950, save for such provisions as have been validly repealed by the procedures set in Article 100 of that Constitution, but including every provision validly added by way of constitutional amendment under Article 100;
> (ii) Every unrepealed Act of the Legislature validly enacted under, and otherwise consistent with, the provisions of the Constitution of 1950;
> (iii) Every provision by way of delegated legislation validly made under a power validly conferred by any unrepealed Act of the Legislature;
> (iv) Every ruling on any question of law made by the Supreme Court or the Court of Appeal established by the Constitution of 1950, save that the Supreme Court may reverse any of its own prior rulings and those of the Court

of Appeal, and the Court of Appeal may reverse its own prior rulings; and save that no judicial ruling inconsistent with any provision covered by criteria (i), (ii), or (iii) is valid to the extent of such inconsistency;

(v) Every rule accepted as law by the custom and usage of the citizens of the state, either by way of general custom or local and particular custom, such being applicable either generally or locally so far as not inconsistent with (iv) above; and

(vi) Every rule in force in the state prior to the adoption of the Constitution of 1950, save for any such rule inconsistent with any rule valid under (i)–(v) above.

This is a fictitious 'rule of recognition', admittedly set in a form more likely to be found in a Manual of Law than recited in its entirety by any judge. It contains six 'criteria of recognition'; but it is according to Hart's conception *one* rule containing six criteria ranked in lexical priority—none lower in the list takes effect until all higher are satisfied. Certainly, the official practice, usage, and attitudes that its existence would presuppose would have to be both 'complex' and 'concordant'. But no one familiar with the operations of any modern *Rechtsstaat*, i.e., constitutional state, can doubt that such complex practices are possible.

Now we have a puzzle. It seemed to have been established earlier that Hart's theory of 'secondary rules' is stuck in a vicious circle. But the fictitious model rule of recognition not merely seems a possibility, it has all the ring of actuality for modern constitutional states. The point, however, is that one must still ask by virtue of what a person can act as a judge and be a member of a court able to exercise jurisdiction. The answer can only be that the constitution must contain some provisions about the exercise of judicial power and about the appointment of judges, including provisions about the power of Parliament (or whoever) to legislate in detail concerning administration of courts and the like. Even if we wanted to use the United Kingdom as an example,[7] assuming the traditional conception of United Kingdom constitutional law, we need only drop out the criteria numbered (i) and (vi) and re-number the others accordingly, amending (iv) to allow for the various court systems and hierarchies within the United Kingdom, all now established under Acts of Parliament.[8] Again, the judges whom the rule of recognition clothes with duties to respect these criteria can exercise jurisdiction because of rules enacted by the legislature. These in turn are valid because of the rule of change enabling Parliament to change the law and because enactment by Parliament is a high-level criterion of validity. Is there a vicious circle here?

There certainly appears to be something paradoxical about the interrelation of rules here, each of which seems to presuppose at least one of the others. But the paradox should perhaps not deter us from accepting the overall account. We have found here what some sociologists consider to be a necessary feature of all developed social systems. They have become self-referential, in the sense that legal agencies always refer to the law itself as settling issues of the validity of what they do. Law validates law and becomes in this sense a kind of self-making or 'autopoietic' system within the whole system of social relations.[9] On perhaps similar grounds, Joseph Raz denies that in a developed legal system the ostensible circularity of reasoning among the trio of Hartian secondary rules is intellectually troublesome.[10] He argues that there need not be a means of identifying the legal institutions that are bound to uphold the rule of recognition that is independent of the rule itself. He says that potential rules of recognition are represented by 'any proposition of the right form'—we might assume that the model above is an example of the right form. Such a proposition, says Raz, 'is the Rule of Recognition of a country [if it] meets the following two conditions. (1) The institutions it refers to do exist. (2) They actually follow a rule whose content is that proposition.'

This makes the important point that validity of law in the real world depends on some constitution being actually in force and functioning as the genuine normative framework of governmental activity in the state. This in turn depends on effective coordination of the different organs of government within some scheme of separation or distribution of powers. Each has to respect the exercises of power that others validly carry out under the conditions prescribed in the constitution, whether concerning the conduct of the executive branch, the legislature, or the judiciary. There also has to be reasonable compatibility between each branch in terms of the interpretation of the provisions that confer and distribute the powers and settle the relative priorities among them. The rule of recognition observed by the courts as a binding common standard is not itself the whole of the constitution, but a part of it;[11] there has to be respect for the whole constitutional order for Raz's first condition to be satisfied.

A further point to notice is that in any state which has a formal or 'written' constitution, it seems necessary, as in the model 'rule of recognition' presented earlier in this chapter, that the criteria of recognition include the norms of the constitution as highest level binding norms for the courts. The claim[12] that the rule of recognition plays a radically different role from Kelsen's '*Grundnorm*' or 'basic norm' is to that extent doubtful, for each concept has to do with what makes it obligatory to treat constitutional norms as valid grounds for decision making. That Kelsen treats this as a matter of simple 'presupposition' while Hart insists on its conventional character is significant in terms of their rival conceptions of sound jurisprudential methodology. But the idea that something lies behind the formal constitution is significantly a point they have in common, and Hart may have been somewhat overinsistent on the extent to which he transcended Kelsen's ideas. It can even be argued that the upholding of a settled constitutional order depends on a norm commonly observed by all officeholders and sustained by the expectations of politically aware citizens that the constitution ought to be respected. Rules of recognition can then be considered as special norms governing the judiciary in its various branches, with possibly different criteria for different courts within a complex system, especially but not only in federal systems of government.

All in all, it is necessary to propose some pretty substantial amendments to Hart's original version of the theory about primary and secondary rules. The theory can, however, be adapted to accommodate these amendments. As a framework for the comprehension of legal phenomena, it can be reconstructed in a highly plausible way. In a thoroughly adapted form,[13] it yields the extensive explanatory powers claimed for it by Hart.

JUDICIAL ROLE AND JUDICIAL DUTY

Some readers may consider that the solution developed out of the ideas by Raz and Luhmann to the problem of the apparently circular or paradoxical quality of the main Hartian secondary rules is altogether too glib. It leaves unchallenged the historically back-to-front character of Hart's introduction of rules of recognition, adjudication, and change. To deal with such worries, it remains of value to re-present ideas that took front place in the first edition of the present book in attempting to deal with this problem, but to do so in a way that takes account of valid criticisms of the earlier version.[14]

The first question to ask is whether it is really true that one could not conceive of any kind of adjudication without a preestablished power-conferring rule of adjudication. This does not seem to be so. We must return in thought to a society supposed to live solely by primary social standards. By these standards, says Hart, there must be some conception that violent acts by humans against humans are wrong. But not every such act can be wrong, by Hart's argument. For there must be exception at least for individual and collective acts of self-defence, for acts necessary to the taking of amends for wrongful acts of violence, theft, etc., and for those acts that are otherwise deemed legitimate expressions of social pressure against wrongdoing. The trouble with that, as Locke long ago pointed out in his *Second Treatise of Civil Government*[15] and as Hart observes in conjuring up the 'inefficiency' of pre-legal social order, is that the exceptions will tend to eat up the rule. My violent act, I claim, was just retribution for your violent act. That act, you claim, was itself just retribution for my previous violent act, which I in turn claim to have been a retaliation against an earlier act of yours. And so on. My family and friends back me, your family and friends back you, and our shared standards turn out to be not much guarantee against life being, after all, nasty, brutish, and short.

No doubt indeed, societies can subsist over periods of time despite internal warfare, feud, and vendetta. The history of the Hebrides after the fall of the Lords of the Isles provides a graphic example.[16] But very many, possibly all, 'primitive' societies do have provisions that run counter to this undesirable state of affairs.[17] The exceptions to the prohibition on violence may be more guarded than we envisaged. It may well be held that all violent acts save those in immediate and necessary defence of self, family, and property are wrong unless they are by way of enforcing compensation or retribution against one who is *adjudged* to be a wrongdoer. But adjudged by whom? That will itself depend on a customary standard which must as a minimum impose a certain *duty* on those who present themselves in the role of victims of a wrong. The duty in question is the duty to seek peaceful satisfaction of the alleged wrong by agreement with the alleged wrongdoer, failing which, either to abandon the allegation or to make one's complaint about the matter to (say) the elders of the village. I choose elders for my example, on the supposition that they might be people defined solely by customary reference to a natural characteristic (age), not by anyone's appointment. In turn, the elders of the village before whom such a complaint is made have, by the same custom, a duty to pass judgment on the matter. Has this man been wronged as he claims?

Thus phrased, the elders' duty has necessary though inexplicit reference to the customary standards of wrongdoing current in the community. They alone make meaningful the question for judgment—"Has this man been wronged?"—as a question arising in a community of the primitive sort envisaged. It is possible, but it is not necessarily the case, that both parties to a complaint are held to have a duty to abide by the elders' judgment. It is not necessary because, if the complainer wins, he falls within the exception to the requirement against violence. This may sufficiently motivate the other party to give voluntary satisfaction. If the complainer loses, he falls outside the exception, so the other party has in principle nothing more to fear than he had before the elders passed judgment.

Whether or not the last mentioned duty exists, this picture of an imaginary but not improbable social order[18] is one to which our theoretical concept of 'normative power' is inapplicable. Like the modern British manufacturer of goods, various parties because they are in certain roles have certain duties. They do not get the duties by invoking any rule, nor do they discharge the duties by performing acts that involve the invocation of a distinct power-conferring rule. They discharge them respectively by making complaints about what they say are wrongful acts according to customary standards and by expressing judgments on whether the acts said to be wrongful did happen and on whether in that case they were by any standard wrong. No more does that involve an exercise of normative power than does this case: boys playing football in a park have a dispute whether something one of them did was a foul, so they ask a spectator to give his opinion, he gives it, and they accept it. Only if more complex arrangements exist or come into existence would the concept of judging as a juristic act such that it may be validly or invalidly performed become relevant and applicable.

The elders of the village in our analytical example have a duty combining two elements:

> (a) to make a judgment upon a disputed complaint;
> (b) to make their judgment by reference to standards of right and wrong conduct whose existence as standards is not determined by the present choice or decision of the elders themselves, though interpretation of the standards necessarily rests with them.

And that duty falls to be exercised against a background of primary social requirements including this one:

> (c) Violence by anyone against anyone else is wrong unless in necessary self-defence or against an adjudged wrongdoer who does not give voluntary satisfaction.

Of the points noted, (b) and (c) imply that the elders' duty is a secondary one. The duty-standard (we can even call it a 'duty-imposing rule') has reference to and is thus, in the Hartian sense, 'parasitic upon' other standards, primary social standards.

Points (a) and (b) together imply (i) an elementary 'rule of adjudication', but one concerning merely a *duty* to decide questions, and (ii) an elementary 'rule of recognition'—the elders' duty is to apply all and only the customary standards of the village in passing their judgments.

Point (c) makes the judgment of the elders the final authoritative determination whether any act of violence is a justified act. Even in cases of alleged self-defence—although the first judgment is that of the person who uses violence thinking it 'necessary self-defence'—the question whether his judgment was correct can be referred *ex post facto* to the elders for their judgment. That judgment, if sought and given, is final. Thus the elders have a monopoly *over*, though not a monopoly *of*, the justified use of force.

It will be useful to call the role which our imaginary elders play a 'judicial role',[19] a theoretical term I define for my purposes as follows:

The judicial role is the role of any person, persons, group of persons, organized group of groups of persons, or any person(s) belonging to such group(s) who for any reason—

> (a) has/have a duty to pass judgment on any disputed or disputable complaints of wrongdoing made to them, with or without limit as to subject matter;
>
> (b) has/have a duty to make their judgment by reference to standards of right and wrong conduct whose existence as standards is not determined by their own present choice or decision, except in so far as they must interpret or extrapolate from existing standards in justifying their decision (this varies slightly from the rudimentary case of the envisaged village elders above; for a full justification of these variations see chapter 11);
>
> (c) has/have a monopoly over the justified use of force in a human society by the standards prevalent in that society. (Notice that where, as in a modern state, jurisdiction is divided among several courts (or groups of groups of persons) the 'monopoly over the use of force' depends on an *organized* hierarchy of courts and enforcement officials. That organization requires the existence of Hartian 'rules of adjudication'. Individual judges or courts belong to an organized group of groups of people which as an organized group has the relevant monopoly though no single individual has it.)

By that definition, my village elders have a judicial role. So does the Supreme Court of the United States and all its members, so does the *Cour de Cassation* in France and all its members, so do the Lords of Appeal in Ordinary, so do Court of Session judges, so does the Sheriff at Stornoway. The International Court of Justice and its members do not constitute a perfect case, because they fail on condition (*c*). They have no monopoly over the justified use of force in international relations, since it is not obligatory upon states to refer every otherwise irresolvable dispute to them.

Interestingly, it would *not* be an objection in the last mentioned case (the ICJ) that the rules (or other standards) of international law are mainly customary in character. The existence of such rules is *not* dependent on the present choice or decision of those who pass judgment on them, though it is reinforced by every act of judgment. And indeed the ICJ and its members *are* duty-bound to apply customary rules of international law, as provided in Article 38 of the Statute of the Court.

Hart, in his treatment of international law, pours cold water on Kelsen's idea[20] that there could be some such 'basic norm' of international law as that 'states should behave as they have customarily behaved'.

> For it says nothing more than that those who accept certain rules must also observe a rule that the rules ought to be observed. This is a mere useless reduplication . . . (*C.L.* p. 236)

What Hart overlooks is that *his* theory of a 'rule of recognition' is a theory concerning a rule about the standards that it is obligatory for *judges* to observe. And in that case it is no mere useless reduplication to say that certain judges, when states voluntarily refer disputes to them, must decide according to the standards of 'international custom, as evidence of a general practice accepted as law' (see Article 38 of the Statute of the ICJ). Nor is it useless reduplication to say either that the elders of my imaginary village have a duty to apply the standards customarily observed in the village, nor that the High Court in England and Wales has a duty (albeit under a now subordinate criterion of recognition) to apply proven customary rules when these are not contradicted by statute or binding precedent. That is just as well, because a part of Hart's case against Austinian jurisprudence is that it can give no adequate account of the genuinely binding quality of customary law (*C.L.* pp. 45–8).

Be that as it may, the definition I have suggested of the judicial role enables us clearly to distinguish it from that of a mere arbiter (who tries to find a solution based on what seems to him fair and reasonable *ad hoc* as between disputing parties) or that of a mediator (who tries to bring disputing parties to a compromise). A judge, someone who occupies a judicial role, must decide by reference to independently existing standards. That is possible only if there is some criterion, be it custom or be it some other, for identifying the relevant standards. It cannot then be said that the *validity* of rules or other standards as such is determined by the rule of recognition or that the rule of recognition is the ground of validity of, or determines the existence of, the rules or other standards to which it refers. 'Criteria of recognition' determine what are valid *as grounds for judicial decisions*.

If we say that the rule of recognition settles what is 'binding law', and if we say, as Hart says, that it is a rule determining judges' duties, then we can *only* mean that it settles what rules are *binding upon judges* as bases of justified decisions on questions of right and wrong. Equally, if we wanted to say that custom is a source of valid law, we could only mean that custom is a source of rules valid as legal grounds for decisions by judges. Since acts which constitute custom are not power-exercising acts, it is meaningless either to say or to deny that these acts 'validly' create law. Either the acts 'add up to' legal custom or they do not. Validity of the sort that attends procedurally proper exercises of power by properly qualified persons does not enter into the picture of custom at all.

Conversely, if in a constitutional state one criterion of recognition of rules binding on judges is that they be rules validly enacted by the legislature, the 'validity' of a legislative act does not depend on the rule of recognition itself directly. Legislation is validly enacted if it satisfies the constitutional provision (a Hartian rule of change) governing the legislature's power. As such, it yields a valid or binding ground of judicial decision. This in turn implies a judicial duty to apply the constitutional provision. It does not follow that the rule of recognition makes the constitution 'valid' in any other sense. These are important distinctions.

POWERS OF ADJUDICATION AND OF LEGISLATION—A FEUDAL MODEL

So far it has not been necessary to speak of formally conferred powers of adjudication at all. To give an example of such powers, let us shift the historical focus to a simplified analytical model of a feudal order.[21] In that social order, each free man is either lord or vassal to someone else, and only the king is no man's vassal. Each lord *vis-à-vis* his own vassals has the duty to protect their customary rights and to vindicate them against wrongdoers. The king as the supreme lord has that duty of protection originally only as respects his tenants in chief, and as respects his own 'peace', which later came to be interpreted as the general peace of the community. How is the king to fulfil that duty of judgment and protection? Can he delegate it?

By custom it came to be accepted that he could. So an appointment by him of whomsoever he chose as his justiciar[22] was valid, in that it effectively and of intent clothed that individual with the duty to judge questions of customary right. What that duty amounts to is not necessarily affected by the delegation. But that *this* person must discharge the duty depends on the fact that the king has invested him in this office. This presupposes the customary rule according to which the king has power by such investment to delegate to a justiciar all or some of his kingly duties towards his vassals (and, in respect of 'the king's peace', toward everyone in the realm). By our definition, the delegate then occupies a judicial role.

Of his own free will, or under pressure from the great men of the realm, the king may impose on the justiciar procedural requirements as to how he is to go about judging. It may come to be understood that fulfilling these requirements is a condition of the validity of his judgments. The king or the justiciar or some other official appointed by the king may in turn lay down procedures to be followed by those who make complaints, fulfilment of which is a condition of acceptance of the complaint for consideration by the justiciar's court. Now it is the case that the justiciar is in the position of having a power conferred on him to give valid judgments provided he follows the proper procedure, and provided a complaint has been validly laid before him in proper form.

So the justiciar, who still has the duties definitive of the judicial role, has them by exercise of a royal power of appointment . He must fulfil them by exercising his powers validly in relation to complaints brought before him by parties of appropriate status who exercise validly their power of making a complaint.

Still the range of the justiciar's powers is circumscribed by those subject matters that are covered by the king's duty of protecting his vassals and his own peace. But it may happen (and in England it did happen from an early date) that the prestige and politico-military power of the king, coupled with the relative efficiency of his justiciar's court, give rise to a desire among knowledgeable people to get their disputes into his court if at all possible. One device which was quite early tried out, and which caught on, was to allege that the dispute in question was such that if unregulated it would endanger the king's peace. It would even be alleged of any wrong that it involved resort to force of arms by the defendant. If the court depends on litigants' fees for its income (and it did), the court and the potential litigant have converging interests. Such pleas are made to secure effective remedies; they are accepted without critical scrutiny of the alleged infringement of the peace incidental to the main claim. It becomes possible to get certain questions of common-law rights raised in the king's bench by the simple procedure of alleging armed violence alongside the real ground of complaint. By this means, custom and usage extend the range over which the judicial power is exercisable, the process being one in which the power to raise an action before that court has been transformed.[23]

At some point in such a development it becomes appropriate for the hermeneutic theorist to describe the position in terms of separate power-conferring secondary rules. Once instructions to a justiciar how he is to proceed become conceived as standing instructions or standing rules of a court comprising several regular judges, it will come to be held by participants and interested parties that the judges can exercise jurisdiction validly only by invoking these rules. So, too, the conditions necessary for a party to lay a valid complaint before the court can come to be conceived as a rule stipulating that appropriately qualified people can, in relation to appropriate subject matters, make a valid complaint only if stipulated procedures are observed. Doing that involves invoking the rule. Doing it successfully (i.e., 'validly') involves activating the judicial duty to decide the complaint by the appropriate procedure of hearing and trial, which requires the judge to make valid exercise of his powers.

This presupposes that the king has the ability to give instructions to the justiciar. But a central feature of feudal order is precisely the right possessed by superiors to give binding commands to their inferiors, conditionally or unconditionally vesting duties in them, within the field covered by the superior's rights. This obviously implies a power in the king to confer and regulate judicial powers and judicial duties.

The duty to decide individual complaints about wrongs is not the only duty of a feudal king. He has a duty to protect the customary rights of the community, so he must know what these are. There may be *general* doubts about rights as well as particular complaints about wrongdoing. In that case, the king's duty, in consultation with the members of his Great Council, is to take opinions and settle what the law *is*. 'Statutes', authoritative settlements of these general questions of legal right, are made and promulgated. But, at least ostensibly, this need imply no power of *change*.[24] No doubt all concerned have a lively awareness how their interests are affected by various possible outcomes of this process of legal clarification (clarification of what standards are the prevailing or the ancient customary standards). Unquestionably, attention to such interests affects the outcome. But, in principle, what is at stake is the settlement of doubtful points of *preexisting* law, not of new law.

If, however, a distinct judiciary (persons or groups fulfilling the judicial role) has emerged, the making of a 'statute' has some importance. For the judges, it constitutes conclusive evidence of what the law is. The duty to decide disputes according to the existing customary standards of the community now includes a duty to apply statutes. The other duty to inquire into general or local customs, as evidenced by the prior judicial decisions or by any other means, now applies only where statutes are silent. Until there arise by custom some set of understood procedural and other requirements which must be fulfilled before a general decision on law counts as a 'statute', it is misleading to describe what is going on in terms of 'power-conferring rules'. Rather, the king in fulfillment of *his* duties is (*inter alia*) instructing his judges as to *theirs*; after the consultation he is duty-bound to hold with his peers.

Only when we reach a point in history when the active participants share 'from the internal point of view' an understood set of standards as to the requirements for validity of a 'statute' is it proper to say that there exists a power-conferring rule enabling only *those* people acting by *this* procedure to make a valid statute. Even then, there may be vagueness as to the range of admissible subject matter. Is it only possible to clarify preexisting rights? Or may *anything* be enacted by statute? Are preexisting rights matters of custom simply, or is custom itself only evidence of principles of right reason revealed to men by the light of nature? By the seventeenth century this was a hotly contested question. As against proponents of the absolute power of a divinely or humanly appointed ruler,[25] thinkers of the 'rationalistic' school such as Grotius[26] in the Netherlands, Coke[27] and Locke[28] in England, and Stair[29] in Scotland answered it in favour of the view that there are principles of right reason. Custom is good evidence of these, albeit not absolutely conclusive. This view, like the absolutist view, had important consequences.

THE EMERGENCE OF THE SOVEREIGN LEGISLATURE

The rationalist view upholds custom and common law against royal power; but at a price. For custom is not authoritative *per se*. It is now only held to be evidence of the principles of right reason. That being so, there must be room for those who live in enlightened ages to correct the customs of their less enlightened forefathers. Further, since reason reveals that the purpose of positive law is (as Stair[30] put it) to promote 'society, property, and commerce', the legislator accordingly has a duty to exercise the statute-making power to amend customary rules in order to promote the interests of society, property, and commerce. This is a use of power to further implement principles of right reason, implying no power of abrogating or violating such principles. Nevertheless the restricted reinterpretation of the statute making power as a power to *change* laws for good ends still leaves the main basis of the law as immemorial custom, *now heavily evidenced* by prior judicial decisions. In a legal system in which this view prevails, the criteria of recognition are:

> (i) Statutes, so far as not in conflict with principles of right reason;
> (ii) Judicial precedents, as best evidence of customary rules, so far as not inconsistent with statutes;
> (iii) Customary rules otherwise evidenced, so far as not inconsistent with statutes or with judicial precedents.

That in turn is a picture of law that is necessarily unacceptable to those who do not believe in principles of right reason ('natural law'). They have cause to denounce it, which is precisely what Jeremy Bentham[31] did in the latter eighteenth century. His denunciation involved reinstating the absolutist doctrine in a new form. Statutes are law because decided by those who have power to decide them. The supposed restriction in terms of natural law is not a real restriction. It is a recipe for either anarchy or conservatism according to the 'caprice' of whoever invokes it. Judicial precedents and customs are a mess, lauded only by those who have a political or a pecuniary interest in the obscurity of law; they constitute law only because not repealed by those with a power to repeal and replace them. Hence they exist only by circuitous command of those who have that power. The only criterion for the existence of law is that it is made and sustained by those who have power to make and sustain it: those whose commands are in fact habitually obeyed.

Whatever be its merits and defects as a general philosophy of law, the Benthamite picture of law became in a sense self-fulfilling. Various schools of thought converged in advancing the thesis that every sovereign independent state has in some form a sovereign legislature (an individual or a group) who has power (in some sense) to make or change any law whatsoever. Some, such as Bentham[32] and Austin[33] in Britain interpreted this as a simple factual social power: the power to make one's commands 'stick'; others such as Dicey[34] interpreted it as a legal norm: the *legal* principle of the 'sovereignty of parliament'. Yet others advanced similar views in the clothing of Hegelian metaphysics.[35]

Taking a Hartian view of that, we can say that over a long tract of time there emerged a power-conferring 'rule of change' that stemmed originally from a power to settle conclusive evidence of law. It next grew into a power of limited legal change, and was finally reinterpreted as an unfettered power of change. Parallel with this development were refinements in and modifications of the 'rule of recognition' upheld by the judges as settling the criteria of recognition determinative of their duty to decide according to 'laws', which are for them valid as justifying grounds for their decisions. The judges are thus among those who participate in the redefinition of the power of change vested in the legislator.

But once that redefinition has occurred, it becomes possible that the courts themselves, these ancient institutions originating in long custom, can be reorganized, even reestablished by statutes settling which courts have what powers over what subject matter acting by what procedure. That in fact happened, both in respect of England and Wales[36] and in respect of Scotland,[37] through a series of well-known reforming Acts of Parliament in the nineteenth century. The 'rules of adjudication' became validly enacted new rules, created by exercise of Parliament's power of change. Judges and other senior lawyers and officials were committed to accepting each change as valid because conformable to the developed criteria of recognition accepted by them from the internal point of view.

The discussion has been historically crude and has latterly centered on an extremely sketchy account of a possible process of development, which is reasonably faithful to the broad course of modern legal history with special reference to Britain. Its point, again, is primarily as an analytical model. It shows that rules of recognition, change, and adjudication are indeed necessarily interlocking and interacting, so that change in or redefinition of one must be mirrored by change in or redefinition of another. At a certain point in this development, the mutually self-referential character of the rules emerges, yielding the apparent paradoxes present in all autopoietic systems. This substantially supports the view stated by Raz about the non-troublesome character of the apparent circularity from which this whole discussion commenced.

Provided we avoid the view that judges *cannot* preexist a power-conferring rule of adjudication, provided we accept that the judicial role depends at the deepest level on the concept of 'duty', not on that of 'power', it is possible to see how a legal system can 'get off the ground' and develop. By definition, the judicial role necessarily has reference to at least some rudimentary rule of recognition requiring 'judges' to decide according to certain existing standards independent of their own decision. But the rule of recognition itself concerns duties, not powers.

When 'rules of change' have arisen, they are necessarily reflected in the rule of recognition. Since they confer powers to make valid legal changes, their exercise may in turn lead to a redefinition or reestablishment of the rules of adjudication. They may even, as with the United Kingdom's European Communities Act 1972 alter some of the criteria of recognition within a legal system—for example, by requiring the recognition of European Community law as binding in the United Kingdom even in preference to Acts of Parliament. There may be practical political difficulties about all this. They are not the consequence, however, of logical absurdity or vicious circularity.[38]

CHAPTER ELEVEN

Judicial Discretion and the Judicial Role

REALISM VERSUS FORMALISM

Any theory of law that concentrates on the idea of laws as rules and of legal systems as systems of rules is apt to lay itself open to the charge of 'formalism'. Historically speaking, the heyday of jurisprudential formalism was the middle period of the nineteenth century. In France, this was represented by the 'exegetical' approach to the Napoleonic Codes, which held that the proper attitude of judge or doctrinal expositor was that of striving for the single correct interpretation of the Codes as a logically complete and intellectually coherent body of law.[1] In Germany, the legal task was conceived as being that of explicating the true and inward meaning of the Roman civil law concepts adopted into German law.[2] In Britain there developed an increasingly strict attitude to judicial precedents[3] and a powerful movement towards legislative consolidation or even codification of important branches of law. In the United States the professors of law, confronting a 'common law' increasingly fragmented among the several jurisdictions of the federated States, devoted themselves nevertheless to attempts at formulating ideal versions of the common law and its concepts both as a critical benchmark for testing court decisions in the various jurisdictions and as a prelude to hoped-for codifications which in fact never fully materialized.[4]

Not surprisingly, the latter nineteenth century brought a reaction against such idealized and formalistic conceptions of the law and its rules. F. Gény[5] in France, R. von Ihering[6] and latter the school of 'Freirechtsfindung'[7] in Germany, Salmond[8] and later Allen[9] in England, made their various protests against the false premises of any excessively formalistic legal theorizing. But nowhere was the reaction sharper than in the United States. There J. C. Gray,[10] O. W. Holmes,[11] and Roscoe Pound[12] issued various attacks on the 'ideal legal rules' approach. They stressed the need for attention to the actual, legally dispositive, decisions of the courts. In the 1920s and 1930s their ideas were carried yet further by a younger and more radical set of academic lawyers and judges (most notably, K. N. Llewellyn[13] and Jerome Frank[14]) whom it became fashionable compendiously to describe as 'American Realists'.[15] Their general attitudes Frank apportioned either to 'rule scepticism' or to 'fact scepticism'. The former was a sceptical view of the extent to which decisions were reached by applying rules, or at least chiefly by applying them. The latter was the view that even if 'rules' were applied, the 'findings of fact' by courts did not always bear any close relation to what really happened, but served to derive from the rule a result that seemed acceptable.[16]

In unguarded moments, the realists and their predecessors over-played their hand. There are utterances of both Llewellyn and Holmes that seem to suggest the 'law' is nothing other than the actual decisions of courts and of legal officials, or predictions about them.[17] J. C. Gray[18] attempted a legal theory which distinguished the 'law' as the rules for decision used by judges in deciding cases from the statutes and the precedents from which in their decision making the judges drew the law it seemed to them right to apply. Such unguarded moments apart, the realists and their forerunners nevertheless constructed a powerful critique of the view that 'rules' are all there is to law. (They did much else besides this particular line of criticism of traditional juristic theory. A main point, indeed, was to challenge the narrow case-law and black-letter approach to legal scholarship and teaching. They were interested in the whole range of what Llewellyn called the 'Law Jobs'. Much of their importance is simply missed out of Hart's view of them.)

Hart, therefore, in *The Concept of Law* had a difficult course to steer. On the one hand, his aim was to reinstate the thesis that laws genuinely are rules, explicable as that special kind of social rules we find in a 'union of primary and secondary rules'. On the other hand, he wished no less firmly to discountenance the formalist view of legal rules, and to show that his own theory was far from being a formalistic one. His strategy to this end was one of explaining (in *C.L.* ch. 7) how, although laws are rules, it is in the nature of legal rules that they both do and should leave a considerable scope for the discretion of judges and other officials in dealing with particular cases. His aim was to underscore the errors of formalism identified by the rule sceptics, while at the same time administering a corrective to any radical form of rule scepticism itself.

Whereas Hart represents his theory as a necessary corrective to the excessive rule-scepticism of American realists, the suggestions put forward in the previous chapter for correcting the theory of secondary rules actually involved an adoption and adaptation of some of the ideas of the greatest American realist, the late Karl Llewellyn. My suggestions there focused on the idea of the judicial role as a dispute-settling role, distinguished from mere mediation or arbitration by reference to the proposition that judges properly so-called are those who are duty-bound to apply standards which are independent of their own decisions. This idea closely parallels suggestions made by Llewellyn in an unjustly neglectèd (though somewhat difficult and indigestible) essay called 'The Normative, the Legal, and the Law-Jobs'.[19]

Hart castigates the realists for denying that there are legal rules and for asserting that the law is only what judges and other officials do about disputes. He argues that any strong version of this doctrine is obviously nonsensical because there could not be judges or other officials if there were not at least some reasonably clear secondary rules of adjudication instituting individuals in judicial and other official positions. That, however, is a version of the very argument which leads Hart towards an inextricable logical circle—so if it is not fatal for Hart's position, why should it be for that of the realists? The business of finding out whether there are any 'judges' (under whatever name) in a society requires investigation of the question whether anyone there discharges a 'judicial role' as defined in the previous chapter. Whether, in an advanced legal system, the particular individuals who exercise that role exercise it in virtue of a valid power-conferring rule of adjudication is a subsidiary question. If it were not, there would be a vicious circle in the theory.

Reflection on the judicial role leads us, however, to the quintessentially Hartian question about the rule of recognition. Do the individuals who decide disputes conceive themselves duty-bound to apply predetermined standards or not? Do others in their society share that conception of their duty? And is this *just* legitimizing *talk*, or do the 'judges' really act by and large as required by the publicly announced conception of their duty? It will not be enough to only listen to self-congratulatory speeches by judges or professors extolling the tenacity with which their system upholds the 'rule of law'. It will instead be necessary to check whether in the main judges do seek to decide cases by applying established rules.[20] Hence it is as important for Hart, as for any realist, to attend not only to what judges say, but also to what they do. And the realists' concern to focus on the doings of other legal officials and legal actors is one which Hart ought to have taken more seriously.

What is more, it may prove to be a misconception if we make the dogmatic assumption that criteria of recognition identify *only* valid *rules* as the standards judges are duty-bound to apply. The earlier chapters of this book showed that the Hartian theory of social rules can and should be expanded by following up his own hints about principles and values-as-standards and perhaps yet other standards of conduct and judgment. That being so, it seemed singularly inapposite to speak of the more primitive forms of social ordering as comprising *only* 'primary *rules* of obligation'. Hence, in cases where we confront the judicial role in its most rudimentary form, we shall not be surprised if we discover that those who judge, judge indeed by standards implicit in the community's attitudes but by no means always and only by reference to 'rules' in the specific (and thus useful) sense of the term.

What is true of the simpler case need be no less true of the more complex. It need not be thought that 'rules' exhaust the standards available for judicial application in more developed legal orders, including those under which we citizens of 'postindustrial states' live.

A certain amount of nonsense was talked by, and far more has been talked about, American legal realists and their rule-scepticism. But there was a simple, central message in the rule-sceptical element of the wide-ranging realistic works on law. That message is essentially correct. Formalists who represent legal activity as though it were always and only a matter of the application of clear and perfectly coherent rules to the ascertained facts of particular cases present an ideal view of legal order which never has existed and never will exist anywhere. Realists who examined legal practice and reported on the falsity of the formalist vision were quite right. When, like Oliver Wendell Holmes, Jr., they stressed the practising lawyer's need to be able to predict for her client the likely outcome of some case or another, they spoke truly. They added a further truth when they noted that 'black-letter rules' are rarely on their own a sufficient ground for successful prediction of that sort. They erred only when (or if) they *defined* law as predictions of what the courts will do. At least, they erred when they made statements of a kind that could be read as though they were 'definitions' of law, not that any appears so to have been intended apart from that essayed by J. C. Gray.

Perhaps the gravest deficiency in Hart's *Concept of Law* is the extent to which he gave his hand to perpetuating the caricature picture of the realist teachings and concerns. In fact, these teachings pointed the way to raising the very questions whose importance Hart firmly stresses in his seventh chapter. These are such questions as: *how far* it is possible for rules of law fully to determine what is the correct or legally justified decision in a given case and *what* factors are relevant to justifying (and therefore to predicting) decisions in contested or contestable cases at law. It is true that some of the predictive concerns of some realists drew them away from asking (even when contemporaries like Roscoe Pound and the arch-realist Karl Llewellyn were asking) what standards *other than rules* go into the justification of decisions. It is also true of Hart that in his explicit teachings as distinct from his more or less implicit hints, he failed to develop a full account of this matter.

RULES AND DISCRETIONS

Be that as it may, Hart has a valuable and partially correct doctrine as to the reason why legal rules do not by any means exhaustively ground the decision of every legal problem. It is the doctrine of the vagueness and open texture of legal rules,[21] qualities of rules which follow from the fact that rules are framed and stated in ordinary natural languages by the use of general words and phrases like 'vehicle', 'traffic light', 'manufacturer', 'kill', 'intention', and so forth. For such terms there is a 'core of certainty', that is, clear instances of things, people, acts, and aims of actions which beyond doubt fall properly within the sense of the term in question. But there is also a 'penumbra of doubt', a range of fringe or borderline cases which are not unambiguously or clearly covered by the term used. Edinburgh City at one time had to decide whether skateboards were prohibited 'vehicles' under the bylaws about parks. The House of Lords once had to decide whether a statute prohibiting various forms of discrimination on the grounds of 'national origin' also prohibited discrimination by local authorities by way of excluding persons of *foreign nationality* from admission to municipal housing lists. (The Lords held that it did not: *Ealing LBC* v. *Race Relations Board* [1972] A.C. 342. Parliament subsequently changed the law to include nationality-based discrimination expressly within the prohibitions of the Race Relations Act.)

Over and above the cases of 'open texture' where general terms fail to have clean-cut edges, there are cases of vagueness. For example, a common-law rule or statute often imports some general standard such as that of 'reasonableness' (reasonable care in negligence, for example) or 'fairness' (as statutory requirement of 'fair rents' for dwelling houses covered by the Rent Act, for example). Here, the required degree of carefulness or level of rent is stated vaguely rather than with mathematical precision. The contrast envisaged between the relatively vague and the relatively precise can be highlighted by contrasting older general legal prohibitions of being 'drunk and disorderly' with current rather exact prohibitions from driving motor vehicles while one has more than a certain measured proportion of alcohol in one's bloodstream.

Since legal systems are systems of rules (*per* Hart) and since rules are framed or statable in general language, it follows that, quite apart from other grounds of uncertainty in rules,[22] there is a limit to the degree of determinacy in the guidance they can ever give. For all rules (except very badly drafted ones) there are some clear cases, and for some there are many clear cases. If that were not so, the possibility of any legal system existing anywhere as any sort of guidance of anyone's conduct for any purpose would be nil. Common experience however reveals not merely the possibility but the actuality of legal guidance of behaviour. Every time I drive past a 30 mph sign on the road, I know what is the maximum speed at which I ought to be driving as a law-abiding citizen. And I know the guidance I have been given equally as well in the cases where I regrettably ignore it as in those cases where I virtuously follow it.

But equally, for all or almost all rules there are hard cases. The *Law Reports* are full of reports of these problem cases. Often there arise situations where the classification of facts or alleged facts is disputed, and therewith the applicability of a relevant rule. For example, does it count as 'adultery' if a woman gets herself pregnant by artificial insemination from a donor other than her husband? Often again there arise situations where the correct interpretation of a rule is seriously in doubt. To repeat an example, is 'national origins' in the Race Relations Act 1968 to be interpreted as including or as not including legal nationality? Often again, it is questionable whether the law relevantly bears upon the situation in a given dispute at all. Do manufacturers owe consumers of their products a duty to take reasonable care in preparing and packaging them? As everyone knows, that was an open question in the United Kingdom until the House of Lords settled the point in *Donoghue* v. *Stevenson*[23] in 1932.

In modern legal opinion it has become a more or less commonplace view that in deciding such problem cases, judges do not simply find and apply law, they make it. Hart shares that view. His theory holds that although judges are indeed duty-bound to apply the relevant legal rules in every case in which they are clearly applicable, they necessarily have a wider discretion what to do in the situations for which the rules are not clear. Certainly, they are guided in the exercise of the discretion by reference to persuasive and 'permissive' (*C.L.* p. 294) sources of law, such as doctrinal writing and foreign case-law. Certainly, the proper exercise of discretion is shaped by the need to work out grounds of decision which give some sort of rationality to the instant decision in the difficult case, exhibited in a 'concern to deploy some acceptable general principle as a reasoned basis for decision' (*C.L.* p. 205).

But there is no reason to suppose that recourse to these other sources of guidance can conclusively reveal a single right answer in cases where the rules of law themselves have failed to give clear and determinate guidance. The judge must go beyond the law and (without sacrifice of impartiality) consult her own sense of moral and political rightness, equity, and social expediency in order to come to what seems the best decision on the problem in hand. At least for the parties to the case, she partly *makes* the 'law' that she 'applies'. And if the rule of recognition sets precedent as a binding source of law, she also makes law for the future by her decision. The new-made law, however, is in turn subject to all the difficulty and indeterminacy intrinsic to trying to settle the *ratio decidendi* of the case—the supposed 'rule' in it that is 'binding' for the future.

THE LIMITS OF DISCRETION; THE DIVERSITY OF LEGAL STANDARDS

The foregoing Hartian doctrine, as I have suggested at length in a book called *Legal Reasoning and Legal Theory*,[24] points in the right direction, but does not take us far enough. For there are in legal systems canons or standards of legal reasoning that determine what are satisfactory justifications of judicial decisions where justification by simple deduction from a legal rule and the established facts of the case is inapplicable for any of the reasons we have considered above. Very briefly, these can be summarized for modern legal systems as follows.

First, conformably with the principle of formal justice ('treat like cases alike') a judge ought to base the instant decision on some *ruling* which settles the *type* of case to which the instant case belongs and the proposed decision for that type of case. Second, she ought to *evaluate* that ruling and any possible rival rulings in the light of the *consequences* which would follow from adopting it as a ruling in general application. That evaluation should be made by reference to legally appropriate values, including justice, common sense, public policy, and legal convenience, as the judge sees those. Third, the ruling must be shown to be *coherent* with the rest of the legal system or the relevant branch of it. This depends upon its being either an analogical extrapolation from already settled rules of law or precedents of binding or persuasive character, or a particular application of some general principle already at least implicit in the pre-established law. Finally it must be shown to be *consistent* with the pre-established law in the sense that it does not conflict with any previously established legal rule according to some reasonable interpretation of potentially conflicting rules.

That is perhaps a ridiculously brief summary of a long and involved argument. The point of mentioning it at all in the present context is that Hart did at one time state that in the main he accepted the ideas put forward in *Legal Reasoning and Legal Theory*[25] and thought them consistent with his own views. The *Postscript* (at pp. 272–5) gives a sketch of an approach to legal reasoning and adjudication that is, at the very least, thoroughly compatible with these views. The problem for the present work is how, if at all, such ideas do fit the Hartian theory.

On some points the 'fit' is easy. The requirement of 'consistency' simply repeats the Hartian view that judges do have to apply settled legal rules where they are applicable, adding only the corollary that it is equally obligatory for judges to show that possibly or ostensibly conflicting rules *can* be distinguished to avoid conflict with the favoured 'ruling' in a hard case. On the other hand, one has to stress that this activity of distinguishing and reconciling ostensibly or potentially conflicting rules takes place within a wider argumentative context which is concerned *inter alia* with values, principles, and other standards of conduct. That shows that the Hartian distinction between a rule's 'core of certainty' and 'penumbra of doubt' is by no means an inert and invariant 'given' arising from the purely linguistic properties of rules formulated in ordinary legal language.[26] The possibility of ambiguity in rules is a *resource* available to the judge, who may sometimes have reason to squeeze the 'core' down to the absolute indistinguishable and unavoidable minimum. Yet at other times in other contexts, that same judge (or another one) may have reason to give a broad and liberal reading of the rule so that it captures matters within even its remotest penumbra.

That takes us, as William Twining and David Miers point out, to consideration of the contextual variables.[27] These bring in the very issues of valuation and of principle that figure in 'consequentialist' aspects of legal argument and in arguments from 'coherence' as sketched above. How about the matter of fit with the Hartian theory on these points? The answer is that there is a perfectly comfortable fit with Hart's theory, provided that we give it some such reading as was suggested in chapters 3–5. There I tried to show that Hart's theory of social rules admits of extension to cover prin-

ciples and values as standards in themselves and various other types of social standard. Since legal rules are a species of social rules in Hart's theory,
there is no reason to deny the possibility that there are legal principles, legal
values-as-standards, and other legal standards as well as legal rules.

That is precisely the fact of the matter. 'Law' does embrace these principles, values, and other standards as well as rules of statute law and rules
derived from case law. And a study of legal reasoning reveals them in operation. It is part of the justification of, for example, a decision on a barrister's
liability for negligence in out-of-court work that hurts his client's interests
that there is a general legal principle importing liability for careless acts that
damage persons who will foreseeably be affected thereby. It is a further and
essential part of the justification that there is a value of corrective justice
served by a general ruling in favour of barristers' liability in such cases,
and that such a ruling does not make likely any severely inexpedient consequences for the general administration of justice. This absence of inexpedient consequences serves to distinguish the decision in favour of liability
for out-of-court work from a prior ruling against admission of liability for
alleged misconduct of litigation by barristers in court.[28]

A particular feature of legal reasoning that points to the role and significance of general principles in law is the omnipresent resort to analogical
reasoning. The instant case may not be 'covered' by a rule of statute law or
by any admissible precedent. But in such cases judges and lawyers argue
by analogy with settled rules and seek to make choices between competing
analogies. This exhibits a presupposition that the specific rules and rulings
validated by the 'rule of recognition' are themselves instances or concretiza-
tions of more general principles, namely, the principles whose observation
in the law tends to promote certain valued states of affairs. These principles
and values implicit in the law do then constitute legal standards to which
it is considered legitimate, indeed obligatory, to have recourse where the
more specific formulae of legal rules are lacking or give only weak and in-
determinate guidance.

What is more, the whole enterprise of legal argumentation in hard cases
circulates around the duty of the judge not to give any old decision but to
give a decision founded on some explicit or implicit ruling on the point(s)
of law disputed by the parties. That duty depends on a legal principle of
central importance, the principle of formal justice in decision making: to
decide like cases alike and hence to make decisions on the footing that they
cover any case of an envisaged generic type, not just the singular matter in
hand between the particular parties to the instant dispute. Recognition of

and adherence in some measure to that principle of formal justice is in fact a further necessary element in distinguishing the judicial role as such from that of a mere mediator or arbiter whose decision is peculiar to the instant case between the parties in question.

As I formulated the second element in my definition of the judicial role, it ran as follows:

> (b) [Those who occupy that role] have a duty to make their judgment by reference to standards of right and wrong conduct whose existence as standards is not determined by their own present choice or decision, *except in so far as they must interpret or extrapolate from existing standards in justifying their decision*.

We are now in a position to see the force of the italicized exception, which has been, in a sense, qualified by addition of the duty to have regard to the principle of formal justice. One of the implications of the principle of formal justice is that judges should try to make *rulings* on difficult points. In making such rulings, they do exercise choice. They create new standards for actual application in the instant case and for potential future application. On the other hand, as we have seen, they do so by way of interpretation of and extrapolation from existing legal standards. These standards are not all 'rules' in the specific sense of that term. Hence it is only ostensibly paradoxical to say both that judges in some degree *make* the law in hard cases and yet that they do so by applying existing legal standards.

Although this seems a plain contradiction of the views ascribed by Hart to American realists at large, it is quite compatible with two of the main points made by Karl Llewellyn and his associates. First, judges do not always *actually* observe the standards that they *should* observe. This is true. It helps us to realize that only by considering their prejudices, personalities, and routine professional practices can we have much success in predicting how they will decide when prejudice pulls one way and legal standards the other. Second, just because the standards that are not rules are even vaguer, even more open-textured, than rules, the judges necessarily have a wide discretion in interpreting them even when they are not deviating from the right path. So again, practitioners need to know about judges' predispositions (etc.) in order to advise their clients which way the court is likely to decide.

The second of these points is exactly the one that Hart makes about judicial discretion. It seems obviously to be true. In applying broad standards, judges do have a wide discretion. Suppose that a legal system acknowledges the equitable principle that 'every wrong ought to have a remedy'. That is far more vague and general than, say, the rule that 'a judge must impose a sentence of life imprisonment on any person over 18 years of age who is convicted of murder'. The general principle leaves the judge with a wide discretion. The particular rule leaves the judge with no discretion at all. It sets a mandatory penalty. All this being so, it follows that there are important inquiries about law and its working that go beyond the competence of the analytical jurist. On just this ground, as was said in the Introduction, Hart's work only gives a partial understanding of law even when it is most successful in its own terms. The work of the realists and sociologists of law is *at least* an essential complement to analytical work.

Hence, there is a decided oddity in the criticism of Hart's theory of judicial discretion advanced by Ronald Dworkin.[29] Dworkin says that *because* a legal system is always founded on principles, *therefore* judges do not really have 'strong' discretion. It is not true, he says, that when the rules fail to give a clear answer, the judge has discretion unlimited by any legal standards. That is quite correct in itself. The judge's discretion is discretion to do as seems right and proper consistent with legal principles, legal values, and other relevant legal standards. But that is as strong a discretion as there can possibly be. The decision how it is right and proper to interpret and apply vague-because-general principles involves evaluating consequences of a ruling this way or that. This is a matter of *settling*, not *finding*, priorities within the legal system. Neither is there an actual consensus within states/societies about moral and political priorities; nor is there any reason to suppose that there is some ideal judge's or observer's standpoint from which to establish the *true* moral and political priorities served by the legal system.

Even if it is the case, as Dworkin presupposes,[30] that moral values and principles have objective truth and universal validity, it remains also the case that people inveterately disagree about them, as Dworkin does not deny. Political principles are thus also subjects of inveterate disagreement. Legal systems result from a patchwork of historical assertions of contentious and changing political principles, political compromises, and mere political muddles. That from which laws emerge is controversial; this is true even if some or all of the controversies concern moral issues on which there is, in principle, a single right answer. So the idea could not be sustained that judges have only 'weak' discretion since their task is to 'find' *the* right priority ranking of legal principles and deduce from it *the* right answer—it remains a matter for judgement, not deduction. Though the Hartian theory of judicial discretion does need amendment, and though Dworkin's criticisms do point toward the amendments needed, his own particular reading of these amendments ought not to command our assent.

It is common ground, anyway, that judicial discretion exists only within the framework of some predetermined standards. Where these standards are legal rules, the discretion extends only within rather a restricted field, though rarely eliminated completely. Where the rules give no guidance or give ambiguous or conflicting guidance, recourse may be had to other standards of judgment. But since these standards are all less precise than rules, the discretion involved in interpreting and extrapolating from them is greater. 'Discretions' come not in differences of kind (a view Dworkin imputes to Hart) but in differences of degree (as follows from Hart's admittedly incomplete reflections on the subject). The larger the degree of discretion, the more nearly the judge approximates to a lawmaker in settling his own rulings on disputed points, even though in doing so he is still interpreting and applying relatively vague legal standards. The legislature, by contrast, *can* (though it rarely does) make total innovations radically at odds with previous legal standards.

THE COMMON LAW AND THE CONTROVERSY
ABOUT RULES

These reflections enable us to proceed towards meeting another powerful objection to Hart's theory. A. W. B. Simpson[31] has contended that 'law-as-a-system-of-rules' is a misrepresentation of the English common law. The common law, he points out, comprises lots of elements like the 'doctrine of consideration' which were never introduced by one clear ruling nor reduced nor reducible to a set of rule/propositions laid down in some series of cases. The common law, viewed historically, represents the shared practices and understandings of a professional caste of judges and lawyers and, as such, cannot be captured as a carefully individuated and interrelated system of rules. In a partially comparable way, Scottish legal historians[32] have time and again pointed to the way in which, in its 'golden age' in the century and a half after the publication of Stair's *Institutions* in 1681, Scottish common law was very much a body of principles—not a set of 'rules' extracted by 'induction' from 'precedents'. Such observations might be taken as further evidence in Simpson's favour.

In order to meet such an objection as his, one must press again the argument running through the present work that Hart overstates the prominence of rules in law and understates the importance of other types of legal standard which fit better Simpson's picture of the common law. What has been shown, however, is that the recognition and allowance of other legal standards than rules is fully compatible with his theoretical approach.

It has already been said that in relatively primitive societies 'rules' need not be supposed to feature very prominently among the primary social standards. But that has been shown not to be fatal to the idea that those occupying judicial roles in such societies are really working with a rule of recognition, for example, in the form that they are duty-bound to apply the established standards of the community when deciding disputes. Equally, there is no reason to suppose that the rule of recognition in more developed societies *excludes* recognition of standards other than rules. Common-law systems as depicted by Simpson or (as to Scots common law) by Lord Cooper *must* have among their criteria of recognition criteria allowing for the various standards settled by professional usage and custom among the judges and those who plead before them as legal standards.

This conclusion ties in with another point which needs stating. As a matter of history, it has been controversial *what* part and *how large* a part legislatively enacted rules or strictly binding precedents *should* play within legal systems. The real and lasting Benthamite revolution in legal thinking derived from the attack on the common law[33] on the ground of its lack of clear rules as well as of the sinister interests that sustained it. The French revolutionaries—Bentham's contemporaries—likewise wanted codified rules of law *because* the old reliance on principles, doctrines, standards, and the like left too much discretion to the judiciary.[34] It is not a revealed truth of jurisprudential analysis that legal systems are only systems of rules. It has been an important political tenet, an important doctrine of critical morality, that legal systems *ought to be* largely or entirely recast as 'rules'—clearly formulated prescriptions and proscriptions of conduct.[35] Nor is it accidental that the periods of popularity of that tenet coincide with periods when precedents have been treated as themselves sources of 'rules', so that the distinction between *ratio decidendi* and *obiter dicta* is stressed as being of capital importance. For the *ratio* is the 'rule' laid down in the precedent.

In no sphere has the doctrine that laws ought to be reduced to rules been more hotly pressed forward than in that of the criminal law. There, it is said, the citizen must be free from discretionary punishment. There should be clear advance notice of what is a punishable crime, not retroactive reinterpretation of broad principles of proper conduct. *Nulla poena sine lege* is the battle-cry (and translated with strict accuracy, let us not forget, it means 'no punishment without a *statute*'). Where modern systems do comprise statute law in criminal matters, they do so at least partly because of the success of those who raised the battle cry. Likewise, where they do comprise statute law in commercial matters, they have been recast in that form as a response to businessmen's asserted or supposed needs for clarity and predictability in law and to their opposition to too much equitable discretion in the hands of judges.

If it can be a politically controversial matter how far 'law' *should* be reduced to *rules*, it cannot be a true analysis of law that it comprises *only* rules by its very nature. A study of Hart's views on judicial discretion, coupled with reflection on his rather underplayed analysis of standards other than rules, enables us to administer a necessary corrective to his general theory of law.

HART'S CONCEPTION OF LAW RECONSIDERED

What we are left with after administering the corrective is unquestionably a rich and powerful analysis of legal order. At the heart and centre of it lies Hart's concept of the 'rule of recognition', that without which, it seems, the judicial role as such is inconceivable.[36] Those who occupy it do, in developed systems, owe their position to valid appointment under a complex of 'rules of adjudication', which also define their areas of judicial competence. These rules may be enshrined in a constitution or enacted by a legislature. Where there is a distinct legislature at all, we presuppose 'rules of change', constitutional in nature, which confer appropriate power on the defined legislature. These powers of legislative change by their exercise have the effect of facilitating the statement of *rules* of law in place of what would otherwise be altogether vaguer principles and standards, and of enabling persons in authority to innovate and change legal standards. Hence in modern systems private powers exercisable in law and wrongs proscribed by law do to a large extent owe their definition to legal rules in the strict or narrow sense. What is more, the lawyers' practice of referring to precedents and professional usages comes itself to be assimilated to the practice of reliance on statute. Common law itself grows more 'ruly'.

The ever-increasing tendency of legal order to define itself in terms of more or less precise rules (the move, as Max Weber[37] put it, towards 'logically formal rationality' in law) tends to reduce judicial and official discretions. But, as Hart says, it can never eliminate them entirely, because of the vagueness and open-texture of language. It would not even be desirable, he adds, that we seek to eliminate such discretion by excessively precise legislative draftsmanship. No more than anyone else can legislators foresee the future in its entirety. Nor have they a monopoly in practical wisdom. Judges and officials *should* be left some discretion to act fairly, equitably and sensibly in the light of the needs of cases as they appear to responsible officials when they arise.

From an analytical point of view, the chief defect in Hart's work is his understatement of the essential role played by the other working standards of the law. Since it is possible to take full account of these other standards within the four corners of his theory, the error is not fatal to it. It could, however, be argued that in its analytical style and approach Hart's jurisprudence necessarily passes in silence over some vital matters, the very matters that most engaged the realists' attention. The realists for example wanted to know how far and why the actual practice of the law can and does sometimes deviate from the publicly acknowledged standards and justifying grounds for legal activities. They wanted to know how far and why there arise in practice unofficial rules about how to do things at law over and above the official, publicly acknowledged standards. Contemporary sociologists of law have similar concerns. To understand law in action it is necessary to explore such matters as these by empirical inquiry.

To such an objection, the proper reply must be to acknowledge that work such as Hart's cannot be represented as a complete investigation of all that is necessary for an understanding of law. Certainly, however, it is as yet not proven that Hart's general approach is incompatible with satisfactory answers to the questions into which he himself failed to go.

Sanctions, Punishments, Justice

SANCTIONS, RULES, AND LAWS

Implicit in the very idea of social rules and standards as developed by Hart is the idea of 'critical reactions' to deviant conduct. The internal point of view, involving a preference for conduct according to a certain pattern, logically entails also adverse reactions to conduct departing from the pattern. Hence, it is a logical truth that one who breaks such a rule incurs the disapproval of those who accept the rule. From their point of view, the disapproval is justified disapproval. Many people, we may suppose, are sensitive, some highly sensitive, to the disapproval of others. To be an object of disapproval is disagreeable. Hence, if the somewhat woolly and indiscriminately used term 'sanction' is taken to mean any normally disagreeable experience which a person is liable to suffer on the ground of his being deemed to have contravened some standard of conduct, it follows that there are no rules without 'sanctions' in this wide sense.

It is, however, a wide sense. For what we are considering is logically implicit in our very idea of a rule or standard of conduct. The disapproval in view is not necessarily *expressed* disapproval. It is not disapprobation or criticism or blame *meted out* in order to induce better conformity to the rule. It is not in that way purposive at all. It is a simple matter of what is involved in adherence to some standard whereby doing x in circumstances c is wrong. If I *do* adhere to that standard, I do necessarily disapprove of your doing x in c. (If I don't disapprove, it turns out that I don't adhere to that standard, or not without previously unconsidered exceptions.)

What about expressing disapproval, criticism, blame, and so forth? No doubt it is hard to disguise or suppress one's disapproval entirely. But is there *reason* positively to express disapproval? There certainly is, from the point of view of one who 'strives to teach and intends to maintain' (*C.L.* p. 56) a certain standard. The least one can do with a view to getting others to bring themselves up to the mark is to let them know what one thinks of their doings, and that one holds them to be wrong. This can be true even of purely personal standards or principles, such as those of our vegetarian friend considered in chapter 4. All the more is it so in the case of social rules of groups where, as Durkheim pointed out so forcefully, the solidarity of the group is established and/or reinforced by collective and individual acts of expressing disapprobation of those who transgress against the group's rules.[1] Groups are, after all, *constituted* by people's sharing common rules.

Once one starts considering expressions of disapproval, one cannot but note that there are gradations of disapprobation from mild reproof to angry denunciation, to say nothing (yet) of physical punishments and retaliations. These gradations are related (*a*) to the degree of flagrancy of transgression and (*b*) to the perceived importance of the rule infringed. The severest disapproval is of the grossest and most manifestly wilful transgressions of the most important rules. But that in turn forces us back in thinking of the collectively held *values* which at least implicitly underpin the rules, some relative ranking of such values being presupposed in the notion that some rules have greater importance than others. Hart's fundamental key to the concept of morality, it will be recalled, was this criterion of the relative importance of its rules and other standards. Furthermore, in his view, the primary elements of law always include standards regulating the most important conditions of individual and collective survival. Hence it ought to follow from his analysis that the strongest expressions of disapprobation are reserved for wilful infractions of moral standards and of the central primary elements of law.

Closely related to disapprobation is resentment. In the nature of the case, infractions of moral or basic legal standards concerning honesty, respect for possessions, avoidance of physical harm to others and the like commonly involve direct harm to specific other persons. The person harmed may disapprove the act done as an infringement of an appropriate standard of conduct. She will then surely also *resent* the harm wrongfully done to herself, and, if she does resent it, she has from the 'internal point of view' *justification* for her resentment. Hence, although this is not logically entailed by the 'primary standard' infringed, a secondary standard requiring some remedial action by the wrongdoer to assuage the justified resentment of the person harmed is commonly and naturally adhered to as an essential ancillary standard. Breach of this secondary or remedial requirement is in its own turn 'sanctioned' by the disapprobation of group members-at least those who willingly accept the standards of the group.

All these above points are necessary elements in Hart's theory of social rules, though not all are given quite the prominence one might have expected. At two or three points in his argument, however, Hart (as will be recalled) does expressly argue that there are reasons why the relative peace and likely survival of social communities calls for more than simple individualized expressions of disapproval, however severe, for breaches of primary standards. The same goes for refusals to comply with remedial requirements. In small face-to-face communities, these individual reactions may be enough to secure reasonable conditions of order, says Hart. But in larger, less 'closely knit' communities, there is a standing risk that those who do voluntarily conform to the common requirements and standards may find others taking unfair advantage of their conformity. These others willingly take the benefit of the relative security of life and of expectations that is promoted by general conformity to basic standards. But they do not play their fair part in maintaining the general conformity.

Since that is so, there is a risk that those who do voluntarily conform find themselves being effectively exploited by those who do not. The social institution which most effectively counters this risk, according to Hart, is the organization of effective coercive 'sanctions' imposed upon those who break the rules (or violate other important standards, we may add). The existence of an organized system of sanctions functions as some kind of guarantee to those who bear the burdens of social existence willingly that others cannot take the benefits, neglect their part of the burdens, and get away with it. This ties in neatly with Hart's point as to the 'inefficiency' of a régime of pure 'primary rules of obligation' sustained only by diffuse social pressure, and with his theory that the evolution of 'secondary rules of adjudication' can be represented as a 'remedy' for that 'inefficiency'. It also ties in with the point made in chapter 6 about the necessity for a hermeneutic analysis of the concept 'penalty'.[2] Resort to penalties, it was said, can be justified from the internal point of view as a matter both of expressing forcefully and seriously an adverse judgement on conduct held to be wrong and of discouraging repetition of that conduct.

The development of adjudicative institutions in societies is precisely what marks off the separate domain of law, since 'law' for Hart comprehends only those rules and standards which those who bear the judicial role are duty-bound to apply in view of their 'rule of recognition'. Since the use of force interpersonally is justified only subject to judicial control (where the judicial role exists in its fully developed form), it follows that forceful reactions to wrongdoing are within the province exclusively claimed for law. From the internal point of view relative to any given legal order, sanctions for wrongdoing exacted by physical force are justified only subject to legal provisions as interpreted by judges. (For even questions of lawful self-defence or of lawful use of force in quelling disorder, riot or insurrection are subject to *ex post facto* judicial scrutiny.)

There is accordingly good reason why in the history of legal theory many thinkers have been tempted to treat the provision of coercive sanctions as a necessary and defining feature of law, whether by insisting that *every* true law is backed by a sanction or, more credibly, by insisting that every true law must belong to a system of rules *some* of which provide for coercive sanctions. The development of law includes indeed a development towards a legal and indeed an official monopoly in the justified use of force to sanction wrongdoing. Such a temptation Hart, however, discountenances. For it confuses the fundamental nature of law as a system of regulative and facultative rules (and other standards) with an ancillary albeit practically necessary method of securing the rights and enforcing the duties laid down by the system. Human nature might develop in such a way that resort to force ceased to be or to be thought necessary for securing conformity to the law's requirements. But that would by no means entail that orderly and cooperative social existence coupled with an extensive division of labour could go on without continued reference to a 'system of primary and secondary rules'. Such a system would still have to maintain the technique of legislative change to cope with social and technological developments, and would still need to have adjudicative institutions to determine disputed or difficult questions of law, fact, and right.

These arguments deserve to command assent, though subject to addition of the aforementioned rider that in a *wide* sense, 'sanctions' (viz., disapprobation of behaviour contrary to appropriate standards) are a logically necessary element of any rule or standard of conduct falling within the Hartian analysis. Presumably, indeed, the prospect of a withering away of coercive sanctions would depend on the possibility that avoidance of disapprobation, including above all self-disapprobation, might come to be for most people most of the time a sufficient motive of law-abiding conduct even when other motives were lacking.

Anyway, such a utopian world is not our world. Modern legal systems do provide for, and their officials do resort to, the use of force in at least three ways: for the anticipatory quelling of riot, insurrection, and other like threats to public peace and established order; for the imposition of punishments on those who commit 'criminal offences'; and for the enforcement of court orders in the way of 'civil remedies' awarded to those whose rights have been infringed as against those who have infringed them. It is a standing defect in juristic discussion that it largely ignores the first of these, and unduly assimilates the latter two. An award of compensation for a civil wrong is not at all like the imposition of a criminal punishment, even a fine. There is a 'sanction' of coercion *behind* the order for civil compensation and it is brought to bear if the wrongdoer refuses to pay up when he can. Criminal punishments are 'sanctions' in themselves.[3]

Preventive, punitive, and compensation-enforcing uses of public force by legal officials are then salient features of modern legal systems. For the very reason that legal systems are founded on the principle (among others) that violence ought to be repressed, there arise moral and political problems concerning the justification of, and proper limits on, the public and official use of force and violence in these ways. Modern states indeed command coercive organizations that can deploy coercive power on a scale beyond the dreams of primitive people in their simple societies. Perhaps we have purchased the 'efficiency' reposing in our 'rules of adjudication' at too high a price?

Among the greatest of Hart's contributions to legal, moral and political philosophy has been his work on one aspect of this problem, that concerning the nature and justification of legal punishment. In turning to consider, all too briefly, this part of his work, we bring into view his critical moral philosophy alongside of his analytical theorizing about an important legal institution.

PUNISHMENT: DEFINITION AND GENERAL JUSTIFYING AIM

Those who think that an approach to philosophical questions by the method of 'linguistic analysis' necessarily trivializes them and substitutes a complacent conservatism for serious political thought[4] should read, or re-read, Hart's collection of essays on *Punishment and Responsibility*. The message shining through these beautifully written essays is that careful analysis of the terms and concepts in current use within the relevant social practices is an *essential* preliminary to entering upon the questions of moral and political values posed by critiques or justifications of those practices. The former is not a substitute for the latter. But careful analysis is a necessary precondition of any *rationally* persuasive discussion of the value questions.

Nowhere is this point better taken than in Hart's insistence on the need to distinguish questions of the following kinds:

> (i) As to the *definition* of punishment: What do we *mean* when we speak of punishing people; how are we to understand and use that term?
>
> (ii) As to the *general justifying aim* of punishment: If that defined practice of 'punishing' exists in a society, what aim or objective might be ascribed to it that would justify retaining such a practice (or introducing it, if it did not previously exist)?
>
> (iii) As to the distribution of punishments: On what ground can it be justifiable to punish particular individuals (the question of *title* to punish) and *how much* can it be justifiable to exact by way of punishment (the question of *amount*)?

His point is that attention must be given to each of these as a question distinct from the others. Care should be taken to avoid the use of what is truly a definition of punishment as though it were itself an answer to a (value-) question about justification of the practice or about justified distribution of punishments. Equally, we must be alive to the possibility that principles of general justification and of justified distribution may be different and potentially conflicting principles, as he himself holds.

As to definition, Hart subscribes to the widely held view that the 'central case' of punishment has five elements. These are that punishments are: (i) unpleasant experiences; (ii) inflicted for breach of legal rules; (iii) meted upon actual or supposed offenders on the ground of the offence committed; (iv) intentionally administered by human beings as an expression of disapproval of the offence committed;[5] (v) constituted as authorities within *that* legal system. (See *P.R.* p. 5). There are, however, other cases that Hart considers penumbral ones beyond this core. In relation to point (ii), families, schools, and so forth also have rules and also punish those who break them. In relation to point (iii), we can find instances of 'collective' or 'vicarious' punishment, and other cases of 'punishment' of scapegoats who neither are offenders nor are supposed to be offenders by those who 'punish'. In relation to point (v), in some legal orders there are 'decentralized sanctions' imposed by people who are not themselves officials of the legal system.

In making this characteristic reminder that definitions of standard cases must also allow for a wider 'family' of non-standard, fringe, or penumbral cases, Hart warns against resort to a 'definitional stop' in discussion of general justifying aim or distribution. For example, utilitarians argue that what justifies punishment is its social utility.[6] The threat and the enforcement of punishment for offences deter people from commission of offences. Hence, although punishment involves the wilful infliction of harm on those who are punished, this is justified by the greater good secured by resort to punishment, namely that fewer harmful offences are committed than would otherwise occur. Persuasive though that argument is, it opens up the following well-known problem: Why then punish only offenders? Sometimes great good might come of knowingly convicting and punishing an innocent person for a notorious offence, in order for example to cool off a lynch mob intent upon finding and killing some innocent people (e.g., black people) as scapegoats for the offence.[7]

It is not open to utilitarians simply to say that that question does not arise just because of the definition of 'punishment'. They cannot thus resort to a 'definitional stop' to dodge a genuine question about the practices which their principles apparently justify. Neither would the practice of occasionally punishing an innocent scapegoat fall clearly outside of any reasonable definition of punishment. Certainly, it is only a fringe instance of punishment, yet the practice would not lack utilitarian justification if the only relevant consideration in this field were the aim of securing a balance between harm done and harm averted.

As to the general justifying aim of punishment Hart himself does mainly adhere to a utilitarian view. He starts from the assumption that punishment is in itself an evil. It is so because it involves human suffering, both the suffering of the offender actually punished and the suffering of those others who are put in fear by the prospect of such punishment. Those who are so put in fear cannot but find their liberty of action restricted by their fear of liability to punishment for doing as they would otherwise wish. What is more, these evils result not from the chance of natural accident, but from the intentional human choices of those who make or sustain the system of criminal law, and of those who impose its penalties. In all this, Hart is of the same mind as Jeremy Bentham and John Stuart Mill:

> These thinkers held that the use of the criminal law is an evil requiring justification and that it is not justified by the mere fact that conduct which the criminal law is used to punish is an offence against the accepted moral code of the community. For the justification of punishment . . . it must be shown that the conduct punished is either directly harmful to individuals or their liberty or jeopardizes the collective interest which members of society have in the maintenance of its organization or defence. (*M.C.L.* pp. 31–2)

Since punishment is in itself an evil, it can be justified as a social practice only to the extent that it can be shown to produce some greater good than the evil which it itself constitutes; and that good should be of a kind commensurable with the evil in question. By that test, the harms involved in punishment should be counterbalanced by a diminution in the amount of suffering in the community, achieved by deterrence of those activities whose harmful character justifies treating them as criminal offences.

The mode or 'mechanism' whereby such deterrence might work is uncertain. To Hart's view, some of the theorizings of Bentham and Austin (John Austin) about criminal motivations seem excessively rationalistic. It is, as he rightly says, unrealistic to suppose that persons on the brink of committing an offence pause and calculate the amount of pleasure their act will bring them, subtract the amount of pain involved in their punishment multiplied by the probability of detection and conviction, and go ahead only if the balance of accounts is on the credit side. Hart's view on this is set out in the context of his various discussions of the rationale for including some forms of negligent, as distinct from wilful, actings in the calendar of criminal offences. *Ex hypothesi*, when people act negligently, they act unthinkingly (and may thoughtlessly do great harm). Since no one decides to act negligently, no one's decision whether or not so to act can *at that moment* be guided by contemplation of the pains of punishment as a counter-motive. But, in a wider way, the threats implicit in the criminal law 'may cause you to think'; certainly, in this way, the law operates 'more like a goad than a guide'. The same may hold good even in case of crimes whose definition requires intention, not mere negligence.

> But there seems to me to be nothing disreputable in allowing the law to function in this way, and it is arguable that it functions in this way rather than in the rationalistic way more frequently than is generally allowed. (*P.R.* p. 134)

For Hart the primary general justification of the practice of punishment for breaches of the criminal law is that it is in this way a means of deterrence by threats whereby those types of potentially harmful conduct which are criminal offences are discouraged. This does not conflict with other utilitarian objectives such as disabling the offender, at least temporarily, from repeating the offence during a stretch of imprisonment. It does however sit in some degree uneasily alongside schemes for the reformation of offenders, and here, for the present, the legal system has settled for a compromise.

> What makes the compromise seem tolerable is the belief that the influence which the threat and example of punishment extracts is often independent of the severity of punishment, and is due more to the disgrace attached to conviction for crime or to the deprivation of liberty which many measures of reform at present use in any case involved. (*P.R.* p. 27)

This aside about 'disgrace attached to conviction for crime' raises a point of weakness in Hart's theory. The introductory section of this chapter pointed out the analytical connection in Hart's general theory between somebody's breaking a rule and their suffering the disapproval of any others who accept the rule. The point about 'disgrace attached to conviction' squares well with that. Hart at various points admits that there is a partial analogy that obtains between legal punishment and moral blame. This admission reinforces the point. All in all, there must surely then be an expressive element in punishment, which may be relevant to its justification. For it would appear that as a social practice punishment is (among other things) a means of expressing disapprobation or condemnation of the acts of those who offend. Being a conventional practice, it is a mode of attaching conventionally understood degrees of reprobation to offences, judged both by the flagrancy of the offence and the importance of the values attacked (as was said in the introductory section of the chapter). This operates at two levels. At the legislative level, there is some exhortatory-cum-denunciatory force in the very act of legislating to the effect that such and such acts shall be offences, punishable with legal penalties. At the trial level, the particular act of a particular convicted offender is the focus of a specific 'condemnation'.

Hart nowhere gives much countenance to this view of punishment, though he does allow that it could be relevant to a broadly utilitarian view of its justification, or at least that it 'trembles on the margin' of such a view (*P.R.* p. 235). Yet in truth it seems a more credible account of the possible general deterrent operations of the criminal law than even Hart's heavily qualified rationalism. Followers of the sociological tradition set by Émile Durkheim[8] might well argue that precisely what punishment of offenders does is to reinforce 'social solidarity' by upholding a collective sense of the moral importance of the rules of criminal law. It is the conventional and ritualized practices of legislative prohibition and then of trial, conviction and sentence that both express and sustain the common conviction that offences are in their varying degrees *wrong*. Further, it is this sense of wrongness, even revulsion, that restrains people from offending, far more than any rationalistic arithmetical calculation of pains that one risks set against the pleasures one anticipates. Durkheim's view has on the face of it great intuitive plausibility. It seems most surprising that Hart does not eagerly adopt it both in its own right and as further support for his theory of legal rules as social rules, with which it has been shown to be thoroughly compatible.

In his essay, 'Social Solidarity and the Enforcement of Morality' (1967) Hart directly confronts Durkheim's theory as to the connection between social solidarity and punishment in its expressive aspect, and shows reasons to doubt it. Nevertheless, he does at another point in his argument admit the force of these Durkheimian considerations. Distinguishing present practices of punishment of offenders from rival schemes for non-punitive treatment of persons with dangerous propensities, he remarks that:

> unlike a medical inspection followed by detention in hospital, conviction by a court followed by a sentence of imprisonment is a public act expressing the odium, if not the hostility, of society for those who break the law. As long as these features attach to conviction and a sentence of imprisonment, the main objection to their use on those who could not have helped doing what they did will remain. On the other hand, if they cease to attach, will not the law have lost an important element in its authority and deterrent force-as important perhaps for some convicted persons as the deterrent force of the actual measures which it administers? (*P.R.* p. 209)

He does not, however, make a great deal of this point, and there seem to be two reasons why he does not. The first is his libertarian opposition (discussed fully in the next chapter) to undue moralization of the criminal law. Such moralization has to be resisted on account of the view he holds in common with Bentham and Mill that the only justified use of criminal law and punishment is against harmful behaviour. Harmfulness in behaviour has to be distinguished from qualities of behaviour that merely offend against 'the accepted moral code of the community' (*M.C.L.* p. 32). The second, closely related, reason is his utilitarian opposition to any principle that endorses 'retribution' as a general justifying aim of punishment. 'Retribution' in its most exact legal sense, Hart suggests, should be taken as meaning:

> that the justification for punishing men [proportionately to the gravity of their offence, which must itself be a voluntarily committed moral wrong] is that the return of suffering for moral evil voluntarily done, is itself just or morally good. (*P.R.* p. 231)

As he points out, few if any people now subscribe to the classical Kantian[9] or Hegelian[10] versions of this principle, dependent as they are on the metaphysical thesis that punishment in such a case somehow 'nullifies' the offence, restoring the offender to communion with his true and rational self. Rather, the concentration of contemporary retributivism is upon 'the value of the authoritative expression, in the form of punishment, of moral condemnation for the moral wickedness involved in the offence' (*P.R.* p. 235).

That this is of value in itself Hart denies. His denial of its value is variously pursued in *The Morality of the Criminal Law* and *Law, Liberty and Morality*, in both of which he particularly draws attention to the widespread support which belief in such a value enjoys and has enjoyed among English judges. A major illustrative example he cites is from Lord Denning's evidence to the Royal Commission on Capital Punishment: 'The ultimate justification of any punishment is . . .that it is the emphatic denunciation by the community of a crime'. To this Hart's reply is that

> It represents as a value to be pursued at the cost of human suffering the bare expression of moral condemnation, and treats the infliction of suffering as a uniquely appropriate or 'emphatic' mode of expression. But . . . is the mere expression of moral condemnation a thing of value to be pursued at this cost? (*L.L.M.* p. 65; *q.v.* also for the quotation from Lord Denning).

In short, Hart's conviction as to the evils of the suffering involved in the deliberate threat of and the deliberate infliction of punishment debars him from accepting this modern variant on retributivism as a morally adequate justification of punishment. If punishment served no purpose in discouraging harmful behaviour, its own harmful character would require us forthwith to abandon it. There could be no sufficient countervailing value in the mere expression of condemnation *by this means*. Those who agree with Hart's opinion on that last point may nevertheless take leave to doubt whether he himself does not seriously under-play the expressive aspect of punishment. Surely this must be a major element in any success that punishment can have in reinforcing the determination of the law-abiding to avoid the 'disgrace' of criminal conviction. We may also doubt whether he has sufficiently applied his own hermeneutic method to analysing the concepts of penalty and punishment, along the lines sketched in chapter 6.

Despite all that, Hart's own principles of punishment are by no means out-and-out utilitarian ones. Though he is insistent on a utilitarian position as to the general justifying aim of punishment, his whole attitude is only

> the kind of qualified utilitarian attitude which appears to me to accord (as an unquestioned utilitarianism does not) with the moral convictions which most of us share. (*P.R.* p. 88)

The qualifications in question depend on certain of the principles of justice upon which retributivist critics of utilitarianism in punishment have always insisted. But Hart considers that these principles are ones that impose side constraints on a practice which is positively justified by its utility; they are principles governing the just distribution of punishment, not justifying the practice itself.

Before turning to consider the distribution of punishments, we should note one aspect of justice which both in *C.L.* and in *A.A.N.R?* Hart mentions as relevant to the general justification of punishments but which finds no place in his essays on punishment and responsibility. As we saw, Hart holds that law-abiding citizens ought to have some guarantee that their self-restraint is not exploited by others. Hence some coercive sanctions are a normally necessary feature of legal orders. But are they merely necessary in fact, or is this a requirement of fairness to the law-abiding citizens? If the latter, there is a non-utilitarian general justification of punishment implicit in Hart's view, and it is regrettable that he did not anywhere consider how this might fit in with his utilitarian doctrine. Perhaps the right answer is that what fairness demands is for punishment *as such* only to be used where and when it is *also* useful as a restraint on harmful behaviour.

THE DISTRIBUTION OF PUNISHMENT: JUSTICE AND RESPONSIBILITY

A standard Kantian objection to utilitarian theories of punishment is that they (immorally) justify the treatment of some human beings as means to others' ends. The person who is punished, is punished *pour encourager les autres*. His or her suffering is a deterrent example to others like-minded. Deterring them saves yet other people from becoming the victims of the offences they are deterred from committing. The achievement of this desired end for those saved from being crime's victims flows through a particular mechanism: the suffering of the person who was punished. In thus making persons and their suffering a cog in the mechanism for protecting others we dehumanize them. This is of the essence of immorality. Yet utilitarianism presents itself as a moral theory that can succeed in justifying punishment.

On this, great importance attaches to Hart's work on the elucidation of the nature of criminal responsibility and in explaining why it ought to include an element of *mens rea* or 'guilty mind'. This effectively establishes the materials for a persuasive reply to a Kantian critique of his utilitarian principles concerning the general justifying aim of punishment. In simple terms, his argument is that we do not use people as means to others' ends when we punish them, so long as it is truly a matter of their own choice whether or not they make themselves liable to punishment. This implies upholding a morally imperative constraint upon any practice of punishment: *You may only punish those who had a choice whether or not to break the law, and who exercised that choice in favour of breaking it.*

In its terms, that is a principle guiding what Hart calls 'distribution' of punishment. It limits the *title* we have to impose punishment on people, whatever short- or long-run good we think some use of punishment might tend to bring about. No one is morally entitled to impose suffering on others in order that good may come of it, except if by some free act of their own these others have taken upon themselves the risk implicit in liability to punishment. Then they are sufficiently the authors of their own misfortune to have against those who punish them no just complaint that they are being used merely as a means to others' ends. To this might again be added the Hartian point that those who do exercise self-restraint in keeping the law would for their part have a just complaint if those who voluntarily break it got off scot-free. Hart rightly represents the requirement that voluntary conduct is a prerequisite of title to punish as a requirement of justice, not a mere corollary of the utilitarianism which he proposes as the general justifying aim for the practice of punishment. The relevant principle of justice is independent of, and not derivable from, utilitarianism.

To prove this mutual independence of the principles, Hart cites the instance of those offences of 'strict liability' which are admitted in modern law, mainly 'regulatory offences'[11] as they are often called. The cases where either strict or vicarious liability is imposed (e.g., for the sale of adulterated food or milk or the supply of alcohol to persons already intoxicated) may be justified by reference to the harm which they avert. In admitting strict or vicarious liability in such cases, the law relieves the prosecution of any need to prove *mens rea*, and so also deprives accused persons of the opportunity to excuse themselves by showing that the offence occurred despite their best efforts to prevent its occurrence. But since such excuses can sometimes be dishonestly manufactured, the deterrent effect of the imposition of strict or vicarious liability may indeed be greater than if the normal excuses which negative criminal liability were admitted. The good thereby procured may be considerable (e.g., in the reduction of instances of poisoning by adulterated foodstuffs). But the good here is purchased at a cost of some injustice to some defendants. It may be acceptable to hold that such relatively minor injustices are a price worth paying for saving people from poisoning. But this is not merely a part of the 'harm' always involved in punishment, outweighed by the good procured by the practice. Reflection on the particular unease one feels about the exaction of this price shows that what is involved is the overriding of a principle distinct from that of utility. (See *P.R.* pp. 76–8)

Normally, it is right to insist strictly on observance of that principle of justice. For certain justifications and excuses are normally available to an accused person even when she admits, or when it is proved, that by her acts she was 'causally responsible' (*P.R.* pp. 214–15; and cf. Hart and Honoré, *Causation in the Law*) for some event whose voluntary commission is an offence. The justifications and excuses depend on the stated principle of justice. Indeed, the basic idea of being criminally responsible only for one's voluntary acts is properly to be understood only in terms of the absence of any justification or excuse. The rationale of this rests not on the postulated existence of some mysterious form of 'act of will' controlling muscular movements. Rather, according to Hart, it rests in the first instance on the more commonsense view that 'he did it, but he couldn't help doing it' is a valid excuse for what one has done, however untoward 'its' outcome may be. That commonsense view has a deeper rationale than appears at first sight.

> It is illuminating to look at the various excuses which the law admits, like accident or mistake, as ways of rewarding self-restraint. In effect, the law says that even if things go wrong, as they do when mistakes are made or accidents occur, a person whose choices are right and who has done her best to keep the law will not suffer. (*P.R.* p. 182)

What we are dealing with, then, is a principle of justice that disallows punishment of the innocent. It also disallows punishments in most cases where the defendant was not a voluntary wrongdoer, that is, was acting neither intentionally nor recklessly (nor negligently, in cases where a person 'should have thought about what he was doing'). This principle is concerned with giving people a fair opportunity to plan their lives and to avoid official intervention in their affairs. The value at stake is liberty in one's actings. The distributional principle is that all people ought to have the same equal opportunity to secure their own liberty of acting. They can have this equal opportunity only if the principle that criminal responsibility normally attaches solely to voluntary acts is rigorously sustained in the criminal law.

Hence there is a parallel here with the 'facilities' that the private power-conferring secondary rules of the civil law secure to individuals. A fair system of criminal law gives a negative guarantee that people can plan their lives without fear of official interference, provided that they avoid intentional infractions of the criminal law and cultivate the virtue of self-restraint. Parallel to that, a fair system of civil law provides positive facilities that enable people to plan their activities with reasonable security as to the validity and outcome of the transactions they undertake, provided they attend to any legally required formalities.

This argument from fair equality of opportunity is one which Hart thinks holds good regardless of one's view on the 'determinism *versus* free will' debate as a topic of general philosophy. It justifies a requirement of voluntary acts as preconditions of criminal liability without at all presupposing that human beings either have or have not 'a will' that is free in the sense that the choices they make are not fully determined by necessary and sufficient anterior conditions.

Yet more importantly, the same argument serves for Hart to distinguish his principle of distribution of punishment from closely similar 'retributive' ideas. For it is not a necessary, or any, part of Hart's case that punishing a person is morally justified only when she or he has voluntarily committed some immoral act, as classical retributivism (or modern denunciatory retributivism) claims. There is, he observes, an

> important distinction between the assertions that (1) it is morally permissible to punish only voluntary actions and (2) it is morally permissible to punish only voluntary commission of a moral wrong. (*P.R.* p. 40)

His case supports the former, but not the latter, of these assertions. On the one hand, not everything which positive morality — or ideal morality — condemns as wrong is or ought to be criminally punishable. On the other hand, for social utility, the law justifiably admits of many regulatory offences that no moral code condemns. The moral principle of fairness in distribution of punishment only requires voluntariness as a condition of liability for all or most legal offences; it does not require that they be also moral offences.

Thus having distinguished himself from pure retributivism in the matter of *title* to punish, Hart further distinguishes himself from pure retributivism on the question of the *amount* of punishment that is justified in respect of particular offences. Here utilitarian principles do have a part to play, by way of settling an outward limit. No punishment (however effective) ought to be admitted if it does itself cause more severe suffering than the offence in question causes or would cause if the lawmaker refrained from prohibiting it. Yet if some punishments, say those involving torture, are too barbarous to be admitted whatever the harm they might be thought likely to avert, then it appears that there are also non-utilitarian restrictions on the admissible severity of punishments.

On these arguments alone, there is and ought to be some proportionality between the supposed gravity of an offence (the harm which its commission is likely to involve) and the severity of the punishment that can be imposed. But this does not entail acceptance of the retributivist's traditional idea of a matching in moral terms between the degree of guilt or wickedness manifested by an offender in offending and the degree of suffering meted out in repayment for the offence. This is the kind of matching of which a caricature version can be found in 'an eye for an eye and a tooth for a tooth'.

There is, however, also a requirement of justice, the formal justice of treating like cases alike and different cases differently, that bears upon this matter of justifying amounts of punishment. Again, this principle of justice is neither derivable from nor identical to the principle of utility. If ever it is justifiable for courts in particular cases of special notoriety to hand out exceptionally severe 'deterrent' sentences so as to enhance the disincentive against committing some socially dangerous crime, those who suffer thereby have to that extent suffered an injustice. That doing so *may* in some cases have a sufficient utilitarian justification does not mean that after all there is no injustice done. It merely means that there are occasions when even injustice might be an acceptable price to pay for social peace. But that is a claim whose credentials need the severest examination on any occasion when it is advanced.

CONCLUSION

Hart's theory of sanctions and of punishments as here sketched stresses their functional aspects, perhaps at too much cost to a hermeneutic appreciation of them. Laws may have to be backed by organized sanctions, given the present state of human society. But, at least in the form of coercive sanctions, they are to be seen as practical necessities of social peace and order, not conceptual requirements for the very existence of law. In the form of criminal punishments, legal sanctions involve the imposition of evils upon people. Hence the practice calls for special justification, and the justification must be in terms of the commensurable good it does, set against the evil it necessarily involves.

This justification cannot be founded on an unqualified utilitarianism. As to distribution of punishments, there are irreducible requirements of justice that disqualify us from punishment of the innocent and of those who offend involuntarily. They also require us, as against critics like Baroness Wootton,[12] to sustain the traditional requirement of *mens rea* in the definition of all save relatively trivial offences. They also disqualify us from any ventures into reformative 'treatment' that stray too far from the justice of treating like cases alike. All these constraints of justice follow from an appreciation of the moral values of liberty and of fair equality of opportunity to enjoy that liberty.

We may point out in conclusion of this chapter that these values of liberty and of fair opportunity are for Hart connected with a principle that also underpins the 'hermeneutic' method involved in his analytical jurisprudence. It is the 'important general principle' that:

> Human society is a society of persons; and persons do not view themselves or each other merely as so many bodies moving in ways which are sometimes harmful and have to be prevented or altered. Instead persons interpret each other's movements as manifestations of intention and choices, and these subjective factors are often more important to their social relations than the movements by which they are manifested or their effects. . . . If as our legal moralists maintain it is important for the law to reflect common judgements of morality, it is surely even more important that it should in general reflect in its judgements on human conduct distinctions which not only underly (*sic*) morality, but pervade the whole of our social life. This it would fail to do if it treated men merely as alterable, predictable, curable or manipulable things. (*P.R.* pp. 182–3).

It is a matter of some importance that those who reject Hart's hemeneutic approach address themselves to the questions whether human society is not indeed 'a society of persons', and whether this does not require adoption of a method of analysis such as Hart uses.

CHAPTER THIRTEEN

Law, Morality, and Positivism

PRELIMINARY

This chapter returns to a consideration of Hart's principles of critical morality. It is concerned with his argument that in principle the coercive restraints of the law ought to be used only within a limited sphere, and thus with his argument that the citizens of a civilized state do, and ought to, enjoy an extensive liberty of conscience, speech and action. We are concerned in short with his views as to the moral relevance of law. To a consideration of those views must then be subjoined final consideration of his opinion as to the analytical and conceptual distinctness of morality and law. This will complete our review of Hart's legal theory as a certain kind of 'legal positivism.'

THE LIBERTARIAN PRINCIPLE AND THE CRITIQUE
OF LEGAL MORALISM

Hart was a stalwart defender of human and civil liberty, even if at the end of his life he disowned his own earlier attempt (in *A.A.N.R.*?) to derive from conceptual analysis of rights and obligations the thesis that 'if there are any moral rights at all, it follows that there is at least one natural right, the equal right of all men to be free.' His celebrated lectures on *Law, Liberty and Morality* start from assertion of the general critical principle that the use of legal coercion by any society calls for justification as something *prima facie* objectionable, something to be tolerated only for the sake of some countervailing good (*L.L.M.* p. 20). That principle is also, it will be recalled, the basic presupposition of Hart's philosophy of punishment and responsibility.

The dialectical context of the appeal to that principle in *L.L.M.* is well known. In 1957, the Report by the Wolfenden *Committee on Homosexual Offences and Prostitution* had put the case that the proper function of the criminal law is only to prevent public disorders and indecency and to protect people from harmful or offensive behaviour. It had contended that beyond these functions 'there must remain a realm of private morality and immorality which is, in brief and crude terms, not the law's business'.[1] The distinguished judge Lord Devlin (Patrick Devlin)[2] had responded with a vigorous critique of the Committee's views. His counter-argument was (*a*) that a substantial part of the existing English criminal law does go beyond the limited ambit prescribed by the Committee, being concerned with sustaining the existing moral standards of English society at large; and (*b*) that this is quite acceptable since a society has every right to enforce its moral code through the criminal law.

The justifying reason offered for this societal right was that maintenance of a common moral code is an essential element in the maintenance of a viable society. Hence, just as the criminal law may justifiably be used to protect a society from treason, so it may be used to protect it from destruction by flagrant disregard of its common moral code. That does not entail treating every moral lapse as a proper matter for criminal punishment. But it does justify sustaining criminal liability for those forms of immoral behaviour (whether or not conducted privately) which arouse in the ordinary representative citizen (the 'right-minded man', in Lord Devlin's words) 'intolerance, indignation, and disgust'.[3]

It is easy to see how and why that view connects with the modern denunciatory form of retributivism in the justification of punishments. Criminal trial, conviction and sentence are the conventional and ritual mode of expression of societal condemnation of wrongdoing. Since whatever is held to be gravely wrong must needs be condemned as such, the sanction of the criminal law is rightfully applied to any case of gravely wrong conduct. A part of Hart's response to Lord Devlin's argument is thus to be found in what has already been said about his critique of retributivism in that form. But his more fundamental case is against any version of the view that it is right for criminal law to be considered as or used as an instrument for upholding the 'positive morality' of a society at large, that is, of the dominant section(s) of it, or even of the majority within it.

Upon this point, he consciously joins forces with John Stuart Mill,[4] adopting in a qualified form Mill's classical proclamation of the rights of individuals and of minorities against moral tyranny whether by powerful oligarchies or by democratic majorities:

> The only purpose for which power can rightfully be exercised over any member of a civilized community against his will is to prevent harm to others. . . . His

own good either physical or moral is not a sufficient warrant. He cannot rightfully be compelled to do or forbear because it will be better for him to do so, because it will make him happier, because in the opinion of others, to do so would be wise or even right.[5]

Hart somewhat tentatively allows that there may be a qualification added to this proposition. The qualification concerns self-harming activities, such as use of highly addictive drugs, or cases of consent to serious or deadly assaults. Here, says Hart, the law withholds permission from activities involving bodily harm even to a consenting subject. But this, if justifiable, is justifiable not by an appeal to the positive morality which holds such practices to be sinful. It is justifiable (if at all) by reference to the principle of paternalism, the principle according to which people can rightfully be restrained from opting for what may seem immediately desirable at irreparable cost to their long-run physical integrity or mental autonomy.

Hart as critical moralist urges upon his reader the manifest harms to individuals involved in criminal punishment. Punishment can and often does involve physical loss of liberty and moral degradation, possibly also deliberately inflicted bodily pain, even death. People who are punished suffer. Their suffering is deliberately inflicted by state agencies acting in the name of the whole citizen body. That ought not to be done unless to ward off some evil similar in kind. There are forms of human conduct which involve evils similar in kind. These include acts that involve deliberate, reckless or careless imposition of physical suffering on people, ones that exploit their weaknesses in a way that harms them (especially in the case of younger persons, or persons of unsound mind), ones that expose young people to sexual activity (heterosexual just as much as homosexual) at an age at which they are in the main too immature to be capable of forming a considered judgment of their own acts, ones that deprive people of their free use of property lawfully acquired, and ones that contravene norms of public decency. These and other similar forms of harmful conduct can without injustice be prohibited under the threat of penal sanctions, and those inclined to commit them can justly be deterred by punishments.

This notion of deterrence reminds us again of the other, wider, sense in which punishment imposes suffering. To the extent that the general threats of the criminal law put people in fear or otherwise form a discouraging factor in deliberation, they inhibit people's freedom to act as they would wish. Especially in the areas covered by prohibitions of sexual conduct reproved by a positive morality, this may face individuals with agonizing choices. They must choose to restrain and repress powerful feelings and thus forego expression of deep-seated elements in their personality.[6] In the alternative, they have to take the risk of acting in ways that break the law, and consequently living in fear of punishment—to say nothing of ancillary possibilities of blackmail, public prying on and intrusions into privacy, and so forth. In the case of conduct which does no one harm of the relevant kind, making it liable to punishment *solely* because it infringes a positive moral code (even a majority one) cannot be justified. The suffering imposed is balanced by no sufficient countervailing good.

What about the 'good' suggested by Lord Devlin? What about the thesis that social cohesion and solidarity depend on sustaining (among other means by solemn and symbolic acts, as in a criminal court) a common morality? Surely to encompass the subversion of a society is grave harm? Yes, says Hart, it is. But there is no *evidence* that legal toleration of private immorality, or indeed of moral pluralism, in fact does or even tends to dissolve the social bond. It is not merely not proven that diversity or deviance is truly destructive of social cohesion. It is not even on the face of things plausible that this is so. First advanced in *L.L.M.*, this argument was restated by Hart in a yet more thorough and thoughtful way in his 1967 essay, 'Social Solidarity and the Enforcement of Morality'. There, he extended it to cover Durkheim's theory of social solidarity,[7] to which Devlin's bears close resemblance.

It might be argued, however, that the call for evidence is misplaced. It might, for example, be asserted as an analytical truth that 'a society' is defined by a specific moral code. In that case, *that* society would indeed be subverted if any substantial change occurred in its moral code. It would be replaced by a new one, defined by *its* moral code. There need be nothing alarming in that, however. The moral attitudes of people in societies *do* change over time, especially in circumstances of free discussion. There can be many moralities among the myriad of overlapping groups and communities whose members are all in the legal view citizens of a single state. Anyway, ought we not to be deeply suspicious of the tendency to *equate* 'states' with 'societies'? This seems essential to the Devlinite argument, when one considers Lord Devlin's remark that 'A recognized morality is as necessary to society's existence as a recognized government.'[8]

It is, in Hart's view, a matter of positive good that there should be freedom of discussion and of experimentation in living and hence some pluralism of attitudes as between the different people and groups that coexist under a single legal system. This is good not because it necessarily implies change, but because moral virtue involves *free* self-restraint from what one takes to be wrongdoing, not merely coerced constraint into an outwardly proper mode of behaviour. Free self-discipline in the face of moral demands is of the essence of responsible moral personality. To give mature people *equal* freedom to develop moral personality is thus a requirement of justice. Legal coercion is rightfully used to repress as far as reasonably possible the forms of illicit coercion which in the absence of law some might use against others. Such illicit coercion could deny them the equal freedom which is rightfully theirs. Legal coercion beyond that point is both cruel and unjust. All that is subject to one other point:

> Further, freedom (the absence of coercion) can be *valueless* to those victims of unrestricted [economic] competition too poor to make use of it; so it will be pedantic to point out to them that though starving they are free. This is the truth exaggerated by the Marxists whose *identification* of poverty with lack of freedom confuses two different evils. (*A.A.N.R.?* p. 53)

Hart, as was remarked in the opening chapter, belongs in the camp of social democratic liberalism rather than that of pure classical liberalism. For he insists that we ought to recognize the moral imperative of securing to all persons the conditions of the *value* as distinct from the mere *existence* of liberty.[9] The same considerations perhaps also account for his willingness to accept some degree of paternalism into his critical principles.

Next, however, a fresh objection arises: Hart's whole case falls, it may be said, because of a single, central confusion. This lies in his assumption that 'harm' is a morally neutral concept.[10] But the assumption is false. In deciding what is 'harmful' to a person, we necessarily make an evaluation, and the evaluation belongs to morality. Either Hart accepts the concept of 'harm' implicit in some positive morality, or else he smuggles in some purely utilitarian conception of 'harm' and in that case all he is arguing for is the adoption and legal enforcement of a utilitarian rather than some other morality. One way to meet this objection is to stress, as I have been doing to an extent perhaps unauthorized by Hart's texts, that there should be some commensurability of kind as between the harm done by legal punishments and the harm thereby averted. This seems a sound line of argument, though it interestingly blurs the line between utilitarianism and retributivism. It introduces a condition of just commensurability over and above the simple utilitarian criterion that harm done should be outweighed by harm averted.

There is, however, a second argument of Hart's on the present point (which includes at least passing allusion to the 'just commensurability' point):

since all social moralities, whatever else they may contain, make provision in some degree for such universal values as individual freedom, safety of life, and protection from deliberately inflicted harm, there will always be much in social morality which is worth preserving even at the cost in terms of these same values which legal enforcement involves. (*L.L.M.* p. 70)

In short, Hart does not argue that 'harm' is a morally indifferent notion. He argues that it covers a range of infringements of values which are, however, *universal* in the sense that they are intrinsic to *all* social moralities 'in some form'. Nor does he deny that the law in condoning and punishing harmful activities does and should condemn them as morally wrong in addition to being legally prohibited. And he positively asserts that:

the spirit or attitude of mind which characterizes the practice of a social morality is something of very great value and indeed quite vital for people to foster and preserve in any society. (*L.L.M.* p. 71)

As Hart says in 'Social Solidarity and the Enforcement of Morality', all this can be tied up with his theory about the 'minimum content of natural law'. That theory, we recall, insists that there are basic primary elements of law, shared also with all modes of positive morality, whose common observance is essential to the survival of human beings in social communities. The claim about 'universal values' made above depends on the same testable anthropological evidence as the claim about the minimum content of natural law.

Perhaps, however, in his whole approach Hart does under-play and at critical points ignore the truth that criminal legislation and criminal trial and punishment do *unavoidably* have that precise morally denunciatory force which his judicial opponents ascribe to it. It is this moral force that accounts for the 'disgrace' Hart sees both as being inherent in punishment and as being so large an element in the deterrent effect of the criminal law. That this denunciatory element is present flows necessarily from the theory that legal rules are a species, however specialized, of social rules. Hence breach of them entails necessarily 'criticism' by those who for some reason accept them. Judges accept them by virtue of the rule of recognition. Hence they apply the lawful modes of 'criticism' of those who infringe them. According to current legal practices, these range all the way from verbal admonition through fines to sentences of life imprisonment, and still, in some countries, even the death penalty. If we are to apply the hermeneutic method we cannot ignore what judges say about what they take themselves to be doing in passing penal sentences—especially not when it squares so exactly with the hermeneutic account of rules.

From the point of view of a Hartian critical morality this need not be thought embarrassing. For the very question of critical morality is: "When *ought* the punitive machinery of the law to be used?" not "When is it used, and when do judges or legislators think it should be used?" The idea to which Hart sometimes seems to object most strongly is any suggestion that the criminal law encapsulates any morality. But on his own view of universal values and the minimum content of natural law, it seems that the law *ought* to encapsulate a set of requirements that are always also in some form moral requirements. And for these requirements, I should suggest, it is and ought to remain the case that the legal punishment of infractions of them is, and is seen to be, also a somewhat authoritative moral denunciation of them. The same goes for legislation in the sphere of criminal law. On a qualifiedly Durkheimian view, this would obviously be necessary to social cohesion and solidarity across all or most of the groups making up a state. This at least Hart is willing to accept.

> [T]he decay of all moral restraint on the free use of violence or deception would not only cause individual harm but would jeopardize the existence of a society since it would remove the main conditions which make it possible and worthwhile for men to live together in close proximity to each other. (*S.S.E.M.* p. 9)

Provided that this is not taken as licensing (as it tends to be abused for licensing) the legal enforcement of the totality of some particular positive morality, the Hartian demand for moral liberty and moral pluralism within modern states can be fully satisfied. That demand is one that can be supported by powerful reasons of principle, in at least the ways recounted in this section of this chapter, and others as well.

THE MORAL RELEVANCE OF POSITIVE LAW

For those who join in asserting the Hartian principle in favour of moral liberty and moral pluralism within the coercive legal ordering of a contemporary state, the law is always and necessarily morally relevant. For it is always subject to moral criticism. This is a feature that any system of positive law shares with any positive morality, since both constitute social constraints on acting, the legal constraints being also physically coercive.

The mere fact that a legal system and a positive moral order make some provision for the 'universal values' is by no means inconsistent with the possibility that either is unjust in the distribution of its protection or unjustifiably cruel in its modes of reproof or of punishment. Laws always include

some rules that express what are also moral requirements, and legal punishments outside and sometimes even inside the sphere of pure regulatory
offences (*mala prohibita*, in the old phrase[11]) are inevitably morally loaded.
This very fact makes it imperative that criticism be brought to bear on them
by those who have sought to give rational consideration to moral values
and principles. Otherwise, it is likely that great moral wrongs will be done,
the worse for being done in the very name of 'the morality of our society'
(or 'nation' or 'country' or 'people' or whatever).

It is not because law does *not* encapsulate, at least in part, a morality, that
it is open to moral criticism. That it *does* always and unavoidably encapsulate some elements of positive morality is a powerful additional reason why
it *must* always be subjected to the searching criticism of critical moralists.
Positive law is always relevant to morality *both* for that reason *and* for the
special reason that the law invokes force and fear, at least in its contemporary manifestations. If allowance of the former reason goes against the letter of Hart's writings, it seems to me to belong better to their general spirit
than do his express utterances on this point.

There is a second respect, not less important than the first, in which law
is always morally relevant to one who holds moral views at all like Hart's.
This depends on a basic principle of fairness among people to which he
gave the name of 'mutuality of restrictions':[12]

> [W]hen a number of persons conduct any joint enterprise according to rules
> and thus restrict their liberty, those who have submitted to these restrictions
> have a right to a similar submission by those who have benefited by their sub-
> mission. The rules may provide that officials should have authority to enforce
> obedience and make further rules. . . . but the obligation to obey the rules in
> such circumstances is *due to* the cooperating members of the society, and they
> have the correlative moral right to obedience. (*A.A.N.R.?* pp. 6–12)

So far as this principle is applicable, people do have moral obligations of
respect for the law. Such obligations are no doubt defeasible, and there will
be many persons to whom and many circumstances in which it fails to apply.
Nor was it ever Hart's view that this is the only possible moral reason for
obeying law, nor did he ever consider that it is a conclusive and overriding
reason, excluding all possible considerations against obeying the law in given
cases. It does not necessarily apply to all the subjects of a state, but only to
those who *have* benefited by others' submission. One does not need elaborate imaginings to call to mind cases of slavery and race persecution where
the submission of a majority or even a powerful minority to rules has been
gravely detrimental rather than beneficial to the slaves and the persecuted.

Nevertheless, morality must take account of the law on the ground that often moral obligations to obey the law are owed mutually among citizens within a legal system's jurisdiction, on the principle of mutuality of restrictions. If this principle is accepted, it is the more, not the less, important that the law's requirements be subjected to perennial and permanent moral criticism. For it increases the agony of choice in the face of an unjust or oppressive law that those who break it, even conscientiously, thereby find themselves in breach of obligation to their fellow citizens from whose prior submission to laws they have benefited. This may even extend to cases where those others considered themselves bound in conscience to put up with some injustice in meeting the law's demands.

It deserves to be noticed that what Hart says on this point does not conflict with his claim that law ought not to embody any positive morality as such in its entirety. He is not saying that one has a moral obligation to fulfil legal duties because these are already, from the viewpoint of some morality, subsisting moral duties. He is saying that it is a breach of moral principle to take the benefit of others' submission to whatever the law might require and thereafter to fail in reciprocating that benefit. Because the law secures for some at least of its subjects the conditions of individual and communal survival and flourishing, it has to be the case that there are some who owe to others the obligation arising from mutuality of restrictions. But the bare existence of a legal order and its guaranteeing for some the protection at least of the minimum content of natural law does not imply that all the subjects are justly treated.

Once one sees all this in the round, taking a synoptic view of Hart's whole philosophy of law, one cannot but reject—reject even with indignation—a certain aspersion cast upon Hart as legal philosopher by the late Lon L. Fuller. In the revised edition of his *The Morality of Law*, he claimed that Hart's legal theory was, by accident or design, an essentially 'managerialist' theory of law.[13] Fuller's criticism latches on to various of Hart's remarks about the minimum conditions for the efficacy and existence of a legal system, such as the following:

> In an extreme case the internal point of view . . . might be confined to the official world. . . . [O]nly officials might accept and use the system's criteria of legal validity. The society in which this was so might be deplorably sheeplike; the sheep might end in the slaughter-house. But there is little reason for thinking that it could not exist or for denying it the title of a legal system. (*C.L.* p. 114)

Nobody who gave five minutes' cursory thought to Hart's various but largely self-consistent reflections about the moral relevance of positive law could even entertain the supposition that he commends the officials-sheep-and-slaughterhouse model of a legal system. Nobody could suppose that he is any less an enthusiast than L. L. Fuller for promoting the vision of a society in which freely communicating individuals willingly collaborate in their common social enterprises and freely grant each other friendly tolerance in their more particularistic or individual activities, and in which the resort by officials to means of mere coercion is minimized. Nobody could deny either the reality of his concern for justice or the firmness of his contentions that a precondition of justice as defined within his critical morality is the existence of a well working legal system and that a consequence of a just legal system's existence is the establishment of a network of mutual moral obligations of respect for law among the citizens within that jurisdiction.

Despite holding all these views in his stance as a critical moralist, Hart does not suggest that legal systems either do, or in their own essential nature tend to, realize justice or respect for human rights to liberty of thought and action or other such values. Legal systems can and should be geared to realizing noble ideals. A 'legal system' is not, however, itself the name of a noble ideal. (It is not, in its essence, either a nightmare or a noble dream,[14] but human actions can make real laws tend more toward one or other pole.) Legal systems can indeed be 'managerial' or for that matter straightforwardly tyrannical. To suggest that Hart commends such systems or that his philosophy makes straight the way for them is, however, a travesty. We shall further see why in considering his 'legal positivism'.

HART AS LEGAL POSITIVIST

Historically speaking, the movement in thought which we have come to call 'legal positivism'[15] was associated in the English-speaking world particularly with the names of Jeremy Bentham and John Austin, Thomas Hobbes being in a way their seventeenth-century forerunner. This movement was founded on the particular assertion that no law can exist unless deliberately laid down or 'posited' by some rational and volitional being possessed of power over other such beings. That assertion countered the theory that some standards or principles of conduct exist independently of any voluntary 'positing' of them, and that 'law' is, includes, or derives from such principles or standards. Such principles of law were 'natural' principles of right, (*ius naturale* in Latin) lying behind the rules posited (*ius positivum*) by persons holding authority subject to natural law. Some, but not all, believers in natural law held it to be a logical consequence of a belief in natural principles of right that positive 'laws' laid down by human authorities which conflicted with natural law could not be truly laws at all.[16]

It was against this last-stated implication or supposed implication of natural law teachings and associated doctrines of inalienable natural rights, that Bentham and Austin directed their arguments. In Austin's words, 'The existence of law is one thing; its merit or demerit another.'[17] Hence jurists ought to distinguish carefully two tasks. One task is that of elucidating what are the prerequisites of any law's existence, coupled with a description of the laws that actually exist. The other task is that of reviewing the moral merits and demerits of existing laws, coupled with advancing proposals for reform of the unmeritorious ones. As utilitarians, Bentham and Austin both held, though on differing grounds, that there was an objective test of moral merit and demerit (viz., that contained in the 'greatest happiness principle').

Hart clearly does not agree that all law is in the relevant sense 'posited' by some deliberate legislative decision. He explicitly developed his theory of legal rules as social rules in juxtaposition with and in preference to Austinian or other like accounts of laws as commands of sovereigns. What he does hold is that legal rules as social rules have social sources, being entirely rooted in the actual practices (doings, sayings, and thinkings) of persons in society. Legal rules neither are, nor include, nor derive from objectively preexisting and valid natural standards of human conduct. They derive exclusively from social practices. A corollary of this, as we saw in chapter 11, is that judges have certain discretion in applying the law. In exercising that interpretive discretion they sometimes do, and perhaps have to, have recourse to moral standards *quite distinct from* legal rules and standards in reaching what seems the best decision of a hard case. Of course, it is possible that a system's rule of recognition includes what are effectively moral norms among the norms it requires judges to apply in deciding cases, for example on account of a Bill of Rights woven into a state's constitution. Some legal systems do have this character, but not all do, and it is not a necessary feature of legal systems. (On this account, Hart is what is sometimes called a 'soft' or 'inclusive' positivist.[18])

Nobody can suppose that actual social practices including the elaboration of a system of primary and secondary rules will in all cases at all points conform with justice and the other requirements of an enlightened critical morality. Therefore it is an open question whether we can call unjust or otherwise immoral rules and rule-systems 'laws' and 'legal systems' or not.

This, says Hart, ought not to be treated as a lexicographical sort of question. The issue is not as to the weight of English usage of the word 'law' (or German, of the word *Recht*, or French, of the word *droit*) for or against using that word to include or not include unjust or evil rules. Established usage is uncertain on just this point, and differs in emphasis between different languages anyway.

> What really is at stake is the comparative merit of a wider and a narrower concept or way of classifying rules, which belong to a system of rules generally effective in social life. If we are to make a reasoned choice between these concepts, it must be because one is superior to the other in the way in which it will assist our theoretical inquiries, or advance and clarify our moral deliberations, or both. (*C.L.* p. 205)

On both theoretical and moral grounds Hart opts for the thesis that moral value ought not to be treated as a necessary condition of legal validity.

In the first edition of *The Concept of Law*, the theoretical ground that Hart offered for this thesis was a rather thin and unsatisfactory one. It was that we should not exclude from the discipline of jurisprudence study of any modes of governance exhibiting the complex characteristics of 'a union of primary and secondary rules'. It is as important, he says, to study the abuses as to study the good uses of such systems. So it is. But it seems a pretty far-fetched idea that jurisprudence would have to stop studying them if we decided to stop calling evil systems 'legal systems' and evil rules 'laws'. On any view, it would remain vital to consider the formal and structural analogies which obtain as between *Recht* and *Unrecht*.

When he came at the end of his life to work on the '*Postscript*' now printed in the second edition of *The Concept of Law*. Hart gave a somewhat different account of his position as a positivist, in asserting that his theory was both 'general' and 'descriptive'. It was general because it applied to law as an institution used in the organization and governance of all manner of states, not only the theorist's own. Despite variations of content, such that some states might have systems containing iniquitous laws while others were more morally respectable in content, states have it in common that they maintain government through law, and use similar conceptual and institutional structures in doing so. "What is the law?" is a system-relative question, and on similar issues different legal systems may yield very different answers. The theorist as critical moralist may wish to praise or otherwise uphold some such answers, but to criticise others—for example, on the question whether the law permits or even requires capital punishment in the case of some crimes (and, if so, what crimes). But in the descriptive phase of this enterprise, the issue of the moral status of (for example) capital punishment does not arise at all.

Hart's own latest conclusion thus overshadowed somewhat the moral argument he had previously stated in favour of the 'positivist' approach. That argument was as follows:

> So long as human beings can gain sufficient cooperation from some to enable them to dominate others, they will use the forms of law as one of their instruments. Wicked men will enact wicked rules which others will enforce. What surely is most needed in order to make men clear-sighted in confronting the official abuse of power, is that they should preserve the sense that the certification of something as legally valid is not conclusive of the question of obedience, and that, however great the aura of majesty or authority which the official system may have, its demands must in the end be submitted to a moral scrutiny. (*C.L.* p. 206)

As of 1963, this final appeal of Hart's was, as is plain, to the autonomy and supremacy of critical morality. It was an appeal to every concerned person to reject any theory which suggests or implies that whatever is 'law' properly so-called is *conclusive* of the moral question what I am to do. Law is indeed morally relevant. But it is never, and should never be deemed, morally conclusive. What has been done in the name and 'in the forms' of law has often been appalling moral iniquity. The least unreliable way of opening human eyes to the possibility of such iniquity, and of keeping them open to and alert against its occurrence or recurrence, is to teach that 'laws' get their name because of the structural and functional properties of the system to which they belong. They do not get it because they are or can be presumed to be demands of an enlightened morality.

Paradoxical as some may find it, this reason offered by Hart for insisting on the conceptual separateness of 'law' and 'morality' was a moral reason. Hart was a positivist because he was also a critical moralist. His aim was not to issue a warrant for obedience to the masters of the state. It was to reinforce the citizen's warrant for unrelenting moral criticism of the uses and abuses of state power. This stance was not re-stated in the *Postscript*, but neither was it withdrawn or, even implicitly, disowned.

The argument is an attractive one, though some natural lawyers have protested that it is question-begging. That a state's officials enshrine some odious practice 'in the name and forms of law' would not encourage obedience if citizens were alert to the risk of iniquity being done by officials. But the natural lawyers' advice to them to deny the character of 'law' to such iniquity might be at least as effective as the candid stance that Hart's positivism offers them.[19] Perhaps the choice whether or not to adopt the natural lawyer's more restricted conception of law or the positivist's more inclusive one must after all rest on other grounds.

However that may be, when we reexamine here towards the end of our deliberations the whole theory of and about law which Hart presented to the world, we cannot, I think, agree that law as he analysed it stands in a merely contingent relationship with morality.

By Hart's own view of it, a legal order is, in the sense of 'positive morality', a moral order. It comprises rules and other standards accepted and operated from the internal point of view at least by a cadre of officials. Whatever else it does iniquitously or unjustly, it builds in, at least in favour of some citizens, the minimum content of natural law. In its practices of punishment and enforcement it uses the language of rights and wrongs, crimes and offences, and the eloquent testimony of judges shows that its practice of punishment can never be dissociated from moral condemnation. This is not troubling in itself, though it becomes more than troubling in the cases where the critical moralist can persuasively argue that either the mode or the act of official state condemnation is unjust. But what is wrong is the state's moral condemnation of what it is not the right of the state morally to condemn. When evil is done in the name of the law, the greatest evil is that whatever is done in the name of the law is also and inevitably done in the name of a public morality.

Hence it seems simply inconceivable that appeals to law, even to iniquitous law, can ever shed their moral load. That is and has to be one of the messages emanating from a hermeneutic study like Hart's of laws as special social rules. Hence it seems inconceivable that it will ever be thought other than virtuous, albeit at a modest point on the scale of virtue, for a person to be 'law-abiding', even when the law by which he or she abides contains much of evil. By the same token, the lawbreaker, however conscientious, will be stigmatized by the legal officials as a moral wrongdoer and a moral danger.

Over and above this, we cannot but notice Hart's acceptance of Fuller's argument that even bad laws have a certain inner morality,[20] this being a (possibly much distorted) manifestation of formal justice. To the extent (an extent exaggerated as much by Fuller as by Hart) that laws have to be *rules* belonging in a system of rules which are published, prospective, capable of fulfilment and duly implemented by officials according to the terms in which they are promulgated, there is at least some intrinsic moral virtue in such systems. Certainly, as Hart observed in respect of these and the other elements in Fuller's 'inner morality of law', the minimum procedural content of formal justice is compatible with great iniquity in substantive law, as also is observance in some form of the minimum substantive content of natural law. But this gives us further ground for recognizing that and recognizing why 'law' is always a morally loaded as well as morally relevant institution.

There is good reason for this. Law, like morality in either of its senses, concerns what is to be done, and what can be done *justifiably*. Hence law and morality belong within the domain of practical reasoning. As the common terminology of legal and moral discourse indicates, the elements of moral and legal reasoning share a common framework even though they have considerable differences of internal detail. This means exactly that there is at least one necessary conceptual link between the legal and the moral, namely that legal standards and moral standards both belong within the genus of practical reasons for action, whatever be their weight as such.[21]

This does not contradict Hart's proposition that criteria of legal validity neither are identical with nor necessarily include criteria of moral value. The mistake, if any, lies in his supposition that such is the only possible conceptual overlap that might obtain between law and morality. While the distinction between legal validity and moral value is the very point of conceptual distinctness on which modern positivists have centrally insisted, it is not a point which all or most 'natural lawyers' have actually denied. This John Finnis showed quite clearly in his *Natural Law and Natural Rights*, first published in 1980.[22]

The truth is that there is no single grand divide between those who call themselves positivists and those who call themselves natural lawyers. The points of deep significance in the various debates there have been between members of these two camps have variously ranged around quite disparate questions on the nature and obligatory quality of standards for human conduct. The debates, in short, have concerned the nature and foundations of practical reason, including the question whether 'reason' can be 'practical' at all. Since people who have called themselves positivists and people who have called themselves natural lawyers have had at least as acute differences with those in their own camp as with those in the other camp, it is pointless to suppose that the mere appellations 'positivist' and 'natural lawyer' in themselves point to important defining attributes of any writer's work. We must look to that work in itself and examine what it really says.

The important defining attributes of Hart's work are these. He characterizes laws as a special case of social rules deriving from social practices, explicable only by a hermeneutic method. His account is capable of elaboration and extension to cover the types of legal standard other than rules that belong to legal systems as a union of secondary rules, primary rules, and other standards. The nature of such rules and standards is such as to make possible only limitation but not elimination of official discretion. The criteria of validity of legal rules and criteria of recognition of other legal standards do not amount to or necessarily include a guarantee against injustice or iniquity in legal rules or standards or their modes of enforcement. This is compatible with the truth (insufficiently acknowledged by Hart) that legal systems are always not only morally relevant but also morally loaded both in their content and in the tone and terms of their enforcement. One reason for insisting on the distinctness of legal validity and moral value is a moral reason. The moral reason is the principle that every order of positive law or positive morality ought always to be subjected to the critical judgment of an enlightened morality which seeks to make rationally coherent and explicit the values and principles inherent in moralities as such.

The last point is Hart's most persuasive assertion about the issue of law's place in practical reasoning. It is the basis of the social democratic liberalism intrinsic to Hart's thought. It accounts for the fact that, in addition to being an analytical philosopher of the first rank, his writings made no mean contribution to the politics of his times.

CHAPTER FOURTEEN

Epilogue

The preceding chapters have aimed to achieve a fair and accurate, but also constructively critical reading of Hart's main contributions to legal theory. This is a reading that displays the materials in a way that makes them constitute the most attractive theory of law that fits with the texts. There is, however, a problem. To leave matters at this point would be to risk underplaying developments in Hart's thought subsequent to the publication of the present book's first edition in 1981. As was noted in the Introduction, Hart at least once said that he considered himself a more thoroughgoing positivist than he appeared according to my reading of his work. The point of this Epilogue, akin to Hart's own *Postscript* perhaps, is to give due attention to those elements, especially in his later writings,[1] that most clearly encapsulate his outlook as it developed in his later years.

There are several points of interest. First of all, we must consider his view that it is both possible and methodologically appropriate to give a detached and neutral account of a concept like law. This would imply describing law without expressing any commitment to law as an ideal element in social order, and without express or implied endorsement of the content of any particular legal system or one or another possible interpretation of the materials it contains. This leads into a consideration of the difference between 'detached' and 'committed' statements about the law that is in force somewhere. Next, supposing that such a view of the proper method of inquiry is sustainable, we need to look yet again at the precise character of Hart's theory about the nature of law and how he excludes any necessary moral element from the law. It remains, however, questionable how far the justification for his view about the character of law can be sustained without any appeal to substantive value judgements about the impact of one theoretical approach set against some other or others. We shall reflect on this in the process of contrasting his view with that of one powerful restatement of classical natural law theory. Then we shall consider the central points of Ronald Dworkin's critique of the methods used and the conclusions reached by Hart's jurisprudence and the final response by

Hart to this in his own *Postscript*. To conclude the chapter, there will be a brief review of subsequent developments in jurisprudence in response to Hart's work.

METHODOLOGY

How far, if at all, can a theoretical account of legal systems be a neutral one? Can it apply equally to more than one actual legal system and without triviality illuminate in similar terms features that are common to many in a way that makes no positive or negative assumptions about the values any such system embodies or fails to embody? If so, how can this be achieved? These are central issues for Hart in his *Postscript*. There, he returns to the point that we must assume some normal or standard instance of what counts as law or as a legal system. He already gave his view on that at the beginning of *C.L.* In the *Postscript* (p. 240), he draws fresh attention to the relevant passage. He suggests there are certain elements that any ordinary, reasonably well-informed but nonexpert person might suppose to be significant elements of law:

> They comprise (i) rules forbidding or enjoining certain types of behaviour under penalty; (ii) rules requiring people to compensate those whom they injure in certain ways; (iii) rules specifying what must be done to make wills, contracts, or other arrangements which confer rights and create obligations; (iv) courts to determine what the rules are and when they have been broken, and to fix the punishment or compensation to be paid; (v) a legislature to make new rules and abolish old ones. (*C.L.* p. 3)

As he points out, each distinct 'country' such as England (*sic*) or France or the United States or Soviet Russia (as of 1961) appears to have a legal system with at least these features.

Hart therefore sets out to work with what he considers to be this 'central' or 'standard' case of a legal system, found in arrangements of contemporary states that exhibit these five characteristics. His analysis of the concept of law in terms of the legal system that is a 'union of primary and secondary rules' can be seen as a systematised and more detailed explication of the way in which the five elements hang together. It also facilitates providing an account of the meaning of many concepts typically used in expositions of law, like 'ownership', 'contract', 'right', 'duty' and many others. Not everything that is appropriately called law has all these features, but different forms of 'law' can be appreciated by the extent of their resemblance to the presumed standard case.

Some values are obviously involved in this presentation of the 'standard case'. It has to be supposed that for the expositor's purposes and for the presumed purposes of the audience addressed, greater importance attaches to law as it is manifested in the internal arrangements of contemporary states than to other forms of social ordering that can also be called 'law'. This is not, however, an issue of moral value, but more a matter of professional orientation.[2] It does not concern any particular value, especially any particular moral value, ascribed to any particular legal system or to legal systems as such. One can regard it as important for the improvement of understanding to study a particular object, institution, or set of institutions without ascribing particular moral value to the object or institution(s) studied. Granted that most or perhaps all states have in some degree a legal system of the complex Hartian type, nothing follows concerning the degree to which the laws in them satisfy demands of justice, humanity, or general welfare among citizens of the state in question. Law is always open to moral criticism and to campaigns for improvement of it, and merely to establish what law exists somewhere is not to say anything about what law ought to exist on a given topic there or anywhere else.

This, however, already makes it obvious that from the point of view of persons active within any given state, their law is of real concern to them. This leads into what Hart means by the 'internal point of view'. The laws that exist are standards whereby persons judge their own conduct and that of others. Laws represent the outcomes of political value judgements and the outcomes of political struggles and contests, settled sometimes by elections and sometimes by even more forceful means. Laws are often grounded in judgements about what is right—morally right—or what is just or expedient, or they may depend on a view concerning the principles of critical morality that ought to inform lawmaking. The outcome of any particular political contest represents usually some more or less acceptable balance of the right and the expedient. When it comes to applying and interpreting law, account must be taken of the way in which laws express values and how a particular law meshes or fits with other established laws, so as to come to a reasonable conclusion on a matter in dispute. To understand them at all, one must understand how they could function to guide citizens' conduct and to ground critical appraisals of what people do or fail to do.

Critical to Hart's enterprise, therefore, is the possibility of sustaining what in earlier chapters we have called the 'hermeneutic' approach to legal scholarship. (It might be more accurate to call this 'Hart's version of the hermeneutic approach', since there are others, notably that of Ronald Dworkin). Hart acknowledges that the content of law is a matter of concern, of strongly value-laden concern, to those whose law it is. It is a standard for their behaviour and for critical judgement of it. If this cuts against the grain of their moral convictions, the situation is an unhappy one for them, but not if moral conviction and legal requirement are for them in reasonable harmony. The position of Hart, or the Hartian jurist, is to take full account of the 'internal point of view' of the insiders. Such a jurist may, however, abstain from engagement with it in terms of the jurist's own personal opinions on the substantive issues of morality and expediency put in issue by the laws. The laws can be described, in outline or in detail, as laws that make a certain sense to (or raise objections among) those who administer them and those who live by them. The jurist need not—should not—endorse or condemn, but merely observe. One's job as jurist is one thing, one's job as exponent of a critical morality is another. (Hart, it will be recalled, himself undertook both jobs.)

We are here considering a development in Hart's later thought that derived from his attention to work by Joseph Raz, namely his deployment of the distinction between committed and detached statements of legal rights or duties, or of the content of legal rules.[3] He also acknowledged that such detached statements can be considered as made from a 'hermeneutic' point of view.[4] This is fully compatible with the account given about social rules in chapter 4. Unfortunately, when Dworkin came to write *Law's Empire*[5] and to advance his own 'interpretive' theory of law, presenting it as a development of hermeneutics in legal theory, he passed this over in silence. He seems to have failed to notice the original suggestion by Peter Hacker, adopted in this book by myself and subsequently confirmed by Hart, that Hart's account of rules essentially involves a hermeneutic approach.

But is it possible to pursue detachment in interpretation? The question is of considerable significance in its bearing on the tenability of Hart's method of doing jurisprudence. Hart argues that faithful reports can be given about the character and content of some body of law even by somebody who has no commitment to the particular values in which these laws are grounded. Certainly, such a person has to take full account of the meaning of the rules and other standards from the point of view of those whose rules and standards they are. This requires sensitive attention to the values they perceive in them. But the theorist or jurist need not, and perhaps should not, share in the committed stance of the one who, working as an insider, applies the law. It is enough that the reporter fully grasp the 'internal point of view' and express it in any report that she makes. On this view, there can be perfectly accurate, dispassionate and indeed 'descriptive' reports about some law, laws, or indeed a whole legal system. If, for example, somebody wants to consider whether the European Union should change its competition law to assimilate it to U.S. antitrust law, they will need to have some explanation about the latter. This would best be done, it seems, in the style of Hartian reportage, not as if arguing a practical conclusion to some disputed point about antitrust law, such as the *Microsoft* litigation.

The often-criticised remark by Hart that his work could be considered as a form of 'descriptive sociology' at least becomes intelligible in the light of the foregoing discussion. For he is telling us that nearly all the different societies that constitute different sovereign states or substates do have it in common that they possess a working legal system. Each such legal system can illuminatingly be shown to consist in a variant on the structure of primary and secondary rules expounded in *The Concept of Law*. Though he did not adduce detailed empirical evidence to this effect, it is not a claim that has ever been disputed on the basis of contrary evidence—some may think the structure is wrongly described, or that practices within states are nowhere well described in this way. They may object that what is sociologically of interest about law and claims to legality or legitimacy is not captured by this theoretical approach, and that quite different programmes of study need to be implemented in order to achieve a sociologically significant understanding of law.

Yet, for all that, it remains a serious claim that the Hartian analysis reveals a significant set of features to be found in many different states. This does not involve a claim about the current semantic criteria whereby the word 'law' is correctly used in speech or writing in the English language. It does, however, suggest that study of central cases of what it is commonly acknowledged as correct to call 'law' reveal common systemic and structural properties. The claim is a strong one, and if it were false it would surely be easy to falsify it. Some at least of subsequent endeavours in the way of socio-legal study have indeed found Hart to provide a valuable starting point for empirical and theoretical approaches to social inquiry in the legal domain, though with various changes of emphasis or direction from Hart's own line.[6]

In response to Dworkin's allegation that his theory relies on a kind of 'semantic sting',[7] Hart denies that his variety of positivism offers a kind of 'plain fact' semantic account of law. What the law is on a given point in a given jurisdiction may depend on identifying a relevant rule by reference to the rule of recognition, but the meaning of the concept 'law' is not derived from or determined by a conventional rule of recognition. In expounding the theory of law as a union of primary and secondary rules, one is offering an explanation of law and how it works and hangs together.[8] One is not explaining the meaning of the word 'law', nor does one's explanation of law depend on the linguistic conventions that dictionary-makers record when establishing current usages of words in the English language.

THE CONTENT OF THE THEORY

To adopt the method of giving a detached and descriptive account of legal systems as discussed above is one thing. Another thing is to justify the account given in applying the method. Hart reaffirms in his later writings, with renewed emphasis, that there is no *necessary* moral element or moral minimum in any legal system according to his analysis. It is true, he says, that some legal systems do introduce, for example through a constitutional bill of rights or charter of rights, criteria for legal validity that put in place a kind of moral filter. For example, it may be forbidden for the state's agencies to resort to 'cruel or unusual punishments' or to impose on persons 'torture or inhuman and degrading treatment'. In such circumstances, the validity of a proclaimed piece of law—say, a criminal statute enacted by a congress or parliament—will not only depend on the formal validity of its passage through the lawmaking process. It will also depend on its not being the case that any punishment prescribed in the statute is 'cruel or unusual' or 'inhuman and degrading'. Judgement whether or not 'cruelty' or 'degrading quality' is present implicates moral judgement, even if it also involves reviewing legal precedents and other technical-legal source materials.

Hart considers such provisions to be perfectly possible under his version of legal positivism and his conception of the kind of criteria of recognition that may be included within a rule of recognition. Particular legal systems have their own criteria of recognition (or of validity) of laws. If some states have adopted negative conditions such as those exemplified above, that is what their law actually is. But other states may not have adopted similar substantive criteria of validity and may solely rely on formal, source-based tests. Nothing in the concept of law dictates that one or other of such approaches to validity is necessary—the choice is a matter for constitutional politics, not for conceptual analysis. On this account, Hart considers himself to be a 'soft' or 'inclusive' positivist, rather than an 'exclusive' one, in terms of a controversy that arose among followers of his theoretical approach concerning what is the correct understanding of positivism.[9] Exclusive positivists see substantive criteria of the kind considered to be a matter of lawmaking rather than one concerning the recognition of what is already law. That is, they hold that criteria of this kind confer a negative lawmaking power on constitutional tribunals or other highest level courts.[10] Only after they have applied a judgement about 'cruelty' or whatever and either allowed or disallowed the validity of the legislation in question, is there applicable law on the matter in dispute. Hence moral criteria of the kind in question are never themselves law except in the form of conditions affecting the exercise of legal power by judges.

Hart himself, to the end of his days, remained professedly agnostic on the question of the 'objective' status of moral values or principles. He certainly considered issues of moral right and wrong to be weighty matters on which any reflective person has a considered opinion, but he left open the question whether such differences of considered and reasonable opinion are in principle resoluble. He remained unsure whether one must be objectively better than another, with some opinions being objectively correct and others erroneous. Only if the objectivist view prevails is there (in his view) any practical difference between inclusive and exclusive positivism.[11]

Anyway, inclusive positivists such as Hart do consider it possible that moral criteria be embodied in law, and possible that they authorise seeking and applying the right or best version of moral values written into the criteria of recognition. What they deny is that every possible legal system necessarily does embody such criteria in its law.[12] Some legal systems incorporate some moral criteria. Others may incorporate other moral criteria, yet others no moral criteria at all. Hence there is not a necessary moral element in whatever constitutes a legal system—the presence or absence of such criteria is a contingent one and depends on issues of constitutional design and constitutional politics. Again, we see Hart setting out a basis for comparison and description of actual legal systems, all having 'legal' character in common, but exhibiting significant differences of content and parallel differences of structure (for example, in respect of the relative finality of decisions by legislatures and by courts).

THE CHALLENGE OF NATURAL LAW

Turning to broader debates about the Hartian approach thus clarified, we might commence by noting the rediscovery of natural law that took place partly in response to *The Concept of Law* and spearheaded by John Finnis, himself one of Hart's earliest doctoral students. In *Natural Law and*

Natural Rights (1980), Finnis showed the error of attributing to St. Thomas or other mainstream natural lawyers crude versions of the idea that unjust laws are not laws at all. Law and morality are indeed distinct, precisely in that laws are ordinances laid down by whoever has the care of (that is, exercises effective power in) a community. Like all human activity, however, lawmaking is oriented to some good. There are objective and mutually incommensurable goods for all persons, but in the context of a community, one can try to secure that each has a fair opportunity of pursuing the good alongside of others. Whatever can be done to secure that this is so belongs to the 'common good' of the community.[13]

This idea of the common good is relevant to jurisprudence because of the bearing it has on what was earlier said about Hart's methodology. Rather than defining 'law' by reference to necessary and sufficient conditions for what counts as law, Hart proposes that we consider the 'central case' of a working legal system, that of a modern state, and show how it characteristically combines primary and secondary rules. Other less central or standard cases can then be understood by reference to and by comparison with this 'central case'. A part of Hart's argument for positivism is that the bare existence of a legal system as a system of rules carries no guarantee concerning the substantive justice or moral satisfactoriness of the content of these rules and procuring the conditions for this.

This may indeed be true, says Finnis. But the problem is that Hart has not taken the idea of a 'central case' far enough. The 'focal meaning' of any conceptual term dealing with matters of human interest identifies something that is a really good, healthy, or well-working example of the object of study.[14] We cannot understand medicine without considering that the practice of medicine is in principle geared to the promotion of health. This is so, whatever disputes there may be about the causes of bad health, the prospects for dealing with them, and, indeed, the best understanding of what it is to be in good health. Similarly, education is a practice that makes sense given the assumption that knowledge and understanding of the natural and human worlds are goals worthy of pursuit. So too with law: we should start from a conception of what makes legal systems work well and be thoroughly satisfactory. This is fully compatible with acknowledging that many instances of law in the real world will fall short of this focal meaning or ideal type, and some may even be so grossly inadequate as to be merely a 'corruption of law'.

If we take this methodological precept seriously, it can be argued most persuasively that law must in principle be oriented toward the common good of the community whose law it is and seek to realise justice among its members. This is a view that should in no way blind us to the many defects in all actual legal orders, even while acknowledging, however, that there are considerable variations across the range, from the most satisfactory to the least acceptable among the legal orders in the world about us. In the most extreme cases, there will only be corrupt laws that carry no element of genuine obligation with them, though they may be backed by coercion enough.

Hart acknowledges the persuasive and attractive character of this restatement of a Thomistic 'natural law' theory. But in response, he warns against this idea of law in its 'focal meaning'.

> [T]he identification of the central meaning of law with what is morally legitimate, because orientated towards the common good, seems to me in view of the hideous record of the use of law for oppression to be an unbalanced perspective, and as great a distortion as the opposite Marxist identification of the central case of law with the pursuit of the interests of a dominant economic class. (*E.J.P.* p. 12)

Here, be it noted, there is no appeal to the need for scientific clarity or linguistic accuracy. At issue, again, is the question of what it is important for the jurist to study, and what makes it important. Hart's warning addresses the risk of moral complacency about the uses of the concept of law. To this extent, his later thoughts remain congruent with the reading of his position that was offered in chapter 13. His positivistic methodology apparently remains grounded in practical, indeed moral, concerns, not purely epistemic ones. It has been controversial[15] among Hart's successors whether it is either necessary or tenable to base one's methodology on a claim about the moral basis for insisting on detached juristic inquiry. It does not, however, seem that, even in his latest writings, Hart was able to escape making such a claim himself. For my own part, I have come to consider that Finnis's concept of 'focal meaning' is one that ought to be adopted by the legal theorist, and in my own most recent work, I have sought to achieve this.[16]

DWORKIN'S CHALLENGE

Ronald Dworkin would by no means criticise Hart for having practical values at the foundations of his methodology. His critique would more likely be that Hart did not take this approach in a sufficiently radical way and perhaps tended to draw back from his earlier position in later writing.

According to Dworkin, a practical concept like 'law' is necessarily an 'interpretive' concept, for whenever we apply it we have to consider what is the most attractive possible conception of it. The problem we must address in thinking about government under law is the question in what circumstances a state is justified in using coercive force against persons within its jurisdiction. The legalist's answer is that this can only be justified on the basis of public decisions taken prior to the coercive act, whether decisions by way of judicial precedents or lawmaking decisions by a legislature. But what do such decisions mean, and what do they really authorize? That, says Dworkin, depends on interpretation of them, and the interpretation of them that makes best sense and best expresses the overall integrity of the legal community as a community of principle is the one that will most satisfactorily justify the use of force. This is so, even though the justification will not necessarily be fully convincing, if (as is likely in any human community) the materials for interpretation are themselves less than ideal.[17]

Dworkin's argument depends crucially on a claim about the character of any interesting question that asks, "What is law?" A supporter of Hart's methodology will consider that this question directs us to looking for some kind of descriptive account of what societies living under law all have in common. What is it that goes by the name of 'law' or 'droit' or 'Recht' or 'diritto' (assuming that all such terms are at least partially adequate translations of the others)? This way of asking what is law differs sharply from what is going on when a person with a problem, for example, about an injury or illness attributable to using some form of patented drug or medicine, asks, "What is the law about this?" Such a "What is the law?" question is always a local question. (Hence we should take note of the more than verbal distinction between asking 'What is Law' and asking 'What is *the* law [in relation to such and such a practical problem]'.) The latter is a question localized to some courtroom and its legal jurisdiction. The questioner asks how the law in force here determines whether the defendant has done a wrong to the questioner, and, if so, what damages or other compensation are due. In the event of litigation concerning the misadventure in question, it will fall to the court to decide what the law does provide about this problem and how the litigation should be dealt with in fidelity to the law.[18]

Dworkin challenges his readers to think how a court could possibly decide 'What is *the law*?' if it had not already an answer to the question 'What is *law*?' Yet this may be too speedy. Those who can give learned, insightful, and wise answers to a practical question of law in the course of deciding cases are certainly confident in their usage of the word 'law' and its cognates, and they clearly have a sound understanding of the concept of law. It does not, however, follow that they have a carefully thought out general theory of the nature of law, or indeed that they would be better at answering the practical questions they face if they did. Dworkin's argument is that an answer to the abstract question "What is law?" has to be sustainable as a prelude to answering the second, local, and concrete question "What is *the* law on this concrete question for determination between these parties?" Even if this is so, it does not follow that in other respects the kinds of arguments relevant to pursuing the former have to address anything like the same considerations as apply to the latter.

Answering practical legal questions obviously calls for what may be a controversial interpretation of the relevant legal materials—texts of statutes and precedents read in the light of guiding principles and underlying conceptions of justice and common good. So answering the abstract question must duly allow for the kind of interpretation required in answering the latter. Dworkin concludes that any satisfactory answer to the abstract question will itself have to be posed in terms of the general values that the more particular question engages.

Hart's reply to this is to deny, in terms similar to those already stated here, that the answers to the two lines of inquiry are as closely bound up as Dworkin contends. If legal systems have the general character that Hart ascribes to them, then indeed practical legal questions, issues in litigation, will arise that call for interpretation of the available legal materials. Such interpretation will interrogate the relevant materials 'from the internal point of view'. It will ascribe values to the materials and deploy principles implicit in them or, perhaps, explicit in judicial and doctrinal discussions of prior cases in the same domain. The local and concrete question "What is the law on this matter?" will be answered in ways that deploy materials of a kind whose relevance indeed follows from the understanding of law established through consideration of the general and abstract question "What is law?" But answering the latter question, though it will explain the role of values in any legal system viewed from the internal point of view, will not itself declare a committed stance for or against any specific set of values.

LEGAL REASONING AND THE THEORY OF ADJUDICATION

It is relevant to this discussion to consider how Hart over time moved his position in respect of the relevance of 'linguistic philosophy' to legal interpretation. He never abandoned his basic account of vagueness and open texture in the words of statutes and precedents, these being words in use in ordinary language. Such linguistic flexibility is indeed a source of judicial discretion in hard cases. But he latterly acknowledged that not all problems of ambiguity in law, or difficulty of interpretation, stem solely from these characteristics of words in natural languages.[19] Some arise because of conflicts of value or purpose, or of conflict between an apparently literal reading of a rule and a sensible practical interpretation of it. (Of course a bylaw saying 'no vehicles in the park' does not make it illegal to place a World War II army truck on a plinth in the park by way of a war memorial.) He acknowledges that his account of judicial discretion and judicial reasoning ought to have allowed properly for this.

It is worth remarking, however, as others have,[20] that Hart offered at most a sketchy or skeletal theory about the character of adjudication and of legal reasoning in *C.L.*, and did not subsequently develop any extended account of these matters. The direction of his inquiry was always more toward a structural explanation of the elements of a legal system and of its systemic character as such. It is a bit perverse to read his book as though it centrally addressed questions that are somewhat peripheral to its main concerns—and this is perverse, even if the critic thinks these are the most urgent issues jurisprudence should address. Most of what Hart had to say about adjudication was developed as a part of his attempt to steer a course between formalism and rule-scepticism, and was not a main topic of his writing. In response to criticisms by L. L. Fuller and his followers and by Ronald Dworkin, Hart indeed confessed that there was need to develop a more elaborate theory of legal reasoning than he was ever able himself to do.

In chapter 11 (note 25) I drew attention to the part Hart played as general editor of the Clarendon Law Series in encouraging me to write *Legal Reasoning and Legal Theory*.[21] He did, I think, substantially agree with the general lines of that account of legal reasoning, and I certainly intended in writing it to provide the best account of legal reasoning that could be constructed on the basis of Hartian assumptions about the nature of law. However that may be, Hart himself remained insistent that a satisfactory account of legal reasoning cannot but reveal an inevitable scope for judicial discretion in choosing (and justifying the choice) between rival positions each of which can be supported by sound and acceptable legal arguments. For in his view there were no stable meta-principles that would allow objective ranking of different and occasionally conflicting legal principles such as would reveal the single right answer to even the most problematic case where these come into conflict. It is then a matter for practical reason.[22]

Going back to the text of *The Concept of Law*, one may indeed say that this involves displaying what Hart called the judicial virtue of a 'concern to deploy some acceptable general principle as a reasoned basis for decision'. This passage continues:

> No doubt because a plurality of such principles is always possible it cannot be *demonstrated* that a decision is uniquely correct: but it may be made accept-able as the reasoned product of informed impartial choice. In all this we have the 'weighing' and 'balancing' characteristic of the effort to do justice between competing interests'. (*C.L.* p. 205)

One of Dworkin's responses to critics of his 'right answer' thesis was to ac-cuse them of assuming nothing could be right if it was not demonstrably so.[23] In that light, it seems that the gap between his view and Hart's is slight indeed. Moreover, the idea of weighing and balancing of interests aimed at doing justice between them seems in small bulk to prefigure, rather than to be contradicted by, the earlier criticisms by Dworkin of Hart's work, if not all of his later ones.

HART'S LEGACY

Legal theory in the widest sense and the philosophy of law in a more specialist sense have changed out of all recognition in the years since Hart took up his Chair in 1952. In law schools, there has been a great deal of activity concerning Hartian jurisprudence and the debates it has provoked. Natural law theory has come back to life as a serious rival to legal positiv-ism. Other forms of legal theory have sprung up in radical denial of the whole approach of analytical positivism. Critical legal studies, feminist le-gal theory, and many strands of postmodernist thought have been brought to bear on issues about law and state. Legal reasoning and the theory of adjudication are lively sites of ongoing controversy. Empirical socio-legal studies and both theoretical and empirical approaches in sociology of law and the economics of regulation have yielded many new insights into the workings of the law. The 'law in context' movement has sought to ensure that work of this kind remains accessible and relevant to the concerns of doctrinal legal scholarship.[24]

Whether as a starting point for new inquiries, as a target for criticism and refutation, or as a general background inspiration, Hart's work retains a high relevance to a very large part of what is most fruitful and interesting in contemporary theoretical work about law. Both in philosophy departments and in law schools, his texts remain points of frequent reference. Ideas have moved on. Many who started as relatively uncritical disciples of Hart have responded to ongoing debates in ways that have opened up some distance, sometimes a large distance, between their current stance in legal theory and Hart's own stance even on a benign interpretation of it.

Still in 2007, fifteen years after his death and one hundred since his birth, even after reviewing all the debates and arguments of the preceding half century, those who embark upon the study of jurisprudence are wise to acquaint themselves in good depth with Herbert Hart's contribution. In its day it exercised incomparable influence, and thus in its afterlife it continues to have great relevance. It is in this belief, and in reverence for his memory, that I offer to the reader a new edition of this simple (but not stupid) introduction to his work and his thought.

Notes

CHAPTER ONE

1. Jenifer Hart, *Ask Me No More* (London: Peter Halban, 1998) pp. 61–79.

2. Ruth Gavison (ed.), *Issues in Contemporary Legal Philosophy: The Influence of H.L.A. Hart* (Oxford: Clarendon Press, 1989).

3. Cf. Nicola Lacey, *A Life of H.L.A. Hart: The Nightmare and the noble dream* (Oxford: Oxford Univ. Press, 2004) pp. 11–4, 268–71, 358–9. It is important to acknowledge the pervasive influence of Lacey's book on almost all points at which the present edition of this book goes beyond its predecessor.

4. Neil MacCormick, "The Concept of Law and *The Concept of Law*," (1994) 14 *Oxford Journal of Legal Studies* 1–23.

5. J. Hart, *Ask Me No More* (*op. cit.* ch. 1 n. 1).

6. Gavison (ed.), *Issues in Contemporary Legal Philosophy* (*op. cit.* ch. 1 n. 2).

7. See, e.g., Thomas Nagel, "The Central Questions," (2005) *London Review of Books*, Feb 3, p. 12.

8. Alfred J. Ayer, William C. Kneale, G. A. Paul, David F. Pears, Peter F. Strawson, Geoffrey J. Warnock, and Richard A. Wollheim, *The Revolution in Philosophy* with an introduction by Gilbert Ryle (London: Macmillan, 1956).

9. Now published as Ludwig Wittgenstein, *Blue and Brown Books* (Oxford: Blackwell, 2nd ed. 1969). The publication of Hart's two volumes of collected papers in respectively blue and brown covers perhaps makes a sly allusion to Wittgenstein.

10 For a vivid firsthand account of such attitudes in the 1950s (and subsequently), see A. W. Brian Simpson, "Herbert Hart Elucidated" (2006) 104 *Michigan Law Review* 1437–60. For a fascinating self-description by Hart toward the end of his life, see David Sugarman, "Hart Interviewed: H.L.A. Hart in Conversation with David Sugarman" (2005) 32 *Journal of Law and Society* 267–93.

11. See Edgar Bodenheimer, "Modern Analytical Jurisprudence and the Limits of its Usefulness" (1955–6) 104 *Univ. of Pennsylvania Law Review* 1680; Hart's reply is in volume 105 (1957) of the same *Review*, pp. 953–75, "Analytical Jurisprudence in the Mid-twentieth Century: A Reply to Professor Bodenheimer."

12. For such a criticism, see Ronald Dworkin, "Hart's *Postscript* and the Character of Political Philosophy" (2004) 24 *Oxford Journal of Legal Studies* 1–37.

13. See H.L.A. Hart and Antony M. Honoré, "Causation in the Law" (1956) 72 *Law Quarterly Review* 58, 260, 398.

14. See Karl-Ludwig Kunz, *Die Analytische Rechtstheorie: Eine 'Rechts'theorie ohne Recht* (Berlin: Duncker & Humblot, 1977).

15. See H.L.A. Hart, "Positivism and the Separation of Law and Morals" (1957–8) 71 *Harvard Law Review* 593–629; and Lon L. Fuller "Positivism and Fidelity to Law—A Reply to Professor Hart" in the same review (p. 630). Hart's further statement on the points in issue appears in chapter 9 of *The Concept of Law* (Oxford: Clarendon Press, 2nd ed. 1994, with *Postscript* ed. by Patricia A. Bulloch and Joseph Raz); Fuller's further statement appears in *The Morality of Law* (New Haven, CT: Yale Univ. Press, revised ed. 1972).

16. See Ronald Dworkin, *Taking Rights Seriously* (London: Duckworth, revised ed. 1978) esp. chs. 2–4. Dworkin's position has since developed into the full-blown 'interpretive' approach to "Law as Integrity" expounded in *Law's Empire* (*op. cit.* ch. 1 n. 24).

17 See, e.g., Duncan Kennedy, *A Critique of Adjudication* (Cambridge, MA: Harvard Univ. Press, 1997) esp. pp. 166–79; Jürgen Habermas, *Legitimationsprobleme in Spätkapitalismus* (Frankfurt/Maine: Suhrkamp, 1973) pp. 135–7; Zenon Bankowski and Geoff Mungham, *Images of Law* (London: Routledge & Kegan Paul, 1976) pp. 10–2; Kunz (*op. cit.* ch. 1 n. 14) pp. 99–118; Judith N. Shklar, *Legalism* (Cambridge, MA: Harvard Univ. Press, 1964); William J. Chambliss and Robert B. Seidman, *Law, Order and Power* (Philippines: Addison-Wesley, 1971) ch. 5, esp. pp. 48, 54; Colin M. Campbell, "Legal Thought and Juristic Values" (1974) 1 *British Journal of Law and Society* 13–30, esp. 26–8; Roger Cotterrell, *The Politics of Jurisprudence: A Critical Introduction to Legal Philosophy* (London: Butterworth, 1989). For a contrary view, see Eric Colvin, "The Sociology of Secondary Rules" (1978) 28 *Univ. of Toronto Law Journal* 195; but see also Eric Colvin, "The Division of Legal Labour" (1979) 17 *Osgoode Hall Law Journal* 595–615; and compare Nigel E. Simmonds, "Practice and Validity" (1979) *Cambridge Law Journal* 361; Denis J. Galligan, *Law in Modern Society* (Oxford: Oxford Univ. Press, 2007); Brian Z. Tamanaha, *A General Jurisprudence of Law and Society* (Oxford: Oxford Univ. Press, 2001) pp. 133–70.

18. See William L. Twining, *Karl Llewellyn and the Realist Movement* (London: Weidenfeld & Nicolson, 1973); and compare E. Hunter Taylor Jr., "H.L.A. Hart's Concept of Law in the Perspective of American Realism" (1972) 35 *Modern Law Review* 606–20. See also Twining's valuable critique of the limitations inherent in Hartian analytical jurisprudence, "Academic Law and Legal Philosophy: the Significance of Herbert Hart" (1979) 95 *Law Quarterly Review* 557; and Robert S. Summers, "Prof. H.L.A. Hart's Concept of Law" (1963) 4 *Duke Law Journal* 489.

19. Hart's writings on John Austin are mainly in his introduction to Austin's *Province of Jurisprudence Determined* (*op. cit.* ch. 3 n. 1); and in *Concept of Law* (*op. cit.* ch. 1 n. 15) chs. 1–5. See also "Legal and Moral Obligation" (*op. cit.* ch. 5 n. 1). Hart's writings on Jeremy Bentham are extensive and were gathered together in *Essays on Bentham* (*op. cit.* ch. 1 n. 20).

20. H.L.A. Hart, *Essays on Bentham: Jurisprudence and Political Theory* (Oxford: Clarendon Press, 1982); *Essays in Jurisprudence and Philosophy* (Oxford: Clarendon Press, 1983).

21. Wittgenstein, *Blue and Brown Books* (*op. cit.* ch. 1 n. 9).

22. See Dworkin, "Hart's *Postscript*" (*op. cit.* ch. 1 n. 12).

23. William L. Twining, "Schauer on Hart" (2006) 119 *Harvard Law Review* 105–13, esp. 107–8.

24. See Ronald Dworkin, *Law's Empire* (Cambridge, MA: Harvard Univ. Press, 1986) chs. 1–2.

25. Michael Martin, *The Legal Philosophy of H.L.A. Hart: A Critical Appraisal* (Philadelphia: Temple Univ. Press, 1987); and Michael D. Bayles, *Hart's Legal Philosophy: An Examination* (Dordrecht, Holland: Kluwer Academic, 1992).

26. Jules L. Coleman (ed.) *Hart's Postscript: Essays on the Postscript to* the Concept of Law (Oxford: Oxford Univ. Press, 2001).

27. Neil MacCormick, *Questioning Sovereignty* (Oxford: Oxford Univ. Press, 1999); Neil MacCormick, *Rhetoric and the Rule of Law* (Oxford: Oxford Univ. Press, 2005); and Neil MacCormick, *Institutions of Law* (Oxford: Oxford Univ. Press, 2007).

CHAPTER TWO

1. One might add that Jenifer Hart, in *Ask Me No More* (*op. cit.* ch. 1 n. 1), ascribes to G. A. Paul (p. 131) a deliberate effort to extend the influence of philosophy into the law faculty through Hart's appointment to the Jurisprudence chair in 1952, notwithstanding the disapproval of quite a few law dons.

2. Hart, "Are There Any Natural Rights?" (1955) *Philosophical Review* 175–91, p. 53 fn. Although Hart disowned this essay in his later writing, I doubt if he wished to abandon this distinction. Compare John Rawls, *A Theory of Justice* (Cambridge, MA: Harvard Univ. Press, 1971) pp. 204–8 on liberty and the 'worth' of liberty. For criticism of such a distinction, see Norman Daniels, *Reading Rawls: Critical Studies on Rawls' A Theory of Justice* (Oxford: Clarendon Press, 1975) pp. 253–81 (Daniels's essay "Equal Liberty and Unequal Worth of Liberty").

3. Friedrich A. von Hayek, *Law, Legislation and Liberty* (3 vols., London: Routledge & Kegan Paul, 1982).

4. Robert Nozick, *Anarchy, State and Utopia* (Oxford: Blackwell, 1974).

5. See Milton Friedman and Rose Friedman. *Free to Choose: A Personal Statement* (London: Harcourt Brace Jovanovich 1980).

6. See, e.g., Bankowski and Mungham, *Images of Law* (*op. cit.* ch. 1 n. 17); Michael Mann, *Consciousness and Action among the Western Working Class* (London: Macmillan, 1973) chs. 4–5; Bob Fine, Richard Kinsey, John Lea, Sol Picciotto, and Jock Young (eds.), *Capitalism and the Rule of Law* (London: Hutchinson, 1979).

7. See Douglas Jay, *Socialism in the New Society* (London, 1962); Douglas Jay, *The Socialist Case* (London, 1937). Compare Lacey, *A Life* (*op. cit.* ch. 1 n. 3) pp. 24–5, 55–6, 283–4.

8. Nozick (*op. cit.* ch. 2 n. 4). See also John Locke, *Second Treatise of Civil Government* in *Two Treatises of Civil Government* (ed. William S. Carpenter, London: J. M. Dent, 1924) chs. 7–8.

9. See Isaiah Berlin, *Four Essays on Liberty* (Oxford: Clarendon Press, 1969).

10. See Ayer, Kneale, Paul, Pears, Strawson, Warnock, and Wollheim, *Revolution in Philosophy* with an introduction by Ryle (*op. cit.* ch. 1 n. 8).

11. Gilbert Ryle, *The Concept of Mind* (London: Hutchinson, 1949). Although Ryle's book had an influence on Hart, he never accepted the 'behaviourist' line taken by Ryle. The passage from Hart, *Punishment and Responsibility* (*op. cit.* ch. 2 n. 18) quoted at page 184 of the present work shows how rooted is Hart's objection to any variety of behaviourism.

12. J. L. Austin's works posthumously published are: *Sense and Sensibilia* (ed. Geoffrey J. Warnock, Oxford: Clarendon Press, 1962); *How to Do Things with Words* (ed. James O. Urmson, Oxford: Clarendon Press, 1962); and *Philosophical Papers* (eds. James O. Urmson and Geoffrey J. Warnock, Oxford: Clarendon Press, 1961).

13. J. L. Austin, *Philosophical Papers* (*op. cit.* ch. 2 n. 12) p. 85. *In vino veritas* means, 'the truth is in wine'; that is, when drinking too much wine, people give away truths that when sober they would prefer to conceal. Rather typically of the period, a classical tag is used to construct a philosophical witticism.

14. J. L. Austin, "Performative Utterances" in *Philosophical Papers* (*op. cit.* ch. 2 n. 12) ch. 10.

15. In "Analytical Jurisprudence in the Mid-twentieth Century" (*op. cit.* ch. 1 n. 11) esp. p. 962, Hart reminds us of the many legal examples of the 'use of language. . . to *do* something.' Examples he gives are 'making a bequest in a will' ("I hereby bequeath") and the language of enactment used by legislators ("It is hereby enacted"). Hart the lawyer thought that J. L. Austin's theory of 'performative' utterances would have been better called one of 'operative' utterances, on the analogy of the 'operative words' of legal documents.

16. Ludwig Wittgenstein, *Philosophical Investigations* (trans. G. Elizabeth M. Anscombe, Oxford: Blackwell, 3rd ed. 1968).

17. See J. L. Austin, *Philosophical Papers* (*op. cit.* ch. 2 n. 12) ch. 6; also published in (1956) *Proceedings of the Aristotelian Society* 1.

18. See Hart, "The Ascription of responsibility and rights" (1948–9) *Proceedings of the Aristotelian Society*; Hart's disowning of this early piece is stated at page *v* of *Punishment and Responsibility* (Oxford: Clarendon Press, 1968). The paper was a forerunner of J. L. Austin's "A Plea for Excuses" (1956–7) *Proceedings of the Aristotelian Society*; it was derived from an earlier session of the same joint seminar. Despite having been disowned, the paper is extremely important as an early indicator of Hart's concern to get at the social rules, not only semantic rules, which lie behind and make sense of our way of talking about responsibility and about rights. As Hart's other early paper (cited in ch. 2 n. 20) points out, this concern with rules and their logic was central to ordinary language philosophy, and important for jurisprudence. 'Defeasibility' remains a topic of considerable interest—see N. MacCormick, *Institutions of Law* (*op. cit.* ch. 1 n. 27) pp. 163–6.

19. It should be remarked, perhaps, that Tony (A. M.) Honoré undertook the preparation of the second edition of *Causation in the Law* (Oxford: Clarendon Press, 1985) on his own.

20. Hart's own view of the state of postwar British jurisprudence is stated in his "Philosophy of Law and Jurisprudence in Britain (1945–52)" (1953) 2 *American Journal of Comparative Law* 355. In this essay, he singles out for favourable discussion work by William Dawson Lamont, Archibald H. Campbell, Wolfgang G. Friedmann, Julius Stone, William Warwick Buckland, Alessandro Passerin D'Entrèves, Frederick Henry Lawson, and Norman S. Marsh, as well as drawing to lawyers' attention the importance of the concentration in 'contemporary philosophy' of 'the notion of a *rule*' (p. 364).

21. Glanville Williams, "Language and the Law" (1945) 61 *Law Quarterly Review* 71, 179, 293, 384; and (1946) 62 *Law Quarterly Review* 387. For Hart's comments on these essays, see the same *Review* "Philosophy of Law and Jurisprudence in Britain (1945–52)" pp. 361–2.

CHAPTER THREE

1. See Jeremy Bentham, *Of Laws in General* (ed. H.L.A. Hart, London: Univ. of London Athlone Press, 1970); and John Austin, *The Province of Jurisprudence Determined and the Uses of the Study of Jurisprudence* (ed. H.L.A. Hart, London: Weidenfeld & Nicolson, 1954).

2. Hans Kelsen, *General Theory of Law and State* (trans. Anders Wedberg, Cambridge, MA: Harvard Univ. Press, 1949); and *The Pure Theory of Law* (trans. Max Knight, Berkeley: Univ. of California Press, 1967). For Hart's response to Kelsen, see "Kelsen Visited" (1965) 10 *Univ. of California law Review* 709; and "Kelsen's Doctrine of the Unity of Law" in *Ethics and Social Justice* (ed. Milton K. Munitz and Howard E. Kiefer, Albany, NY: SUNY Press, 1968) pp. 208–70. See also Stanley Paulson, "Material and Formal Authorisation in Kelsen's Pure Theory" (1980) *Cambridge Law Journal* 172.

3. See Dworkin, *Taking Rights Seriously* (*op. cit.* ch. 1 n. 16) esp. ch. 4; also Dworkin, *Law's Empire* (*op. cit.* ch. 1 n. 24) ch. 3.

CHAPTER FOUR

1. See Hart, *Essays in Jurisprudence and Philosophy* (*op. cit.* ch. 1 n. 20) pp. 13. "[W]hat is needed is a 'hermeneutic' method which involves portraying rule-governed behaviour as it appears to its participants, who see it as conforming or failing to conform to certain shared standards." In these words, Hart effectively endorsed the understanding of his own work proposed in the first edition of this book. Compare Aulis Aarnio, *On Legal Reasoning* (Turku, Finland: Univ. of Turku Press, 1977); and Stig Strömholm, "Legal Hermeneutics—Notes on the Early Modern Development" (1978) *Scandinavian Studies in Law* 215. See also Zygmunt Bauman, *Hermeneutics and Social Science: Approaches to Understanding* (London: Hutchinson, 1978).

2. See works by J. L. Austin cited in ch. 2 ns. 12, 18.

3. Peter Winch, *The Idea of a Social Science and Its Relation to Philosophy* (London: Routledge & Kegan Paul, 1958). Hart cites Winch in the notes at the end of *Concept of Law* (*op. cit.* ch. 1 n. 15; pp. 289, 297 in the 2nd edition) in a way that indicates its importance for him as a source; however, his theory of the 'internal

aspect' of rules makes a *contrast* with 'habits,' thus differentiating his position from Winch's.

4. Wittgenstein, *Philosophical Investigations* (*op. cit.* ch. 2 n. 16).

5. See Max Rheinstein (ed.) *Max Weber on Law in Economy and Society* (Cambridge, MA: Harvard Univ. Press, 1954). Weber's insistence that we must 'understand' (*verstehen*) social actions as they are meaningful to the actors is one of the most important elements in his sociological thought, well discussed in Winch's *Idea of a Social Science* (*op. cit.* ch. 4 n. 3); and in Michael H. Lessnoff, *The Structure of Social Science: A Philosophical Introduction* (London: Allen & Unwin, 1974). Hart's adoption of a variant on this idea appears initially to have been filtered wholly or in part through his reading of Winch (*op. cit.* ch. 4 n. 3) pp. 57–65.

6. Lacey, *A Life* (*op. cit.* ch. 1 n. 3) p. 230.

7. For criticism of this way of proceeding, see Dennis Lloyd, *Introduction to Jurisprudence* (eds. Lord Lloyd of Hampstead and Michael D. A. Freeman, London: Stevens, 4th ed. 1979) pp. 196–7.

8. It may be objected, however, that there is more to 'habits' than Hart admits, and that these also can have an 'internal aspect.' See Martin Krygier, *"The Concept of Law* and Social Theory" (1982) 2 *Oxford Journal of Legal Studies* 155–80, esp. 170–1; and N. MacCormick, *Institutions of Law* (*op. cit.* ch. 1 n. 27) ch. 4.

9. Wherever there is any kind of standard or criterion for passing a judgment about any act, object, or state of affairs (which by reference to which judgment is passed) is in jurists' technical speech 'a norm.' Hence 'normative' means 'pertaining to a norm.'

10. See Peter M. S. Hacker, "Hart's Philosophy of Law" in Hacker and Joseph Raz (eds.) *Law, Morality, and Society: Essays in Honour of H.L.A. Hart* (Oxford: Clarendon Press, 1977), this volume being a *Festschrift* for Hart. On 'hermeneutics,' compare the references in ch. 4 n. 1. See also Hans-Georg Gadamer, *Truth and Method* (New York: Seabury Press, 1975); and Karl-Otto Apel, *Transformation der Philosophie* (Frankfurt/Main: Suhrkamp, 1976).

11. The arguments advanced in this section and the next derive substantially from the Appendix to Neil MacCormick, *Legal Reasoning and Legal Theory* (Oxford: Clarendon Press, 2nd ed. 1994). For a radically opposed reading of Hart, see James W. Harris, *Law and Legal Science: An Inquiry into the Concepts Legal Rule and Legal System* (Oxford: Clarendon Press, 1979) pp. 52–63.

12. See Eerik Lagerspetz, *The Opposite Mirrors: An Essay on the Conventionalist Theory of Institutions* (Dordrecht, Holland: Kluwer Academic, 1996) pp. 30–50 discussing 'mutual beliefs.' See also Neil MacCormick, *Institutions of Law* (*op. cit.* ch. 1 n. 27) pp. 16–8.

13. For criticism of the original version of this paragraph, see Rolf Sartorius, "Positivism and the Foundations of Legal Authority" in Gavison (ed.), *Issues in Contemporary Legal Philosophy* (*op. cit.* ch. 1 n. 2) pp. 41–61, esp. 46–8. Taking up the point about mutual expectations and beliefs as developed by Lagerspetz (*The Opposite Mirrors*; *op. cit.* ch. 4 n. 12) is helpful in defence against this critique.

14. See MacCormick, *Legal Reasoning and Legal Theory* (*op. cit.* ch.4 n. 11) pp. 285–9.

15. John M. Finnis, *Natural Law and Natural Rights* (Oxford: Clarendon Press, 1980) chs. 1–4. Cf. Neil MacCormick, "Natural Law and the Separation of Law

and Morals," in Robert P. George (ed.) *Natural Law Theory: Contemporary Essays* (Oxford: Clarendon Press, 1992) pp. 105–33.

16. See Tony ('A.M.') Honoré's essay "Groups, Laws and Obedience" in A. W. Brian Simpson (ed.) *Oxford Essays in Jurisprudence, 2nd Series* (Oxford: Clarendon Press, 1973) ch. 1.

17. J. Austin, *Province of Jurisprudence Determined* (*op. cit.* ch. 3 n. 1) chs. 1, 6.

18. Jeremy Bentham, "A Fragment on Government," chapter 1 in James H. Burns and H.L.A. Hart (eds.) *A Comment on the Commentaries and A Fragment on Government* (London: Univ. of London Athlone Press, 1977) pp. 428–32.

19. Hart's argument about 'habits' probably applies reasonably fairly to John Austin's idea about the 'habit of obedience,' but many critics have pointed out that it is not a very satisfactory account of habits in general. See Krygier, "*Concept of Law* and Social Theory" (*op. cit.* ch. 4 n. 8); and Sundram Soosay, "Is the Law an Affair of Rules" in Australian Legal Philosophy Students Association, *2005 Annual Publication* (Brisbane, Australia: UQ Vanguard, 2005; order through http://www.alpsa.net/r-annual.htm) 24–40.

20. This claim about the possibility of a detached, 'descriptive' account of law is what Ronald Dworkin considers to be quite impossible. See chapter 14.

21. Yet, when Dworkin came to write *Law's Empire* (*op. cit.* ch. 1 n. 24) some few years after the publication of the first edition of this book and came to write more after the publication of Hacker's 1977 essay, "Hart's Philosophy of Law" (*op. cit.* ch. 4 note 10), he adopted 'hermeneutic' as the description of his own methodological approach without explaining what he took to be the difference or what objection he had to this use of the concept.

22. See, e.g., Jack P. Gibbs, "Definitions of Law and Empirical Questions" (1968) 2 *Law and Society Review* 429; Colin M. Campbell, "Legal Thought and Juristic Values" (*op. cit.* ch. 1 n. 17); Colin M. Campbell and Paul Wiles, "The Study of Law and Society in Britain" (1976) 16 *Law and Society Review* 547. Compare Lacey, *A Life* (*op. cit.* ch. 1 n. 3) pp. 260–2, 333.

23. It would seem preferable to adopt the terminology of Joseph Raz and to call these statements 'normative statements.' See Joseph Raz, *The Concept of a Legal System* (Oxford: Clarendon Press, 2nd ed. 1980); and one may then differentiate 'detached' from 'committed' statements as Raz does and as Hart approved in his Introduction to *Essays in Jurisprudence and Philosophy* (*op. cit.* ch. 1 n. 20).

24. Dworkin, *Taking Rights Seriously* (*op. cit.* ch. 1 n. 16) chs. 2–4.

25. See *Postscript* (*Concept of Law, op. cit.* ch. 1 n. 15) p. 256: "I do not regard [my account of social rules] as a sound explanation of morality, either individual or social."

26. See Hart, *Concept of Law* (*op. cit.* ch. 1 n. 15) p. 205: judges should, in hard cases, be prepared "to deploy some acceptable general principle as a *reasoned* basis for decision" (italics added).

27. Crucial to any critical moral principal is "the assumption that the arrangements of society . . . must satisfy two formal conditions, one of rationality and the other of generality"; *Concept of Law* (*op. cit.* ch. 1 n. 15) p. 183.

28. Compare Hart, *Concept of Law* (*op. cit.* ch. 1 n. 15) p. 229; ". . . legal rules, municipal and international, commonly contain much specific detail and draw arbitrary distinctions . . .." But I disagree with Hart's there stated view that moral rules differ on this point.

29. For a much stronger statement of this thesis, see N. MacCormick *Institutions of Law* (*op. cit.* ch. 1 n. 27) ch. 14.

30. See Herbert James Paton, *The Moral Law* (London: Routledge & Kegan Paul, 1948); this work is a translation of Immanuel Kant's *Groundwork of the metaphysics of Morals*. Compare Richard M. Hare, *Freedom and Reason* (Oxford: Clarendon Press, 1963).

31. See Joseph Raz, *The Concept of a Legal System* (Oxford: Clarendon Press, 1st ed. 1970) pp. 45–9.

CHAPTER FIVE

1. See Hart, "Legal and Moral Obligation" in Abraham I. Melden (ed.) *Essays in Moral Philosophy* (Seattle: Univ. of Washington Press, 1958) pp. 82–107. His criticism is directed at Richard M. Hare, *The Language of Morals* (Oxford: Clarendon Press, 1952).

2. See Richard M. Hare, "Principles" (1972–3) 73 *Proceedings of the Aristotelian Society* 1; and compare N. MacCormick, *Rhetoric and the Rule of Law* (*op. cit.* ch. 1 n. 27) pp. 94–5.

3. See, e.g., Sir W. David Ross, *The Foundations of Ethics* (Oxford: Clarendon Press, 1939).

4. See David D. Raphael, *The Moral Sense* (Oxford: Clarendon Press, 1947).

5. See David Hume, *A Treatise of Human Nature* (eds. Lewis A. Selby-Brigge and Peter H. Nidditch, Oxford: Clarendon Press, 1978) II.iii.3, pp. 417–8.

6. A concept picked up by Hart in *Essays in Jurisprudence and Philosophy* (*op. cit.* ch. 1 n. 20) Introduction, p. 7.

7. The discussion here of 'convention' draws heavily on David K. Lewis, *Conventions: a Philosophical Study* (Cambridge, MA: Harvard Univ. Press, 1969; also Oxford: Basil Blackwell, 1986), though I do not accept his view (see pp. 100–7) that 'rules' is too vague a term to be useful in the present context.

8. See James Bryce, *Studies in History and Jurisprudence* (Oxford: Oxford Univ. Press, 1901) vol. 2, pp. 468–9.

CHAPTER SIX

1. His later view about legal obligations as 'content-independent peremptory reasons' is discussed in the last section of this chapter, and some further implications are discussed in chapter 14.

2. For a classic statement of the 'Scandinavian Realist' view on obligation, see Karl Olivecrona, *Law as Fact* (Copenhagen: E. Munksgaard, 1st ed. 1939) ch. 3; or Alf Ross, *On Law and Justice* (Berkeley: Univ. of California Press, 1959) pp. 52–64, 158–64; or Axel Hägerström, *Inquiries into the Nature of Law and Morals* (ed. Karl Olivecrona, trans. Charlie D. Broad, Stockholm: Almqvist & Wiksell, 1953) pp. 127–200. For Hart's full critique of this school of thought, see "Scandinavian Realism" (1959) 17 *Cambridge Law Journal* pp. 233–40, esp. 236. In Olivecrona's second edition of *Law as Fact* (London: Stevens, 1971) and in Alf Ross's *Directives and Norms* (London: Routledge & Kegan Paul, 1968) there is some movement toward a

view akin to Hart's on the internal point of view, but still in terms of psychological experiences of compulsion or requirement. See esp. A. Ross, *Directives and Norms*, ch. 4.

3. For John Austin's remarks on 'duty' and 'obligation' see *Province of Jurisprudence Determined* (*op. cit.* ch. 3 n. 1) pp. 15–24; also see J. Austin, *Lectures on Jurisprudence* (*op. cit.* ch. 7 n. 14) ch. 22; and Hart's discussion of J. Austin's views in "Legal and Moral Obligation" (*op. cit.* ch. 5 n. 1).

4. For statements by Oliver Wendell Holmes, Jr., on 'duty,' see "The Path of the Law" in Holmes, *Collected Legal Papers* (London: Constable, 1920) pp. 167–202, esp. 173–4. Compare William L. Twining, "The Bad Man Revisited" (1973) 58 *Cornell Law Review* 275.

5. See Kelsen, *General Theory of Law* (*op. cit.* ch. 3 n. 2) pp. 50–64, 71–4; and *Pure Theory of Law* (*op. cit.* ch. 3 n. 2) pp. 114–25. Hans Kelsen's insistence that the legal order is a normative order marked off from others by its specific 'technique' of resort to *organized* sanctions leads him to the view that the *primary* form of law is that of a norm authorizing the imposition of a coercive sanction by a person holding the position of an 'organ' of the legal order. Since that is the primary form, norm statements concerning the duties of ordinary persons are secondary. Hart's concern to elucidate legal concepts in their social context leads him to reject Kelsen's primary/secondary distinction as a direct inversion of the proper order. Law is *primarily* concerned to prescribe duties. Official and other powers are ancillary to that, for they derive from 'secondary rules.'

6. For a more detailed account of these matters, see N. MacCormick, *Institutions of Law* (*op. cit.* ch. 1 n. 27) ch. 6.

7. Rodger Beehler, "The Concept of Law and the Obligation to Obey" (1978) 23 *American Journal of Jurisprudence* 120.

8. Roscoe E. Hill, "Legal Validity and Legal Obligation" (1970) 80 *Yale Law Journal* 47.

9. See Francis de Zulueta, *The Institutes of Gaius* (Oxford: Clarendon Press, 1953) III.13 pt. compare Hart, *Concept of Law* (*op. cit.* ch. 1 n. 15) p. 243.

10. Antony M. Honoré, "Real Laws" (pp. 99–118), in Hacker and Raz (eds.) *Law, Morality, and Society* (*op. cit.* ch. 4 n. 10).

11. I derive the terminology in this and the preceding paragraph from the Kantian idea of a 'hypothetical imperative' that has the form "If you want *x* then you ought to do *y*." These are contrasted with 'categorical imperatives' whereby one ought to do *x* regardless of one's particular desires. See Paton, *Moral Law* (*op. cit.* ch. 4 n. 30) pp. 39 fn., 51, 88–9. Compare Charles Fried, *Right and Wrong* (Cambridge, MA: Harvard Univ. Press, 1978) esp. pp. 11–23.

12. Compare Lon L. Fuller's distinction between 'the morality of aspiration' and 'the morality of duty.' The former concerns ideals of goodness and excellence, ideals to which we aspire. The latter concerns minimal requirements of conduct. We do wrong when we break these, although we do not do wrong in simply falling short of ideal achievement or excellence. See Fuller, *Morality of Law* (*op. cit.* ch. 1 n. 15) ch. 1.

13. Compare Alan R. White's discussion of 'obligation' as a kind of necessity in his *Modal Thinking* (Oxford: Blackwell, 1976).

14. As examples of 'rescue' cases see *Wilkinson* v. *Kinneil Coal Co.* [1897] 24 R. 1001; *Haynes* v. *Harwood* [1935] 1 K.B. 146; and *Baker* v. *T. E. Hopkins and Son Ltd.* [1959] 3 All E.R. 225. See also Arthur L. Goodhart, "Rescue and Voluntary Assumption of Risk" (1934) 5 *Cambridge Law Journal* 192.

15. Dworkin, *Taking Rights Seriously* (*op. cit.* ch. 1 n. 16) ch. 3.

16. Joseph Raz, *Practical Reason and Norms* (Princeton, NJ: Princeton Univ. Press, 1990) pp. 49–58.

17. See Rodger Beehler, "The Concept of Law and the Obligation to Obey" (*op. cit.* ch. 6 n. 7).

18. See Roscoe E. Hill, "Legal Validity and Legal Obligation" (*op. cit.* ch. 6 n. 8).

19. See Justinian, *Digest*, I.ii.2.3–9; Barry Nicholas, *Introduction to Roman Law* (Oxford: Clarendon Press, 1962) pp. 15–6.

20. *Shaw* v. *D.P.P.* [1962] A.C. 223.

21. See Hart, "Bentham and Beccaria" in *Essays on Bentham* (*op. cit.* ch. 1 n. 20) pp. 40–52.

22. See Émile Durkheim, *The Division of Labour in Society* with an introduction by Lewis Coser (trans. W. D. Halls, Basingstoke UK: Macmillan, 1984) pp. 108–9. That Durkheim is wrong as to the historical relationships of repressive and restitutive law is immaterial for present purposes.

23. See Hart's "Commands and Authoritative Legal Reasons" in *Essays on Bentham* (*op. cit.* ch. 1 n. 20) pp. 243–68.

24. See Raz, *Practical Reason and Norms* (*op. cit.* ch. 6 n. 16) pp. 193–9.

25. See Joseph Raz, *The Authority of Law* (Oxford: Clarendon Press, 1979) pp. 18, 21–33.

CHAPTER SEVEN

1. For a discussion of the concept of 'normative power,' see a set of papers by Neil MacCormick (pp. 59–78) and Joseph Raz (pp. 79–102) entitled "Voluntary Obligations and Normative Powers" (1972) *Proceedings of the Aristotelian Society, Supplementary Volumes* 46. See also Joseph Raz, *Practical Reason and Norms* (London: Hutchinson, 1975) pp. 98–104.

2. On this idea that speech acts involve an 'internal intention' (that is, an intention that one's addressee should suppose that one has a certain intention), compare with N. MacCormick, "Legal Obligation and the Imperative Fallacy" in Simpson (ed.) *Oxford Essays in Jurisprudence, 2nd Series* (*op. cit.* ch. 4 n. 16) ch. 5. My discussion of 'obligation' in the latter half of that paper is now superseded by that in chapter 6 of the present work.

3. As to the concept of 'objective' intention in contract, consider the following passage from David M. Walker, *Principles of Scottish Private Law* (Oxford: Clarendon Press, 2nd ed. 1975) p. 605. "Once it has been established what the terms of the parties' contract are, it is for the court to interpret the contract. The court must proceed on the basis that the parties must be taken to have intended what they said and wrote, or what is the natural meaning of the words they used. They cannot be heard to say that they meant other than that."

4. Per Lord Atkin, *Donoghue* v. *Stevenson* [1932] A.C. 562 at p. 599; [1962] S.C. (H.L.) 31 at p. 57.

5. William H. Davies, *The Autobiography of a Super-Tramp* (London: Jonathan Cape, 1952).

6. I derive this point from Raz's "Voluntary Obligations and Normative Powers" (*op. cit.* ch. 7 n. 1) though my own account of powers as deriving from rules that have to be intentionally 'invoked' differs a little from his solution of the same difficulty. Bayles, *Hart's Legal Philosophy* (*op. cit.* ch. 1 n. 25), rejects this idea about 'invoking' rules but fails to solve the problem about the difference between facultative rules and rules that people use to generate facilities in anomalous ways.

7. See Gibbs, "Definitions of Law" (*op. cit.* ch. 4 n. 22).

8. See Raz, *The Concept of a Legal System*, 2nd ed. (*op. cit.* ch. 4 n. 23) p. 72. "The crucial question is what exactly are the principles underlying the jurisprudential division of the law. This I will call the problem of individuation." The problem is to work out how to divide out the statutes, precedents, and other authoritative legal texts into an orderly and comprehensible set of distinct rules. As Raz points out (p. 71), the first author to discover this problem was Jeremy Bentham. It is fair to say that Raz was the first to offer a systematic solution to the problem.

9. "Bentham on Legal Powers" (1972) 81 *Yale Law Journal* p. 799; see *Essays on Bentham* (*op. cit.* ch. 1 n. 20) ch. 8.

10. See N. MacCormick, "Law as Institutional Fact" (1974) 90 *Law Quarterly Review* 102–29.

11. Bayles, *Hart's Legal Philosophy* (*op. cit.* ch. 1 n. 25) p. 28, suggests, erroneously, that the first edition failed to register this point. With respect, the problem of individuation and of what makes it possible to individuate rules in certain ways deserves the more careful treatment it receives here.

12. N. MacCormick, "Law as Institutional Fact" (*op. cit.* ch. 7 n. 10); see N. MacCormick, *Institutions of Law* (*op. cit.* ch. 1 n. 27) chs. 1–3. compare John Searle, *Speech Acts* (Cambridge: Cambridge Univ. Press, 1969) pp. 50–3; and G. Elizabeth M. Anscombe "On Brute Facts" (1958) 18 *Analysis* 78.

13. See *Newborne* v. *Sensolid (Great Britain) Ltd.* [1954] 1 Q.B. 45.

14. See John Austin, *Lectures on Jurisprudence* (rev. and ed. by Robert Campbell, London: J. Murray, 5th ed. 1885) ch. 23; and compare Colin F. H. Tapper, "Austin on Sanctions" (1965) *Cambridge Law Journal* 271 87.

15. See Jeremy Bentham, *Introduction to the Principles of Morals and Legislation* (eds. James H. Burns and H.L.A. Hart, London: Univ. of London Athlone Press, 1970) p. 201.

16. J. Erskine, *An Institute of the Laws of Scotland* (Edinburgh, 1st ed. 1773) I.i.6.

17. J. Austin, *Lectures on Jurisprudence* (*op. cit.* ch. 7 n. 14).

CHAPTER EIGHT

1. Apart from "Definition and Theory in Jurisprudence" (1953) 70 *Law Quarterly Review* 37, Hart's main writings on the subject of 'rights' are: "Theory and Definition in Jurisprudence" (1955) 29 *Proceedings of the Aristotelian Society, Supplementary Volumes* 239; "Are there any Natural Rights" (1955) 64 *Philosophical Review*;

and "Bentham on Legal Rights," alias "Legal Rights" *Essays on Bentham* (*op. cit.* ch. 1 n. 20) pp. 162–93.

2. See N. MacCormick, "Rights in Legislation" (p. 189) in Hacker and Raz (eds.) *Law, Morality, and Society* (*op. cit.* ch. 4 n. 10); also N. MacCormick, *Institutions of Law* (*op. cit.* ch. 1 n. 27) pp. 117–52.

3. W. N. Hohfeld, *Fundamental Legal Conceptions* (ed. W. W. Cook, New Haven, CT: Yale Univ. Press, 1923); for subsequent developments of Hohfeld's ideas, see Walter J. Kamba, "Legal Theory and Hohfeld's Analysis of a Legal Right" (1974) *Juridical Review* 249. See also Rex Martin and James W. Nickel, "A bibliography on the Nature and Foundations of Rights, 1947–77" (1978) 6 *Political Theory* 395; also their "Recent Work on the Concept of Rights" (1980) 17 *American Philosophical Quarterly* 165–80.

4. N. MacCormick, "Rights in Legislation" (*op. cit.* ch. 8 n. 2); and other writings cited in that essay. See also N. MacCormick, *Institutions of Law* (*op. cit.* ch. 1 n. 27) chs. 7–8.

CHAPTER NINE

1. See A. P. D'Entrèves, *Natural Law* (London: Hutchinson, rev. ed. 1970); Leo Strauss, *Natural Right and History* (Chicago: Univ. of Chicago Press, 1965); Finnis, *Natural Law* (*op. cit.* ch. 4 n. 15); George (ed.) *Natural Law Theory* (*op. cit.* ch. 4 n. 15).

2. See Thomas Hobbes, *Leviathan* (ed. Michael Oakeshott, Oxford, 1960).

3. See D. Hume, *A Treatise of Human Nature* Book III, Part ii; *An Enquiry Concerning the Principles of Morals*, sections III and IV, Appendix III.

4. See F. Engels, *Anti-Dühring* in Michael Oakeshott (ed.), *Social and Political Doctrines of Contemporary Europe* (New York: Cambridge Press, 1949) pp. 129–31.

5. See Adam Smith, *Wealth of Nations* (eds. Roy H. Campbell, Andrew S. Skinner, and William B. Todd, Oxford: Clarendon Press, 1976) V.i.6; *Lectures on Jurisprudence* (eds. Ronald L. Meek, David D. Raphael, and Peter G. Stein, Oxford: Clarendon Press, 1978) 8.27, (p. 14). And see A. S. Skinner, "Adam Smith: Society and Government" in Elspeth Attwooll (ed.), *Perspectives in Jurisprudence* (Glasgow: Glasgow Univ. Press, 1977) ch. 11; and P. G. Stein, *Legal Evolution* (Cambridge: Cambridge Univ. Press 1980).

6. Hobbes, *Leviathan* (*op. cit.* ch. 9 n. 2) sec. I.14.

7. See John Locke, *Second Treatise of Civil Government* in *Two Treatises of Civil Government* (*op. cit.* ch. 2 n. 8) chs. 7–8; and compare N. MacCormick, "Law Obligation and Consent: Reflections on Stair and Locke" (1979) 65 *Archiv für Rechts und Sozialphilosophie* 387; also *Legal Right and Social Democracy* (Oxford: Clarendon Press 1982) ch. 4.

8. See Smith and others previously cited (*op. cit.* ch. 9 n. 5). See also Louis Schneider, *The Scottish Moralists on Human Nature and Society* (Chicago: Univ. of Chicago Press, 1967) pp. xxix–xlvii, 99–119.

9. I owe this point to Finnis, *Natural Law* (*op. cit.* ch. 4 n. 15) pp. 215–7. See also Elizabeth H. Wolgast, *Equality and the Rights of Women* (Ithaca, NY: Cornell Univ. Press, 1980).

10. See, e.g., Hume, *Enquiry* (*op. cit.* ch. 9 n. 3) Section III, Part I, at end.

11. See Lacey, *A Life* (*op. cit.* ch. 1 n. 3) pp. 61–2, 73–9, 110–1, 203–5.

12. See Barry Nicholas, *An Introduction to Roman Law* (Oxford: Clarendon Press, 1962) pp. 63, 116.

13. See Marriage (Scotland) Act 1939, discussed in E. M. Clive and J. G. Wilson, *The Law of Husband and Wife in Scotland* (Edinburgh: W. Green and Sons, 1974) pp. 107–22.

CHAPTER TEN

1. Compare Colin F. H. Tapper, "Powers and Secondary Rules of Change" in Simpson (ed.) *Oxford Essays in Jurisprudence, 2nd series* (*op. cit.* ch. 4 n. 16) ch. 10.

2. See N. MacCormick, "Law as Institutional Fact" (*op. cit.* ch. 7 n. 10); and N. MacCormick, *Institutions of Law.* (*op. cit.* ch. 1 n. 27) p. 36.

3. See Friedrich A. von Hayek, *Law, Legislation and Liberty*, vol. 1 *Rules and Order* (London: Routledge & Kegan Paul, 1982) pp. 26–34.

4. Nigel Simmonds and Ian Duncanson have both drawn attention to this point, and I am indebted to their discussions of it. See Ian W. Duncanson, "The Strange World of English Jurisprudence" (1979) 30 *Northern Ireland Law Quarterly* 267; and Nigel E. Simmonds, "Legal Validity and Decided Cases" (1981) 1 *Legal Studies* 24–36. See also Rolf Sartorius, "Hart's Concept of Law" in Robert S. Summers (ed.) *More Essays in Legal Philosophy* (Oxford: Blackwell, 1971) p. 131, 156.

5. See Kelsen, *Pure Theory of Law* (*op. cit.* ch. 3 n. 2) pp. 6–7; compare N. MacCormick, *Institutions of Law* (*op. cit.* ch. 1 n. 27) pp. 56–7.

6. The metre was redefined in 1983 as the distance which light travels in a vacuum in $1/299,792,458$ second. So now there is a standard by which to judge the metre bar—but none by which to judge the new standard itself.

7. The fact that the model chosen incorporates a 'written constitution' and has to be specially varied to accommodate the case of the United Kingdom, shows that Hart's theory *does* fit the normal European legal and constitutional order, even though, as remarked in the Introduction, his own statement of his theory seems to rest mainly on assumptions about English law.

8. For simplicity, I avoid mentioning at this stage the issue of criteria concerning the recognition of European Union law within the United Kingdom, a process which involved a change in the rule of recognition brought about by exercising the legislative power of change. See N. MacCormick, *Questioning Sovereignty* (*op. cit.* ch. 1 n. 27) pp. 81–93; and further discussion in the last section of the present chapter.

9. See Niklas Luhmann, *Law as a Social System* (trans. Klaus A. Ziegert, eds. Fatima Kastner, Richard Nobles, David Schiff, and Rosamund Ziegert, Oxford: Oxford Univ. Press 2004) pp. 381–5; and Gunther Teubner, *Law as an Autopoietic System* (trans. Ruth Adler and Anne Bankowska, ed. Zenon Bankowski, Oxford: Basil Blackwell, 1992) pp. 19–24. Compare N. MacCormick, *Institutions of Law* (*op. cit.* ch. 1 n. 27) pp. 177, 229–30.

10. See Joseph Raz, *Ethics in the Public Domain* (Oxford: Clarendon Press, 1994) p. 289. Rodrigo Sánchez Brigido, *Groups, Rules and Legal Practice*, (Oxford:

Oxford Univ., DPhil Thesis, 2007), contains an extremely ingenious account of the institutional practice of norm-applying officials in terms of a model of collective intentional activities, thereby avoiding the problem of circularity, if it is indeed a problem.

11. See N. MacCormick, *Institutions of Law* (*op. cit.* ch. 1 n. 27) pp. 49–58, 287–8.

12. See Hart, *Concept of Law* (*op. cit.* ch. 1 n. 15) pp. 108–9.

13. for a radical adaptation that seems a better answer than can be achieved by merely tinkering with Hart's ideas, see N. MacCormick, *Institutions of Law* (*op. cit.* ch. 1 n. 27) pp. 49–58, 287–8.

14. Principally M. Martin, *Legal Philosophy of Hart* (*op. cit.* ch. 1 n. 25) pp. 35–8; but see also Bayles, *Hart's Legal Philosophy* (*op. cit.* ch. 1 n. 25) pp. 62–7.

15. Locke, *Second Treatise* (*op. cit.* ch. 2 n. 8) ch. 2.

16. See William H. Murray, *The Islands of Western Scotland* (London: Eyre Methuen, 1973) pp. 178–80.

17. For a critique of Hart's work in its applicability to 'primitive' societies, see G. D. MacCormack, "*Law* and *Legal System*" (1979) 42 *Modern Law Review* 285. I think my suggestions here meet MacCormack's objections.

18. See Chambliss and Seidman, *Law, Order and Power* (*op. cit.* ch. 1 n. 17) ch. 13, on 'the implementation of law in stateless societies.' Although my model case is a purely analytical model, it is not at odds with the anthropological studies discussed by Chambliss and Seidman.

19. In characterizing a 'role' in terms of 'duties,' I depart from the sociological practice of characterizing rules in terms of normative 'expectations.' (See Julius Stone, *Social Dimensions of Law and Justice* [London: Stevens, 1966] pp. 15–23). My reasons for doing so may be gathered from chapter 5. See also Alan Paterson, *The Law Lords* (London: Macmillan, 1982) for applying role-theory in an empirical study of the highest rank of the judiciary in the United Kingdom.

20. See Kelsen, *General Theory of Law* (*op. cit.* ch. 3 n. 2) p. 329.

21. This amateur excursion into the deep waters of legal history (which I excuse as well as I can under the plea of presenting an analytical model) is based on my understanding of such works as S. F. C. Milsom's *Historical Foundations of the Common Law* (London: Butterworth, 2nd ed. 1981) and his *Legal Framework of English Feudalism* (Cambridge: Cambridge Univ. Press, 1976); A. W. Brian Simpson's *Introduction to the History of Land Law* (London: Oxford Univ. Press, 1961); and the Stair Society's *An Introduction to Scottish Legal History* (Edinburgh: Stair Society, 20th vol., 1958). Although grossly oversimplified and schematic, the thesis that formal powers of litigation, of adjudication, and ultimately of legislation in the modern sense emerged from a customary order based on the rights, privileges, and duties of the holders of particular social positions seems to be a reasonably defensible one. See also James H. Burns, "*Winzerus*, a Forgotten Political Writer," (1960) 21 *Journal of the History of Ideas* 124.

22. Compare Milsom, *Historical Foundations* (*op. cit.* ch. 10 n. 21) p. 21: "At the head of [the machinery of central government] was the chief justiciar, the regent in the King's absence, and the centre around which royal justice first grew."

23. On this particular thirteenth- and fourteenth-century development in England, see Milsom, *Historical Foundations* (*op. cit.* ch. 10 n. 21) pp. 245–52.

24. Compare Simpson, *Introduction to the History of Land Law* (*op. cit.* ch. 10 n. 21) p. 40, where it is remarked, even of the seventeenth century that "Clearly the impertinence of Parliament in meddling with the common law had to be kept in some bounds, and so [Sir Edward] Coke only says that the seisin in law has been transferred [by the Statute of Uses]." In 1398, it was established in Scotland that there should be regular sittings of the Scottish Parliament so that the king's subjects might be 'servit of the law.'

25. See Sir Robert Filmer, *Patriarcha: or the Natural Power of Kings* (London, 1680); and Hobbes, *Leviathan* (*op. cit.* ch. 9 n. 2).

26. Hugo Grotius, *De Iure Belli ac Pacis* (trans. Francis W. Kelsey, Oxford: Clarendon Press, 1925) I.i.10–17.

27. "When an Act of Parliament is against common right and reason, or repugnant or impossible, the common law will control it," per Sir Edward Coke (Chief Justice of England's Court of Common Pleas), *Bonham's case* (1610) 8 Co. Rep. 114, 118.

28. Locke's *First Treatise of Civil Government* (*op. cit.* ch. 10 n. 28) is largely a refutation of Robert Filmer; the *Second Treatise* (*op. cit.* ch. 2 n. 8), of Thomas Hobbes.

29. James, 1st Viscount Stair, *Institutions of the Laws of Scotland* (ed. David M. Walker, Edinburgh, 1981) I.i.15–16.

30 Ibid., I.i.18.

31. See Bentham, *Introduction to the Principles* (*op. cit.* ch. 7 n. 15) pp. 21–4.

32 See Bentham, *Of Laws in General* (*op. cit.* ch. 3 n. 1) pp. 18–24.

33. See J. Austin, *Province of Jurisprudence Determined* (*op. cit.* ch. 3 n. 1) chs. 1, 5, 6.

34. Albert V. Dicey, *Introduction to the Study of the Law of the Constitution* with an introduction by E. C. S. Wade (London: Macmillan, 10th ed. 1961) chs. 1, 13; note Dicey's criticisms of John Austin in ch. 13.

35. See, e.g., James Lorimer, *Institutes of Law* (Edinburgh: T. & T. Clark, 1872) ch. 4.

36. Important historical landmarks were the Supreme Court of Judicature Acts of 1873 and 1875.

37 The modern organization of the Court of Session dates from the Court of Session Acts of 1808 and 1825; procedure was substantially reformed by Acts of 1850 and 1868.

38. See N. MacCormick, *Questioning Sovereignty* (*op. cit.* ch. 1 n. 27) pp. 86–93.

CHAPTER ELEVEN

1. See Chaïm Perelman, *Logique Juridique* (Paris: Dalloz, 1976) secs. 16–34 on 'l'école de l'exégèse.'

2. For a discussion of this development in German thought, see Wolfgang G. Friedmann, *Legal Theory* (London: Stevens, 5th ed. 1967) chs. 2–3.

3. See Sir Rupert Cross, *Precedent in English Law* (Oxford: Clarendon Press,

3rd ed. 1977) pp. 22–34; and N. MacCormick, "Can *Stare Decisis* be Abolished?" (1966) *Juridical Review* 197.

4. See Twining, *Karl Llewellyn* (*op. cit.* ch. 1 n. 18) chs. 1–2.

5. François Gény, *Méthode d'Interprétation en Droit privé* (Paris: Librairie Générale de droit & de Jurisprudence, 2nd ed. 1932). See also Gény, "Juridical Freedom of Decision: its Necessity and Method," ch. 1 of *Science of Legal Method: Select Essays by Various Authors* (trans. Ernest Bruncken and Layton B. Register, New York: A. M. Kelley, 1969).

6. Rudolf von Ihering, *Geist des römischen Rechts* (Leipzig: Breitkopf & Härtel, 1898) vol. 2, pp. 309–89; *Law as a Means to an End* (trans. Isaac Husik, New York: A. M. Kelley, 1968).

7. On the school of *Freirechsfindung* see Hermann U. Kantorowicz, *The Definition of Law* (ed. Archibald H. Campbell, Cambridge: Cambridge Univ. Press, 1958); also Eugen Ehrlich, "Juridical Freedom of Decision: Its Principles and Objects," chapter 2 of *Science of Legal Method* (*op. cit.* ch. 11 n. 5).

8. John W. Salmond, *Jurisprudence* (London: Sweet & Maxwell, 1st ed. 1902).

9. Carleton K. Allen, *Law in the Making* (Oxford: Clarendon Press, 1st ed. 1927).

10. John C. Gray, *Nature and Sources of the Law* (Roland Gray, 2nd ed. 1921; reprinted Birmingham, AL: Legal Classics Library, 1985) ch. 4.

11. Holmes, "Path of the Law" (*op. cit.* ch. 6 n. 4) pp. 167–202.

12. See, e.g., Roscoe Pound, "Mechanical Jurisprudence" (1908) 8 *Columbia Law Review* 605–23; and Roscoe Pound, "Law in Books and Law in Action" (1910) 44 *American Law Review* 12–36.

13. See, e.g., Karl N. Llewellyn, *The Bramble Bush* (New York: Oceana, tentative printing and 2nd ed. 1930; reprinted 1960). Note the further development of Llewellyn's position by the time he wrote *The Common Law Tradition: Deciding Appeals* (Boston: Little Brown, 1960) where the stress is on the importance of rules *only subject to other legal factors*. Cf. Twining, *Karl Llewellyn* (*op. cit.* ch. 1 n. 18).

14. See Jerome N. Frank, *Law and the Modern Mind* (English ed., London: P. Smith, 1949; the text dates from 1930).

15. See Wilfrid E. Rumble, Jr., *American Legal Realism: Scepticism, Reform and the Judicial Process* (Ithaca, NY: Cornell Univ. press, 1968); and Twining, *Karl Llewellyn* (*op. cit.* ch. 1 n. 18).

16. Frank, *Law and the Modern Mind* (*op. cit.* ch. 11 n. 14).

17. Llewellyn, *Bramble Bush* (*op. cit.* ch. 6 n. 4) p. 12. But Hart and others ignored the caveats and qualifications he issued in respect of this statement in the 1951 edition (pp. 8–9). See also Holmes, "Path of the Law" (*op. cit.* ch. 6 n. 4) p. 173.

18. Gray, *Nature* (*op. cit.* ch. 11 n. 10).

19. Karl N. Llewellyn, "The Normative, the Legal, and the Law-Jobs: The Problem of Juristic Method." (1939–40) 49 *Yale Law Journal* 1355–1400.

20. For a challenging reassessment of the degree to which, even in the United States, rule-based and essentially deductive reasoning prevails in the reasoning of the judiciary. See James Maxeiner, "Legal Determinacy made in America: U.S. Legal Methods and the Rule of Law" (2006) 41 *Valparaiso University Law Review* 517–89.

21. This doctrine he derived from Friedrich Waissman's "Verifiability" (1945–6) 19/20 *Proceedings of the Aristotelian Society, Supplementary Volumes* 119–50.

22. See William L. Twining and David Miers, *How to Do Things with Rules* (London: Butterworth, 4th ed. 1999) ch. 5, on the various circumstances giving rise to doubt as to the meaning or applicability of a rule. As Hart acknowledged in his later writings, in particular in the Introduction to *Essays in Jurisprudence and Philosophy* (*op. cit.* ch. 1 n. 20), not all problems of interpretation arise simply from vagueness or open texture in language, but can be caused by problems of conflicting values.

23. *Donoghue* v. *Stevenson* [1932] A.C. 532; 1932 S.C. (H.L.) 31. The other examples cited in this paragraph are also from decided cases: *Maclennan* v. *Maclennan* 1958 S.C. 105 (Does AID—artificial insemination by donor rather than husband—constitute adultery?); *Ealing London Borough Council* v. *Race Relations Board* [1972] A.C. 342 (Is nationality the same as national origin?).

24. See N. MacCormick, *Legal reasoning and Legal Theory* (Oxford: Clarendon Press, 1978; 2nd ed. 1994) chs. 3, 5–9. Compare Martin P. Golding, "Principled Judicial Decision-making" (1963) 73 *Ethics* 247–54. For a later view, see N. MacCormick, *Rhetoric and the Rule of Law* (*op. cit.* ch. 1 n. 27), which is, on some points, further distanced from my broadly Hartian position of 1978.

25. The book was published in the Clarendon Law Series, of which Hart was at the time General Editor, and during the preparation of the manuscript we naturally had a number of discussions. subsequently, in his unpublished Austin Lecture to the Association for Legal and Social Philosophy in Liverpool in 1980, Hart endorsed the ideas about legal principles contained in N. MacCormick, *Legal Reasoning and Legal Theory* (*op. cit.* ch. 4 n. 11).

26. On this point, see again Hart's Introduction to *Essays in Jurisprudence and Philosophy* (*op. cit.* ch. 1 n. 20) esp. pp. 3–4.

27. Twining and Miers, *How to Do Things with Rules* (*op. cit.* ch. 11 n. 22).

28. See *Saif Ali* v. *Sydney Mitchell & Co.* [1980] A.C. 198; and distinguish *Rondel* v. *Worsley* [1969] 1 A.C. 191.

29. Dworkin, *Taking Rights Seriously* (*op. cit.* ch. 1 n. 16) chs. 2–4.

30. Ibid., chs. 4–5.

31. A. W. Brian Simpson, "The Common Law and Legal Theory" in Simpson (ed.) *Oxford Essays in Jurisprudence, 2nd series* (*op. cit.* ch. 4 n. 16) ch. 4.

32. See, e.g., Lord Cooper of Culross, *Selected Papers (1922–54)* (Edinburgh: Oliver & Boyd, 1957) pp. 172–209; and Thomas B. Smith, *The Doctrines of Judicial Precedent in Scots Law* (Edinburgh: W. Green, 1952) pp. 1–32. See Stair, *Institutions* (*op. cit.* ch. 10 n. 29).

33. See, e.g., Bentham, *Introduction to the Principles* (*op. cit.* ch. 7 n. 15) pp. 21–4, and esp. 308.

34. The revolutionary dislike of judicial lawmaking survives in Article 5 of the *Code civil* which prohibits judges, under penalty, from making general regulatory decisions under the pretext of interpreting the *Code*.

35. This is very much the point of Tom Campbell's assertion of the case for 'ethical positivism.' See Tom D. Campbell, *The Legal Theory of Ethical Positivism* (Aldershot, UK: Dartmouth Publishing, 1996) p. 79. Compare Jeremy Waldron,

"Normative (or Ethical) Positivism" in Coleman (ed.), *Hart's Postscript* (*op. cit.* ch. 1 n. 26) pp. 411–33.

36. Alan Watson, in *The Nature of Law* (Edinburgh: Edinburgh Univ. Press, 1977) defines law in terms of 'legal process'; by taking a wide view of what counts as a legal process, he avoids the necessity to rest his definition upon the 'judicial role' as here defined and thus avoids the necessity of any rule of recognition. While agreeing with much of what he says about 'legal processes,' I think he casts the net too wide.

37. Rheinstein (ed.) *Max Weber on Law* (*op. cit.* ch. 4 n. 5) ch. 8.

CHAPTER TWELVE

1. See Durkheim, *The Division of Labour in Society* (*op. cit.* ch. 6 n. 22) pp. 105 fn.

2. See ch. 6, pp. 86–7.

3. See "Coercion and the Law" in Neil MacCormick, *Legal Right and Social Democracy* (Oxford: Clarendon Press, 1982) ch. 12.

4. See Ernest Gellner, *Words and Things: An Examination of, and an Attack on, Linguistic Philosophy* (London: Routledge & Kegan Paul, 2nd ed. 1980).

5. The phrase about expression of disapproval is additional to Hart's own analysis, but seems a justified, even necessary, addition. See ch. 12 ns. 11–12; compare with Joel Feinberg, *Doing and Deserving: essays in the theory of responsibility* (Princeton, NJ: Princeton Univ. Press, 1970) pp. 95–118 on "The Expressive Theory of Punishment."

6. The classic English statement of this position is Bentham's *Introduction to the Principles* (*op. cit.* ch. 7 n. 15) chs. 13–15.

7. See, e.g., Edgar F. Carritt, *Ethical and Political Thinking* (Oxford: Clarendon Press,1947) p. 65; and John Rawls, "Two Concepts of Rules" (1955) 64 *Philosophical Review* 3–32, reprinted in Philippa Foot (ed.), *Theories of Ethics* (London: Oxford Univ. Press, 1967) pp. 144–70.

8. See Durkheim, *The Division of Labour in Society* (*op. cit.* ch. 6 n. 22) pp. 108–110; Roger Cotterrell, *Émile Durkheim: Law in a Moral Domain* (Edinburgh: Edinburgh Univ. Press, 1999) pp. 68–78.

9. Immanuel Kant, *The Metaphysical Elements of Justice* (trans. and ed. John Ladd, Indianapolis: Univ. of Indiana Press, 1965) pp. 99–107. For a restatement of a version of Kant's retributivism, see Jeffrie G. Murphy, *Retribution, Justice and Therapy: essays in the philosophy of law/* (Dordrecht, Holland/London: D. Reidel, 1979).

10. T. Malcolm Knox (trans. and ed.), *Hegel's Philosophy of Right* (Oxford: Clarendon Press, 1952) pp. 68–74.

11. Just because such offences are deemed to be 'regulatory' or 'quasi-criminal,' the penalties attached are not viewed as carrying grave moral stigma. Hart's tendency to ignore the expressive or morally symbolic aspect of punishment perhaps makes his discussion of this case somewhat unrealistic. By contrast, the House of Lords is apt to insist on *mens rea* in cases of statutory offences that are 'real' crimes. See *Sweet* v. *Parsley* [1969] 1 All E.R. 347 *per* Lord Reid, p. 357.

12. Barbara Wootton, *Social Science and Social Pathology* (London: Allen & Unwin, 1959) ch. 8; and Barbara Wootton, *Crime and the Criminal Law* (London: Stevens, 1963) ch. 3.

CHAPTER THIRTEEN

1. John F. Wolfenden (chair), *The Report of the Committee on Homosexual Offences and Prostitution* (Cmnd. 247, London: Her Majesty's Stationery Office, 1957) s. 61.

2. Patrick Devlin, *The Enforcement of Morals* (London: Oxford Univ. Press, 1965); the first chapter of this is a reprint of his 1959 British Academy Maccabean Lecture in Jurisprudence published under the same title (Oxford: Oxford Univ. Press, 1959).

3. Devlin, *Enforcement of Morals* (*op. cit.* ch. 13 n. 2) p. 17.

4. John Stuart Mill, *Utilitarianism, Liberty and Representative Government* with an introduction by A. D. Lindsay (London: J. M. Dent, 1910). "[The] interests [of man as a progressive being] authorize the subjection of individual spontaneity to external control, only in respect to those actions of each, which concern the interest of other people" (p. 74).

5. See John Stuart Mill, *On Liberty*, (Boston: Ticknor and Fields, 1863).

6. Nicola Lacey's biography indicates, on the basis of Hart's own private papers, that this is a matter concerning which he was speaking from direct experience. See Lacey, *A Life* (*op. cit.* ch. 1 n. 3) pp. 61–2, 73–9, 110–1, 203–5.

7. See Durkheim, *The Division of Labour in Society* (*op. cit.* ch. 6 n. 22) pp. 105 fn. Discussed in ch. 12.

8. Devlin, *Enforcement of Morals* (*op. cit.* ch. 3 n. 2) p. 13.

9. Compare Rawls, *A Theory of Justice* (*op. cit.* ch. 2 n. 12) pp. 204–5; and Daniels, *Reading Rawls* (*op. cit.* ch. 2 n. 12) pp. 253–81. John Rawls, like Hart, distinguishes between the existence of liberty and its relative worth to individuals; Norman Daniels counterargues that this deprives Rawls's arguments for the priority of equal liberty of any real substance. Daniels's argument, if sound, is damaging to Hart's position also. See also Hart, "Rawls on Liberty and its Priority" (1973) 40 *University of Chicago Law Review* 534–55.

10. On this point, Lord Devlin scores a palpable hit; see his *Enforcement of Morals* (*op. cit.* ch. 13 n. 2) pp. 34–8.

11. See N. MacCormick, *Institutions of Law* (*op. cit.* ch. 1 n. 27) pp. 212–5, 226.

12. Hart's disowning of "Are There Any Natural Rights?" (*op. cit.* ch. 2 n. 2) does not appear to extend to rejecting this principle, of which there are analogues in Hart (*Concept of Law, op. cit.* ch. 1 ns. 15). In the present book's first edition, however, the strength of any obligation to obey the law that is warranted by this principle was overstated. This revision responds also to M. Martin, *Legal Philosophy of Hart* (*op. cit.* ch. 1 n. 25) pp. 221, 304.

13. Lon L. Fuller, *The Morality of Law* (New Haven, CT: Yale Univ. Press, revised ed. 1969) pp. 207–13.

14. Compare Hart's "American Jurisprudence through English Eyes: the Nightmare and the Noble Dream," *Essays in Jurisprudence and Philosophy* (*op. cit.*

ch. 1 n. 20) pp. 123–44, the title of which was deliberately echoed in Nicola Lacey's biography of Hart.

15. On definitions of 'legal positivism,' see Roberto Ago, "Positive Law and International Law" (1957) 51 *American Journal of Jurisprudence* 703–7; Hart, *Concept of Law* (*op. cit.* ch. 1 n. 15) p. 253; Aarnio *On Legal Reasoning* (*op. cit.* ch. 4 n. 1) pp. 29–33; more recently, Wilfrid J. Waluchow, *Inclusive Legal Positivism* (Oxford: Clarendon Press, 1994); and Leslie Green, "General Jurisprudence: A 25th Anniversary Essay" (2005) 25 *Oxford Journal of Legal Studies* 565–80, esp. 570–3. It is important to observe that, as Aulis Aarnio points out, 'legal positivism' is by no means identical with 'scientific positivism' as favoured by Auguste Comte, for example. See also Karl Olivecrona, *Law as Fact* (London: Stevens, 2nd ed. 1971) ch. 1.

16. The classic statement is St. Augustine's "Non videtur esse lex quae justa non fuerit" ("Whatever is unjust is not held to be a law") in *De Libero Arbitrio* I.5—translated as *The Problem of Free Choice*—(trans. Mark Pontifex, London: Longmans Green, 1955). Compare Sir William Blackstone, *Commentaries on the Laws of England: In Four Books* with notes by John Taylor Coleridge (London: A. Strahan, 16th ed. 1825) vol. 1, pp. 38–43; but see Finnis, *Natural Law* (*op. cit.* ch. 4 n. 15) pp. 25–9, 351–66. Finnis rightly observes that this is neither a defining nor a central tenet of 'natural law.'

17. J. Austin, *Province of Jurisprudence Determined* (*op. cit.* ch. 3 n. 1) pp. 184–5.

18. See Waluchow, *Inclusive Legal Positivism* (*op. cit.* ch. 13 n. 15); in the *Postscript* (*Concept of Law*, *op. cit.* ch. 1 n. 15), Hart confirms his own view of himself as a 'soft' or 'inclusive' positivist.

19. This point is powerfully argued in Deryck Beyleveld and Roger Brownsword, *Law as a Moral Judgment* (London: Sweet & Maxwell, 1986) ch. 2.

20. In *Morality of Law* (*op. cit.* ch. 13 n. 13), Lon L. Fuller's argument is that there are certain formal features which must be exhibited in any attempt to subject human conduct 'to the governance of rules.' Although it is not strictly necessary that *every* law be general, be published, be clear, be prospective, be possible of performance, be consistent with other laws, be not subject to frequent change, and be respected by officials, nevertheless these are virtues in laws, and a system would cease to be viable or to have the characteristics of legality if most of these virtues were not most of the time respected by those in charge of governing. Hence, law in its very nature exhibits an 'inner morality,' comprising the eight formal virtues listed. Those who seek to govern according to laws are thus embarked on a moral enterprise.

21. This point is heavily stressed by Robert Alexy, *A Theory of Legal Argumentation* (trans. Ruth Adler and N. MacCormick, Oxford: Clarendon Press, 1988); see pp. 263 for his enunciation of his 'special case thesis,' namely the thesis that legal reasoning is simply a special case of general practical reasoning. Compare Raz, *Practical Reason and Norms* (*op. cit.* ch. 7 n. 1); Finnis, *Natural Law* (*op. cit.* ch. 4 n. 15); and N. MacCormick, *Rhetoric and the Rule of Law* (*op. cit.* ch. 1 n. 27) ch. 13.

22. Finnis, *Natural Law* (*op. cit.* ch. 4 n. 15).

CHAPTER FOURTEEN

1. Such writings by Hart include chapter 10 in *Essays on Bentham* (*op. cit.* ch. 1 n. 20); Introduction in *Essays in Jurisprudence and Philosophy* (*op. cit.* ch. 1

n. 20); *Postscript* in *Concept of Law* (*op. cit.* ch. 1 n. 15); and "Comment" in Gavison (ed.), *Issues in Contemporary Legal Philosophy* (*op. cit.* ch. 1 n. 2).

2. Julie Dickson, *Evaluation and Legal Theory* (Oxford: Hart Publishing, 2001). Compare Frederick Schauer, "The Social Construction of the Concept of Law: A Reply to Julie Dickson" (2005) 25 *Oxford Journal of Legal Studies* 493–501.

3. See Raz, *The Authority of Law* (*op. cit.* ch. 6 n. 25) pp. 153–7; discussed in Hart, *Essays in Jurisprudence and Philosophy* (*op. cit.* ch. 1 n. 20) pp. 9–11.

4. Hart acknowledged the appropriateness of this terminology in *Essays in Jurisprudence and Philosophy* (*op. cit.* ch. 1 n. 20) pp. 13–5.

5. Dworkin, *Law's Empire* (*op. cit.* ch. 1 n. 24) esp. chs. 1–2.

6. See Galligan, *Law in Modern Society* (*op. cit.* ch. 1 n. 17); and Tamanaha, *General Jurisprudence* (*op. cit.* ch. 1 n. 17); but an opposed view is stated in Cotterrell, *Politics of Jurisprudence* (*op. cit.* ch. 1 n. 17).

7. See, e.g., Dworkin, *Law's Empire* (*op. cit.* ch. 1 n. 24) p. 45.

8. See Joseph Raz, "The Nature of the Theory of Law" in Coleman (ed.), *Hart's Postscript* (*op. cit.* ch. 1 n. 26) pp. 1–38. For somewhat conflicting views on this difficult topic, see also in the same volume Timothy Endicott, "Herbert Hart and the Semantic Sting," pp. 39–58; and Nicos Stavropoulos, "Hart's Semantics," pp. 59–98.

9. See Waluchow, *Inclusive Legal Positivism* (*op. cit.* ch. 13 n. 15).

10. See Green, "General Jurisprudence" (*op. cit.* ch. 13 n. 15).

11. Hart's *Postscript* to the 2nd edition of *Concept of Law* (*op. cit.* ch. 1 n. 15) pp. 253–4.

12. See Jules L. Coleman, "Incorporationism, Conventionality and the Practical Difference Thesis" in Coleman (ed.), *Hart's Postscript* (*op. cit.* ch. 1 n. 26) pp. 99–147, esp. 100–2.

13. Finnis, *Natural Law* (*op. cit.* ch. 4 n. 15) p. 155.

14. Ibid., pp. 12–8.

15. For affirmative views on this, see Liam Murphy, "The Political Question of the Concept of Law," and Jeremy Waldron, "Normative (or Ethical) Positivism" in Coleman (ed.), *Hart's Postscript* (*op. cit.* ch. 1 n. 26) pp. 371–409, and pp. 411–33, respectively. For a strongly opposed view, see Andrei Marmor, "Legal Positivism: Still Descriptive and Morally Neutral" (2006) 26 *Oxford Journal of Legal Studies* 683–704.

16. N. MacCormick, *Institutions of Law* (*op. cit.* ch. 1 n. 27) pp. 293–8. In accepting Finnis's argument about 'focal meaning,' I also endorse in a qualified way Dworkin's thesis about 'interpretive concepts' as discussed in the next paragraph of the main text.

17. See Dworkin, "Hart's *Postscript*" (*op. cit.* ch. 1 n. 12) pp. 3–5, 19–22.

18. For a critique of the assimilation of these two different kinds of questions, see N. MacCormick, *Institutions of Law* (*op. cit.* ch. 1 n. 27) pp. 284–5; also Joseph Raz, "Two Views of the Nature of the Theory of Law: A Partial Comparison" in Coleman (ed.), *Hart's Postscript* (*op. cit.* ch. 1 n. 26) pp. 1–37, esp. 27–36.

19. See Hart, *Essays in Jurisprudence and Philosophy* (*op. cit.* ch. 1 n. 20) pp. 4–6.

20. See, e.g., Frederick Schauer, "(Re)taking Hart" (2006) 119 *Harvard Law Review* 852–83, esp. 869–81; and Twining, "Schauer on Hart" (*op. cit.* ch. 1 n. 23).

21. Oxford: Clarendon Press, 1st ed. 1978; 2nd ed. 1994.

22. Hart's *Postscript* to the 2nd edition of *Concept of Law* (*op. cit.* ch. 1 n. 15) pp. 272–6.

23. See Ronald Dworkin, "No Right Answer?" in Dworkin, *Taking Rights Seriously* (new impression with reply to critics, London: Duckworth, 1978) ch. 4.

24. See William L. Twining, *Law in Context: Enlarging a Discipline* (Oxford: Clarendon Press, 1997).

Jurists: Profiles in Legal Theory

GENERAL EDITOR

William Twining